'CATCH YOUR MIRACLE TODAY:
YOUR JOURNEY OF FAITH
AND
DARING DREAMS'

FOREWORD

"CATCH YOUR MIRACLE TODAY:

YOUR JOURNEY OF FAITH AND DARING DREAMS"

Life is a journey with many things to achieve along the way to one's destination called success. No matter how life treats us, we must learn to stay positive and focus on the pursuit of our individual dreams, aspirations, goals, and whatever else we desire.

Life only gives us what we pursue, chase, or reach out to get, not the things we just sit back and wish for. With this in mind, it is never too late to chase and catch your MIRACLES (dreams and success).

Miracles do not just happen; they get activated and attracted to with determination, discipline, and diligence to make them a reality. Whatever miracles we want in life, we must understand they don't come on a silver platter.

From this great and inspiring book in your hands, you will discover that there is no greater time than now to begin to chase, catch, and live your dreams.

The author has outlined steps by which we can all make our dreams come true if we put in the effort and make a reasonable plan. All we must do is know what we really want and take baby steps to be on our path to miracles.

Life has bumps along the way, but if we learn from our setbacks, we will be even more likely to get what we always wanted in the end. Having faith in succeeding in life without putting in the real work to achieve produces failure and disappointment.

The Bible makes it clear that, "For as the body without the spirit is dead, so faith without works is dead also" (James 2:26). Therefore, as we all traverse the varied landscapes of human desires and aspirations, we must add to our faith work to discover the keys to unlock our highest potential and achieve the extraordinary.

Personally, I do not see this book as just one of those motivational or manuals written but as the transformative springboard designed to help or catapult its readers toward their respective divine destinies. It is, therefore, my prayer that as you read this book in your hand, you discover the passion to turn your dream into a burning desire.

Having a strong passion to achieve your dreams, will boost your self-confidence and empower you in pulling through some of the worst hurdles, limitations, and stages of life.

May you gain invaluable insights into moving strategically toward your MIRACLES, embracing the unknown, walking with faith through uncertainties, and dreaming daringly knowing that miracles are not distant occurrences but threads woven into the very fabric of our existence.

Your journey is not just about reaching your goals; it is about experiencing the miraculous along the way and impacting your world positively. Your life is a miracle. Live to let the world know you were here. STEP UP TO CATCH YOUR MIRACLES TODAY.

FERDINARD SENYO LAWSON

(Associate Member of Royal Society for Public Health- England, AMRSPH). MSc in Dementia Care | BSc in Public Health & Social Care |Minister| Author| Transformational Speaker| Leadership and Lifestyle Coach.

TABLE OF CONTENTS

INTRODUCTION

"The best way to make children good

is to make them happy."

Oscar Wilde

Man is born into the world with lots of expectations, dreams, and aspirations. Babies expect to receive constant supply of breastmilk for nourishment and satisfaction while toddlers expect constant attention, tender care, and love till they reach teenage.

Many youth have channeled their need for love and expression of themselves and their strength in different ways just to feel accepted in society. As growing adults, our quest for independence and satisfaction in life keeps growing and varying in diverse ways till we depart the earth.

Our desire for food for example changes from breastmilk to liquid foods, to solid meals, and then to other harder substances as we age.

The desire for security and emotional satisfaction also soars as we grow. The love for power, recognition, and position in society also gallops as the years go by. Man will do everything in their power to realize these desires and cravings in life.

It is this desire to be fulfilled and satisfied in life that led to Abraham Maslow's Hierarchy of Needs Theory which has become a worldwide study and consideration for many decades.

Abraham Maslow's theory of needs, often depicted as Maslow's Hierarchy of Needs, is a psychological framework that explores human motivation and the factors that drive individuals to fulfill their potential.

This theory is often represented as a pyramid with five levels, each representing a distinct category of human needs. According to Maslow, these motivations can be categorized into five levels, each building upon the other.

These are expounded below:

1. Physiological Needs

At the base of Maslow's pyramid are the physiological needs, the most fundamental requirements for human survival. This includes air, water, food, shelter, sleep, and other basic necessities. Until these needs are satisfied, higher-level motivations are less likely to take precedence.

2. Safety Needs

Once physiological needs are met, individuals seek safety and security. This encompasses physical safety, financial stability, health and well-being, and protection from unforeseen threats. Establishing a stable and secure environment allows individuals to focus on higher-level aspirations.

3. Love and Belongingness

Beyond the need for safety, humans crave social connections and a sense of belonging. This includes relationships with family, friends, and a broader community. Love, affection, and a feeling of being valued contribute to emotional well-being and fulfillment.

4. Esteem Needs

As individuals satisfy their lower-level needs, they strive for a sense of self-esteem and recognition. This involves gaining respect from others, achieving personal goals, and feeling competent and confident in one's abilities. Esteem needs drive individuals to seek achievement and validation.

5. Self-Actualization

At the pinnacle of Maslow's Hierarchy is self-actualization, representing the realization of one's full potential and the pursuit of personal growth and fulfillment. This level involves creativity, problem-solving, morality, and acceptance of facts and realities. Individuals focused on self-actualization are driven by a desire to become the best version of themselves.

Maslow's Hierarchy of Needs is dynamic, recognizing that individuals may move up and down the pyramid depending on circumstances and life changes. It provides valuable insights into human motivation, emphasizing the importance of addressing lower-level needs before progressing to higher-level aspirations.

It is a journey, a profound exploration of what it means to be human. By understanding and addressing these needs, we lay the groundwork for a life rich with purpose, compassion, and the continual pursuit of personal growth.

In summary, Maslow's theory serves as a roadmap for understanding the diverse array of human needs and motivations, guiding psychologists, educators, and individuals in their quest for personal development and fulfillment.

No matter who you are or where you find yourself in life, you fall within one or more of these stages of life as outlined above. Till death, man will continue to climb higher on the ladder as postulated by Maslow. There is an inherent element in you that propels you to desire and seek the best in this world as long as you have breath. This is natural and not evil at all.

The way you go about your quest to fulfill these needs determines whether divinity and posterity are pleased and imparted positively or not.

"The purpose of life is not to be happy.

It is to be useful, to be honorable,

to be compassionate, to have it make some difference

that you have lived and lived well."

Ralph Waldo Emerson

"CATCH YOUR MIRACLE TODAY: YOUR JOURNEY OF FAITH AND DARING DREAMS" is designed to enable you to appreciate and achieve the highest and best things in this life and beyond no matter who you are or whatever stage of life you are.

The failures or successes you have chalked should not stop you from going higher and higher till you accomplish your divine mandate on earth and in eternity. There is always a higher or better dimension to accomplish be it in your family, faith, health, finances, academics, ministry, marriage, career or profession, society, nation, globally, etc.

You cannot be one hundred percent or too content until you leave the surface of the earth with the hope of a better life after. From this book, we will discover that the most important commodity you need and must crave is your connection with divinity or the presence of God.

You will learn how to move towards and accomplish your dreams, goals, and aspirations in life. The secrets to fulfilling the best in whatever endeavour are dramatically outlined and explained for you to apply for maximum impact.

The secrets to unlocking your highest potential are not hidden; they are carefully outlined and explained for you. This isn't just a guide; it's a roadmap to apply these insights for maximum impact. As you delve into the teachings within, you'll unravel the keys to fulfilling the best in every endeavor life presents.

In the quest for your greatest desires and aspirations, you'll inevitably encounter dream killers, miracle monsters, and saboteurs —forces that seek to derail your journey. Fear not, for within these pages, you'll discover the art of dealing with these adversaries and overcoming them.

Learn the invaluable skill of handling dream killers with grace, tact and resilience. Unearth the strategies to not only face but conquer these challenges in every sphere of life. Your pursuit of greatness demands a shield and sword against those who aim to thwart your dreams.

As you delve deeper, you'll fortify your faith and resilience, essential tools in preserving and protecting your miracles. Empowered with unwavering belief, you'll find the strength to move mountains that stand defiantly in your path to peace and fulfillment.

So, fasten your seat belt and prepare for takeoff. This isn't just a journey; it's a flight to your divine destination. Together, we'll navigate the skies, confront challenges, and emerge victorious on the other side. Your dreams await, and with every challenge overcome, you draw closer to the fulfillment that awaits you.

"What lies behind us and what lies before us

are tiny matters compared to what lies within us."

Ralph Waldo Emerson

CHAPTER ONE

MOUNTAIN OF MIRACLES

"Life's challenges are not supposed to paralyze you;

they're supposed to help you discover who you are."

Bernice Johnson Reagon

In the heart of Africa, where the sun orchestrates a vibrant symphony upon the rugged landscape, lived Mr. Indigo—an embodiment of resilience, miracles and dreams. His journey to the elusive land of promise had become a testament to the endurance of the human spirit, marked by days of hunger and thirst that wore down his once robust frame.

After five arduous days, destiny led him to the sanctuary of a magnificent Baobab tree, its branches reaching out like ancient arms cradling the secrets of the earth.

As he sought refuge under the Baobab's expansive shade, a sigh escaped his thirsty lips, and his weary body found solace on the bare ground. Disappointment shadowed his gaze as he surveyed the seemingly barren tree, but in the cosmic dance of fate, divinity bestowed upon him a whispered promise—a single fruit, defiantly dangling at the pinnacle.

A beacon of hope emerged, and in response, Mr. Indigo summoned the last remnants of strength within, commencing a climb that reflected the ascent of a soul seeking survival.

Miraculously, he ascended, each branch a testament to his determination, overcoming the hurdles of thick foliage until the life-giving fruit was within arm's reach. Yet, the tapestry of fate took an unexpected twist.

A scavenging bird, a swift shadow against the African sky, swooped in with silent precision, claiming the fruit before Mr. Indigo could grasp the miracle that seemed destined for his salvation. Despair echoed through the leafy expanse.

Heavy-hearted, in the face of desperation, a sharp sting on his neck jolted him from thoughts of surrender. A deadly insect sought the last drops of his life. Battling against these encroaching shadows, he inadvertently snapped a branch.

As he hung suspended between desperation and solitude, a swarm of bees, the custodians of a hidden secret, emerged. The insects, once perceived as adversaries, turned away, revealing a secret crevice dripping with golden honey.

In the dance of despair and redemption, the very environment that had denied him a single fruit unveiled a multitude of honeycombs—a treasure trove that metamorphosed his destiny.

Mr. Indigo, once feeble and desolate, emerged from the shadows, transformed into a wealthy man. The golden honey became not just a sustenance for his own survival but a commodity that connected him to nearby villages and towns, a tangible proof of the miracles often disguised in the struggles of everyday life in the heart of Africa.

"Our greatest glory is not in never falling,

but in rising every time we fall."

Confucius

In the heart of adversity, Mr. Indigo's journey, marked by days of hunger and the arduous pursuit of a better life, unfolds beneath the broad branches of a majestic Baobab tree. His tale reflects the challenges many face in the pursuit of their dreams, with the Baobab serving as a witness to both struggle and potential.

Choosing to climb the Baobab tree despite his weakened state becomes a practical metaphor for actively engaging in the pursuit of a miracle. It echoes the notion that catching a miracle requires not only hope but also intentional effort—taking steps, sometimes challenging ones, toward the opportunities that can bring about transformation.

In the narrative, where a scavenging bird intervenes, introduces a practical truth about the journey to catching a miracle. Obstacles and setbacks are inevitable, and what initially appears as a disappointment may be a stepping stone to a more profound miracle. It emphasizes the need for resilience and adaptability in the face of challenges.

In the unfolding events of Mr. Indigo's journey, the confrontation with the deadly insect and the subsequent encounter with a swarm of bees become pivotal moments, illustrating profound practical lessons. These moments symbolize the inherent unpredictability of life's journey and the simultaneous existence of challenges and unexpected blessings.

The deadly insect represents the harsh and often unforeseen challenges that one may face along the path to catching a miracle. In the face of despair, it appears as though Mr. Indigo is not only battling hunger and fatigue but also a threat to his very existence. This adversity, however daunting, underscores the need for resilience—the ability to withstand and overcome challenges with unwavering determination.

As the swarm of bees enters the scene, a shift occurs in the narrative, revealing an unexpected turn of events. This practical lesson unfolds as a testament to life's unpredictable nature.

In moments of despair, when it seems that all hope is lost, there may be unforeseen blessings waiting to manifest. The bees, initially perceived as potential adversaries, turn away, leading Mr. Indigo to a secret crevice dripping with honey.

The honey dripping from the secret crevice becomes a tangible symbol of the potential abundance hidden within life's challenges. This is a metaphor for the sweetness that can emerge from adversity when one remains open to different possibilities.

The practical lesson here is about maintaining an open heart and mind during difficult times, allowing oneself to see beyond immediate hardships and discover unexpected blessings.

In essence, the encounter with the deadly insect and the swarm of bees underscores the importance of adaptability—the capacity to adjust and find meaning even in the face of unexpected obstacles.

Life's journey, much like Mr. Indigo's, is a tapestry woven with moments of challenge and unexpected sweetness. Embracing resilience and adaptability becomes a practical approach to navigating these twists and turns, ensuring that one remains open to the potential miracles hidden within the folds of life's intricate fabric.

"Every adversity, every failure, every heartache

carries with it the seed of an equal or greater benefit."

Napoleon Hill

Ultimately, Mr. Indigo's transformation from despair to wealth, facilitated by the discovery of honeycombs, reflects the practical reality of catching a miracle. Miracles are often woven into the fabric of everyday life, and recognizing them requires a practical mindset—one that appreciates the value of persistence, adaptability, and a willingness to see blessings even in unexpected places.

The Baobab tree, with its sturdy branches and life-sustaining qualities, becomes not just a witness to Mr. Indigo's journey but a practical guide in the pursuit of miracles amid life's challenges.

Many individuals encounter a parallel account in the journey of life—a cyde of high aspirations and efforts to achieve diverse goals. Every morning brings renewed vigor and dedication to realize these aspirations, only to be met with the inevitable challenges that materialize along the way.

This echoes the human experience captured in Maslow's Hierarchy, where individuals strive for different stages of satisfaction, each accompanied by its own set of difficulties.

Similar to the receding tide and flow of Maslow's stages, our pursuit of satisfaction in various aspects of life is not devoid of hurdles. Disappointments become unwelcome companions, shattering the hopes carefully nurtured.

Relationships, once a source of support, can transform into sources of conflict, and the bonds with family and friends may be strained or even severed, leaving an unsettling void. In these moments, life can feel like it has come to an abrupt halt.

Yet, amidst the storms, I am here to convey a resounding message of hope to you, my precious reader. Despite the setbacks, the disappointments, and the losses, there exists an unwavering promise of hope and divine provision. The trials and tribulations, though formidable, are not the conclusion of your journey. I encourage you not to succumb to despair or surrender your vision.

Life's challenges do not signify an endpoint but rather serve as crucial junctures demanding resilience and perseverance. The disappointments, dashed hopes, and the transformation of relationships do not negate the possibility of a brighter future. Instead, they become integral chapters in a narrative of growth, strength, and eventual triumph.

So, I implore you to hold onto your aspirations and vision. The journey might be arduous, and the path might be obscured at times, but within you resides the power to endure and overcome. In the face of adversity, your unwavering commitment to your dreams becomes a beacon that guides you through the darkest nights.

Remember, just as a seed pushes through the soil to reach the sunlight, your aspirations can find a way to flourish despite the setbacks. Divine provision awaits those who persist, and hope becomes a powerful force that propels you forward, even when the road ahead seems uncertain.

Therefore, my dear reader, do not relinquish your dreams, for within the folds of perseverance lies the potential for miracles.

THE TRIUMPH OF TERERAI TRENT

Dr. Tererai Trent was born in a small village in rural Zimbabwe in 1965. Growing up in a patriarchal society, she faced the harsh realities of gender-based discrimination and cultural norms that limited educational opportunities for girls. Despite these challenges, Tererai held an unyielding passion for learning from a young age.

Her journey took a difficult turn when she was married off at the age of 11, leading to an early interruption of her formal education. However, Tererai's dreams of obtaining an education persisted. With the support of her mother, who recognized the importance of education, she secretly attended school whenever possible.

Tererai's determination to overcome societal barriers intensified when an American visitor, Jo Luck, arrived in her village. Inspired by Jo Luck's encouragement, Tererai began to believe in the possibility of realizing her educational dreams.

In an extraordinary act of commitment, she wrote down her goals on a scrap of paper and buried it in a can, symbolizing her aspiration to achieve higher education, particularly in the United States.

Eventually, Tererai's story reached the ears of Jo Luck, who became a pivotal figure in helping her pursue her dreams. With Jo Luck's support and the assistance of Heifer International, Tererai Trent was able to immigrate to the United States with her family.

In the U.S., Tererai faced a new set of challenges, including adapting to a different culture and educational system. However, her resilience and unwavering determination propelled her through these difficulties.

She earned her GED, followed by a bachelor's degree in Agriculture, a master's degree in Interdisciplinary Studies, and ultimately a Ph.D. in Interdisciplinary Evaluation from Western Michigan University.

Tererai's academic achievements were not only a personal triumph but also a beacon of hope for countless individuals facing adversity. Her story garnered international attention, and she became a sought-after speaker and advocate for education and women's empowerment.

In 2011, Dr. Tererai Trent published her memoir, "The Awakened Woman," sharing her extraordinary journey and inspiring others to pursue their dreams against all odds. Today, she continues her work through the Tererai Trent International Foundation, focusing on providing quality education and sustainable development in impoverished communities, particularly in Zimbabwe.

Tererai Trent's story is a testament to the transformative power of education, resilience, and the unwavering belief in the possibility of one's dreams. From a childhood marked by cultural constraints to becoming a global advocate for empowerment, Dr. Tererai Trent's journey embodies the triumph of the human spirit and the potential for positive change against formidable odds.

"Success is stumbling from failure to failure

with no loss of enthusiasm."

Winston S. Churchill

As we stand at the foothills of the "Mountain of Miracles," the echoes of John 6:1-13 reverberate through the pages of our narrative. In the first portion, the timeless message unfolds, where the meager offering of five loaves and two fish becomes the catalyst for a miraculous feast, a testament to divine abundance.

Now, as we ascend the slopes of this sacred mountain, the inference draws us deeper into the significance of this biblical account. The meager provisions mirror our own perceived limitations, and yet, as the loaves multiplied and the multitude was fed, the mountain becomes a metaphor for the boundless possibilities that unfold when we offer our meager resources to the divine.

In the connection between the message of John 6:1-13 and the unfolding narrative of the "Mountain of Miracles," we bridge the gap between ancient wisdom and contemporary revelation. The mountain becomes not just a geographical location but a spiritual ascent—a journey where our perceived limitations transform into portals of divine abundance.

The miracle at the heart of John 6 becomes the cornerstone upon which the "Mountain of Miracles" stands, inviting us to witness, participate, and ascend into the extraordinary possibilities that await. Let us draw inferences from this story as we shed more light on the Mountain of Miracles.

Reference: John 6: 1-13 (NKJV)

1 After these things Jesus went over the Sea of Galilee, which is the Sea of Tiberias. 2 Then a great multitude followed Him, because they saw His signs which He performed on those who were diseased. 3 And Jesus went up on the mountain, and there He sat with His disciples.

4 Now the Passover, a feast of the Jews, was near. 5 Then Jesus lifted up His eyes, and seeing a great multitude coming toward Him, He said to Philip, "Where shall we buy bread, that these may eat?" 6 But this He said to test him, for He Himself knew what He would do.

7 Philip answered Him, "Two hundred denarii worth of bread is not sufficient for them, that every one of them may have a little."

8 One of His disciples, Andrew, Simon Peter's brother, said to Him, 9 "There is a lad here who has five barley loaves and two small fish, but what are they among so many?"

10 Then Jesus said, "Make the people sit down." Now there was much grass in the place. So the men sat down, in number about five thousand. 11 And Jesus took the loaves, and when He had given thanks He distributed them to the disciples, and the disciples to those sitting down; and likewise of the fish, as much as they wanted.

12 So when they were filled, He said to His disciples, "Gather up the fragments that remain, so that nothing is lost." 13 Therefore they gathered them up, and filled twelve baskets with the fragments of the five barley loaves which were left over by those who had eaten.

1. AFTER THESE THINGS

This is a testament to the fact that despite the many successes that this great man chalked, he left the scene for something different. He was happy for all that had taken place in Jerusalem but was not content and desired to see more people transformed and thus moved to a new location.

Many had been healed including a man healed of an infirmity he suffered for thirty-eight years and had become the talk of the town. Nonetheless, he was willing to leave the praise and challenges behind him and move to another dimension of his ministry.

Beloved there is always a time to make new moves in life after achieving a certain feat. Even if for some reason you are going through a rather unpleasant situation, see that you don't stay in it for too long. Challenges come to strengthen us and not to break us. We do not give up and coil into our shells in the face of opposition.

Sometimes, we need to make a move for the miracle we desire to happen. Like Mr. Indigo, he used all his supplies on his journey and was nearly passing out but mastered all the last strength in him to climb the tree for survival. Though he was not successful with the fruit, his genuine efforts were rewarded with the honey which he saw after the sting.

After getting married, what next?

After buying your dream car what next?

After having that child you prayed for what next?

After building that huge mansion what next?

After starting that company what next?

After completing the master's program what next?

After winning the political power what next?

After surviving that surgery what next?

After that unpleasant situation you went through what next?

After all that you achieved in the years past what next?

'AFTER THESE THINGS' stands as a declaration that our journey doesn't end with successes or challenges. It's a rallying cry for those who refuse to be confined by their current circumstances, who understand that every achievement, every trial, is a stepping stone to something greater.

Precious one, never be content with all that you have achieved nor be dismayed when you face challenges and throw in the towel. This narrative challenges you to look beyond your current chapter in life, regardless of how successful or difficult it may be.

"Don't be afraid to give up the good

to go for the great."

John D. Rockefeller

Complacency has no place here. The talk of the town and accolades may surround you, but don't let them become a comfort zone. Life is a dynamic progression, and 'AFTER THESE THINGS' demands that you keep pushing forward.

Challenges, as formidable as they may seem, are not meant to deter you. Instead, they are opportunities to strengthen your resolve. In the face of opposition, don't retreat. This is a call to rise above adversity, to harness the transformative power of challenges, and to refuse to let them define your narrative.

This text doesn't offer solace in settling for the present. It challenges you to recognize that there is always more to achieve, more to become. The pursuit of greatness is a continuous journey.

'AFTER THESE THINGS' should be etched in your mindset as a relentless pursuit of growth, a refusal to be confined, and an unwavering determination to embrace the miracles that await beyond every challenge. Even after all that you will accomplish on earth, what next for your soul in eternity?

2. SEA OF GALILEE

The Sea of Galilee, also called Lake Tiberias or Kinneret, is a freshwater lake in Israel. It is the lowest freshwater lake on Earth and the second-lowest lake in the world, at levels between 215 metres and 209 metres below sea level.

It is approximately 53 km in circumference, about 21 km long, and 13 km wide. Its area is 166.7 km² at its fullest, and its maximum depth is approximately 43 metres. The lake is fed partly by underground springs, but its main source is the Jordan River, which flows through it from north to south and exits the lake at the Degania Dam.

Galilee truly shines as a spiritual epicenter. It is here that Jesus Christ spent much of his ministry, teaching, healing, and performing miracles. Galilee became the backdrop for some of the most profound moments in the life of Jesus, as he walked its dusty paths, shared parables, and touched the lives of countless individuals.

The region of Galilee was the focal point of many events and teachings in Jesus' ministry. Jesus gave no less than nineteen out of at least thirty-two of his parables delineated in the Bible in this area.

Twenty-five of Christ's miracles were performed in the Galilee area, included his first public miracle at a Cana wedding and his last one given just after his resurrection. This area was also the place where Christ gave the message that is the foundation of true Christianity (Matthew 5 - 7, Luke 6:20 - 49).

Galilee's association with Jesus Christ has imbued it with a sense of reverence and divine connection. It is in this region that Jesus called his disciples, turned water into wine at the wedding in Cana, and delivered the Sermon on the Mount. Galilee became a place of gathering and transformation, where ordinary people were touched by the extraordinary.

Galilee serves as a metaphorical landscape for personal transformation and greatness. Just as Jesus called his disciples to follow him, Galilee invites us to embark on a journey of spiritual growth and renewal. It is a place where the ordinary becomes extraordinary, where the mundane is infused with divine purpose.

Walking in the footsteps of Jesus in Galilee can lead to a profound inner metamorphosis, allowing us to transcend our limitations and embrace a higher state of being.

It is a realm where faith is nurtured, hope is kindled, and love is experienced in its purest form. Galilee beckons us to dive deep into the depths of our souls, to uncover the hidden treasures of our true selves, and to embrace the transformative power of divine love.

The essence of the statement underscores the significance of familiarity, mastery, and comfort in achieving extraordinary feats, drawing inspiration from Jesus' ministry in Galilee. Let's delve deeper and provide practical examples to elucidate this concept.

Familiarity Breeds Miracles

In Galilee, Jesus was not a stranger to the landscape; it was a region he knew intimately. This familiarity allowed him to navigate its terrain effortlessly. Similarly, in our own lives, when we operate in spheres where we are acquainted with the nuances and intricacies, we set the stage for extraordinary accomplishments.

For instance, a skilled musician may find it easier to create beautiful compositions within the genre they have mastered.

In the realm of technology, a software engineer who is intimately familiar with a specific programming language and its intricacies can engineer innovative solutions effortlessly. This familiarity allows them to navigate through challenges seamlessly, fostering an environment where technological miracles, such as groundbreaking software applications, can be created.

Mastery Unleashes Miraculous Potential

Jesus' unparalleled mastery of his ministry in Galilee manifested through a multitude of miracles. Likewise, when we focus on honing our skills and capabilities, we unlock the door to miracles in our own endeavors.

Consider a chef who has mastered the art of blending flavors—each dish becomes a masterpiece, an extraordinary creation born from the depths of their culinary expertise.

Consider the world of sports, where athletes who have mastered their craft showcase extraordinary performances. A tennis player like Serena Williams, with her mastery of the game, consistently delivers miraculous moments on the court, achieving victories that stand as a testament to her unparalleled expertise.

Comfort as a Catalyst for Miracles

In the business circles, successful entrepreneurs often find their comfort zone in a specific industry. Elon Musk, for instance, has shown a remarkable comfort and expertise in the realm of electric vehicles and space exploration. This comfort has been a catalyst for groundbreaking innovations, leading to miraculous achievements in the fields of Tesla and SpaceX.

Galilee was Jesus' comfort zone—a place where he felt at ease in his role as a minister. This comfort served as a catalyst for miracles. Similarly, when we operate within our comfort zones, we tap into a reservoir of confidence and assurance. An entrepreneur comfortable with a specific market may be more likely to innovate and witness remarkable success within that familiar business landscape.

Understanding and Maximizing Personal Capacities

The entertainment industry provides a fitting example. A versatile actor like Meryl Streep understands and maximizes her capacities by taking on diverse roles, showcasing her talent across genres. Her ability to recognize her strengths and adapt to various characters has led to miraculous performances and numerous accolades.

The notion that miracles require a deep understanding of one's capabilities is paramount. In Galilee, Jesus knew where his strengths lay, and he operated within that framework.

Translating this to our own lives, recognizing our unique talents and capacities allows us to focus our efforts where they can yield the most significant impact. An artist who understands their strengths in a particular medium can produce miraculous works of art.

Dedication and Mastery as Precursors to Miracles

The world of science and medicine offers a poignant illustration. Dr. Anthony Fauci, with his dedicated mastery of infectious diseases, has played a pivotal role in navigating public health crises. His expertise and unwavering dedication have been instrumental in orchestrating responses that are, in their own right, miraculous in the face of global challenges.

The phrase emphasizes the need to master one's capabilities with unwavering dedication. Jesus' ministry in Galilee exemplifies that miracles often result from dedicated mastery of one's craft. This principle is applicable across various domains—an athlete who diligently hones their skills becomes capable of achieving extraordinary feats on the field.

In essence, the lessons drawn from Jesus' ministry in Galilee teach us that miracles are not random occurrences. They are cultivated in environments where familiarity, mastery, comfort, understanding of personal capacities, and dedicated effort converge. By recognizing and embracing our strengths, we, too, can create the conditions for miracles to unfold in our lives.

The combination of these factors converge to create environments where contemporary miracles unfold—be it in technology, sports, business, entertainment, or the realm of public health.

3. GO UP THE MOUNTAIN

When the multitudes followed him to see more miracles, he went up the mountain above them. He did not allow them to drown him with their voices nor affect him negatively with their frustrations but rather climbed higher. As the crowd came closer he climbed higher the mountain.

This profound concept encapsulates the idea of continuous growth, resilience, and a relentless pursuit of excellence.

Let's explore and expound on each key aspect:

1. Resisting Drowning Voices

When faced with multitudes and the noise of external opinions, Jesus chose not to succumb to the overwhelming voices around him. Instead, he ascended the mountain, distancing himself from the crowd.

In the modern context, this mirrors the need to resist drowning in the cacophony of external pressures. Successful individuals often rise above the noise, maintaining focus on their goals despite external distractions.

In the world of entrepreneurship, Elon Musk, amidst the noise and skepticism surrounding his ambitious projects, such as SpaceX and Tesla, resisted being drowned by external opinions. He went up to his own metaphorical mountain by consistently pushing the boundaries of innovation, focusing on his vision despite the surrounding noise.

"Don't let the noise of others' opinions

drown out your own inner voice."

Steve Jobs

2. Climbing Higher Despite Proximity:

As the crowd drew closer, Jesus climbed higher. This signifies a proactive stance, a refusal to be complacent even in the face of success. In life, it's easy to settle into comfort zones, but true achievers understand the importance of continuously ascending to new heights. Whether in career, relationships, or personal development, the pursuit of higher dimensions is a hallmark of success.

Serena Williams, one of the greatest tennis players of all time, consistently climbed higher despite being in close proximity to the achievements of her peers. Even as she achieved numerous Grand Slam victories, her determination to break records and surpass her own milestones propelled her to keep ascending to new heights in her tennis career.

"It's not the will to win that matters—everyone has that.

It's the will to prepare to win that matters."

Paul "Bear" Bryant

28

3. Overcoming Present Circumstances:

Malala Yousafzai, after surviving a Taliban attack for advocating education for girls, overcame her harrowing present circumstances by becoming a global advocate for girls' education. She went up to her own mountain by defying adversity and continuing her pursuit of education for all.

The instruction to "go up to the mountain" suggests a mindset of overcoming present circumstances. Jesus didn't allow the current situation to dictate his trajectory. This principle applies universally—whether overcoming challenges, personal limitations, or societal expectations, the path to success often involves transcending present circumstances.

4. Challenging Oneself to Higher Standards:

"Believe you can and you're halfway there."

Theodore Roosevelt

Jeff Bezos, the founder of Amazon, consistently challenges himself and his company to higher standards. The relentless pursuit of customer satisfaction, coupled with innovations like Amazon Web Services, reflects his commitment to setting new benchmarks in the e-commerce and technology industries.

Miracles, according to this concept, happen when individuals challenge themselves to higher standards. It implies that greatness is achieved not in complacency but in the relentless pursuit of improvement.

This idea resonates across various domains—academic excellence, relationship enrichment, business innovation—where individuals strive for higher benchmarks and exceed their own expectations.

5. Sacrifice for Standing Out:

Serena Williams, known not only for her tennis prowess but also her philanthropy, has sacrificed time and effort to stand out beyond the tennis court. Her dedication to various charitable causes showcases the level of sacrifice required to distinguish oneself not just as a sports icon but as a socially impactful figure.

The analogy of climbing a mountain underscores the energy and sacrifice required for standing out. Jesus was willing to invest the effort to distinguish himself.

Similarly, those seeking to make an impact must be prepared to expend the energy required to rise above mediocrity. Success often demands a level of sacrifice and commitment that sets individuals apart from the crowd.

"You have to fight to reach your dream.

You have to sacrifice and work hard for it."

Lionel Messi

6. Stepping Up the Game:

The call to "go up the mountain" is, at its core, an invitation to step up one's game. Whether in education, relationships, or professional pursuits, the principle emphasizes the necessity of continuous improvement. Students must elevate their academic efforts, couples must enhance their relationships, and professionals must consistently strive for excellence.

In the tech industry, Sundar Pichai, the CEO of Google, consistently steps up the game by leading the company through transformative projects like Google's expansion into artificial intelligence and quantum computing. His leadership exemplifies the continuous pursuit of excellence in a rapidly evolving industry.

In essence, "GO UP THE MOUNTAIN" is a powerful directive to transcend limitations, embrace continuous improvement, and strive for excellence in every aspect of life. It serves as a timeless guide for those seeking to achieve extraordinary feats and witness miracles by challenging themselves to ascend to greater heights.

4. THE LAD

This tells you that, no matter who you are or where you are coming from in life, you can still be used by God to make a difference. There is always a package or parcel for everybody on earth. You may look inexperienced and unqualified in the eyes of people but there is still something you can achieve that is unique to only you. A miracle is possible with you and for you irrespective of your present condition.

This also means that you don't need too much experience or exposure to make it in life. All that you have is enough to start something great on earth. Your family background may not be very great but you can make a difference in an area of life.

This principle underscores the universal truth that every individual, regardless of their background or perceived limitations, possesses the potential to contribute significantly to the world.

Let's dig deeper into the inferences of "THE LAD"

1. Everyone Can Make a Difference

This concept emphasizes the idea that there is a unique purpose or contribution for every individual on earth. Regardless of your background or circumstances, there is something meaningful and impactful that you can offer to the world. This aligns with the belief that each person has inherent value and potential.

Helen Keller, despite being deaf and blind from an early age, became a prolific author, political activist, and lecturer. Her achievements underscore the universal potential within every individual, irrespective of physical limitations.

2. Uniqueness in Inexperience

Albert Einstein, known for his revolutionary contributions to physics, exemplifies the uniqueness of contribution. His groundbreaking theories reshaped our understanding of the universe, showcasing how an individual's distinct insights can leave an enduring impact.

The lad in the context implies someone young and seemingly inexperienced. This challenges the notion that one needs extensive experience or qualifications to make a difference. Your uniqueness lies in your individuality, and even in what may be perceived as inexperience, there exists a reservoir of untapped potential waiting to be harnessed.

3. Miracle Irrespective of Condition

Nelson Mandela's journey from imprisonment to becoming South Africa's first black president reflects a miracle unfolding irrespective of adverse conditions. His leadership and resilience in the face of apartheid epitomize the transformative power of determination.

The lad's story suggests that miracles are not contingent upon one's current circumstances. It implies that irrespective of challenges, setbacks, or limitations, everyone has the potential to experience and contribute to miraculous transformations in their lives and the lives of others.

4. Starting Small with What You Have

J.K. Rowling, before achieving global success with the Harry Potter series, started writing in coffee shops with limited resources. Her story illustrates that starting with what you have—a vivid imagination and determination—can lead to extraordinary outcomes.

The lad's offering of five loaves and two fish signifies that you don't need an abundance of resources or a grand background to make a meaningful start. It encourages individuals to begin with what they have in their hands—be it talents, skills, or modest resources—and gradually build upon them to create positive change.

5. No Need for Excessive Experience

Mark Zuckerberg, co-founder of Facebook, started the social media platform in his college dormitory. His success challenges the notion that extensive industry experience is a prerequisite for groundbreaking innovations. Zuckerberg's story highlights the power of youthful entrepreneurship.

The lad's story encourages individuals to offer the best of their abilities, talents, and skills to the world. It underscores the transformative power of genuine, wholehearted contributions. By giving your best, you not only impact your own life but also become a catalyst for positive change in the lives of those around you.

6. Overcoming Family Background Challenges

The lad's story suggests that even if your family background may not be ideal or prestigious, it doesn't limit your potential for making a difference.

You have the agency to carve your own path and contribute positively to society, transcending the constraints of your family history.

Mother Teresa, through her selfless service and compassion, offered her abilities to alleviate the suffering of the poor and sick in Calcutta. Her dedication to humanitarian work demonstrates how individuals can make a profound impact by generously contributing their unique abilities.

In essence, "THE LAD" inspires individuals to recognize their inherent worth, tap into their unique potential, and contribute meaningfully to the world. "THE LAD" champions the idea that every individual is a potential miracle worker, capable of making a significant difference in the world.

It challenges preconceived notions about qualifications and backgrounds, emphasizing that everyone has the capacity to initiate positive change with what they have at their disposal.

"In a gentle way, you can shake the world."

Mahatma Gandhi

5. There is a lad HERE...

To be at the right place at the right time with the right preparation can make a major impact in your life. The lad did not only save his lunch but was present where it was needed in the most crucial moment of time.

Where you are located or the place you find yourself in the pursuit of your dreams and aspirations in life has a great influence in what outcomes you realize. If the lad was not present on the mountain at the time that he was needed, this miracle probably would have taken a different turn or may be would not have taken place.

The assertion that "There is a lad HERE" underscores the significance of being at the right place at the right time with the right preparation, offering valuable insights into strategic positioning and the impact of one's location on life outcomes.

"Luck is what happens when preparation meets opportunity."

Seneca

"Success is where preparation and opportunity meet."

Bobby Unser

1. Right Place, Right Time, Right Preparation HERE

This emphasizes the synchronicity of elements—being in the right place at the right time with the right preparation. The lad's presence on the mountain, armed with his provisions, showcases the importance of alignment and readiness.

An illustrative modern example is Elon Musk's strategic timing in entering the electric vehicle market, demonstrating how precise positioning can lead to groundbreaking success.

In the late 1970s, Steve Jobs, with the right vision and preparation, positioned himself at the forefront of the personal computer revolution. His presence at the right time in Silicon Valley, coupled with the right preparation, led to the founding of Apple Inc., transforming the tech industry.

2. Influence of Location HERE

Martin Luther King Jr. and the March on Washington. MLK strategically chose the Lincoln Memorial as the location for his iconic "I Have a Dream" speech during the March on Washington in 1963. The choice of this symbolic location amplified the impact of the Civil Rights Movement and contributed to transformative change.

The narrative stresses the influence of one's location on the outcomes realized. The lad's presence on the mountain was pivotal for the unfolding of the miracle. Similarly, individuals must be mindful of the environments they navigate in their pursuit of dreams.

A historical example is Rosa Parks, whose refusal to give up her seat on a bus sparked the Montgomery Bus Boycott, illustrating the transformative impact of being in the right place at the right time.

3. Sensitivity and Strategy in Choosing Places HERE

Marie Curie strategically chose her intellectual and scientific gatherings, particularly at the University of Paris, where she conducted groundbreaking research on radioactivity. Her choice of a conducive scientific environment played a crucial role in her revolutionary discoveries.

The passage advises on being sensitive and strategic about the places one frequents. It acknowledges the direct correlation between strategic choices of location and positive outcomes. For instance, a business executive strategically attending industry conferences or networking events may encounter opportunities that significantly impact their career.

4. Strategic Use of Time HERE

The phrase "You location will determine your allocation in life" underscores the relationship between time and outcomes. The lad's allocation of time and presence on the mountain determined the miraculous outcome.

Similarly, individuals who strategically allocate their time to pursuits aligned with their goals often reap the rewards. A modern example could be a budding entrepreneur dedicating time to skill development and networking to propel their business forward.

In 1930, Gandhi strategically allocated his time to lead the Salt March in India, protesting British salt taxes. This symbolic act not only galvanized the Indian independence movement but also showcased the strategic use of time for impactful, nonviolent resistance.

5. Selectivity and Strategic Choices HERE

The passage advocates for selectivity and strategic decision-making in choosing places that positively impact life. It warns against locations that drain, distract, or destroy.

In a contemporary context, successful individuals often attribute their achievements to careful choices in personal and professional environments, showcasing the impact of selective and strategic decision-making.

During his imprisonment on Robben Island, Mandela strategically used his time to educate himself and engage in political discussions with fellow inmates. His selectivity in activities and strategic choices during incarceration contributed to his leadership upon release and the dismantling of apartheid.

Where and what you spend your time and resources on will determine what comes to your life at the end of the day. It is important therefore that we are selective and strategic in choosing wisely places that will have more positive impact in our lives than where we are drained, distracted and destroyed in the end.

"You location with determine your

allocation in life"

In summary, 'There is a lad HERE' stresses the importance of conscious decisions regarding one's presence, emphasizing strategic positioning, and underscoring the influential role of location in shaping life outcomes.

It encourages individuals to be intentional about where they are and how they use their time, recognizing the profound impact these choices can have on the realization of their aspirations.

6. FIVE BARLEY LOAVES

There are five books of Moses which are called the *Torah* or *Pentateuch*. No wonder Jesus starts with five barley loaves. He is transforming the Mosaic Law into something much bigger, greater, and more nourishing. Moses predicted that God would raise up a prophet like himself (Deuteronomy 18:18).

The interpretation of the significance of the five barley loaves in connection with the five books of Moses (Torah or Pentateuch) and the concept of grace is insightful and brings a rich layer of meaning to the biblical narrative.

Let's explore deeper into more significant meaning of the five barley loaves:

1. Transformation of Mosaic Law

The association of the five barley loaves with the five books of Moses suggests a symbolic transformation or elevation of the Mosaic Law. Jesus, by using five barley loaves, could be seen as surpassing the legalistic framework and introducing a new dimension of grace, love and nourishment.

The life and teachings of the Apostle Paul in the New Testament can be considered an example of the transformation of Mosaic Law. Paul, formerly known as Saul, was a Pharisee who zealously followed the Mosaic Law.

However, his encounter with Jesus on the road to Damascus led to a profound transformation. He became a key figure in spreading the message of grace and salvation through faith in Christ.

2. Number Five as the Number of Grace

Connecting the number five with grace underscores the unmerited favor of God. This aligns with the idea that, just as the lad offered five barley loaves, our success and sustenance in life are incomplete without the grace of God.

It emphasizes reliance on divine favor for protection, provision, promotion, and power.

The life of John Newton, the former slave trader who wrote the hymn "Amazing Grace," exemplifies the transformative power of divine grace. Newton's personal journey from a life of sin and cruelty to a life dedicated to God's grace serves as a powerful testament to the unmerited favor that can change lives.

3. Resourcefulness of the Boy

During the Great Depression, individuals like George Washington Carver demonstrated remarkable resourcefulness. Carver, an agricultural scientist, encouraged Southern farmers to diversify their crops and introduced innovative uses for peanuts and sweet potatoes. His resourcefulness helped struggling communities find new sources of sustenance and income.

Highlighting the resourcefulness of the boy in keeping part of his lunch for the journey adds a practical dimension to the narrative. It underscores the importance of being prepared and resourceful in life, even in the face of uncertainties. This principle of preparation can attract more miracles and blessings.

4. Need for a Buffer in Life

The life of Warren Buffett, one of the most successful investors of all time, provides an example of the importance of having a financial buffer. Buffett emphasizes the value of long-term investing, financial preparedness, and having a margin of safety to navigate economic uncertainties and market fluctuations.

The concept of keeping a portion of the lunch for the future emphasizes the need for a buffer in life. It resonates with the idea of having reserves or resources to navigate uncertainties. This principle aligns with the importance of being proactive and having a contingency plan.

Furthermore, the spiritual significance of the five barley loaves can be interpreted in various ways:

a) Symbol of Humility

Barley was considered a more modest and less expensive grain compared to wheat. The use of barley loaves symbolizes *humility and simplicity*. It reflects that God's miracles can arise from the most humble and seemingly insignificant aspects of our lives.

Gandhi, also known as the "Mahatma" or "Great Soul," led India to independence through nonviolent civil disobedience. Despite his pivotal role in history, Gandhi maintained a simple and humble lifestyle, emphasizing the importance of service to others and selflessness.

His commitment to nonviolence and humility made a profound impact on the world, showcasing the transformative power of a humble life dedicated to a greater cause.

b) Surrender and Availability

The lad who offered the five barley loaves demonstrated a spirit of surrender and availability. The small offering he brought to Jesus represents the willingness to give what little one has. This teaches a lesson of surrendering our resources, no matter how limited, to God for His use.

St. Francis of Assisi embraced a life of surrender and availability to God. Renouncing his wealth, he lived a simple life devoted to serving others and embracing nature. His willingness to give up worldly possessions reflects the spirit of surrender.

c) Divine Multiplication

The story of George Müller, a Christian evangelist, showcases divine multiplication. Operating orphanages in Bristol, England, Müller relied solely on prayer and faith to provide for thousands of orphans. God multiplied resources miraculously to meet the needs of the children.

The miracle itself, where Jesus took the five loaves, blessed them, and multiplied them to feed a multitude, symbolizes divine multiplication. It conveys the idea that when we offer our meager resources to God, He can multiply them beyond our expectations for a greater purpose.

   d)   Abundance in Scarcity

The use of five loaves in the midst of a large crowd emphasizes the theme of abundance in scarcity. It teaches that God's provision transcends the limitations of human resources. Even when faced with apparent scarcity, God can provide more than enough.

Corrie ten Boom, along with her family, was part of the Dutch resistance during World War II. They risked their lives to help Jews escape the Nazis by providing them with a hiding place in their home. Unfortunately, in 1944, the ten Boom family was betrayed, arrested, and eventually sent to concentration camps.

In the concentration camp, Corrie and her sister Betsie endured unimaginable suffering. The scarcity they faced was not only physical, with limited food and harsh living conditions, but also the deprivation of freedom and the constant threat of death.

In the midst of scarcity, Corrie experienced moments of grace that defied logic. She and her sister held secret Bible studies in the barracks, providing spiritual nourishment to those around them. Despite the physical scarcity, there was an abundance of spiritual strength and solidarity.

After the war, Corrie faced the immense challenge of forgiving those who had harmed her family and caused immense suffering. Her journey of forgiveness, as documented in her book "The Hiding Place," exemplifies the transformative power of God's grace to bring abundance out of the scars of war.

Corrie ten Boom's post-war life was dedicated to sharing her experiences and spreading a message of forgiveness, reconciliation, and God's love. Her story continues to inspire countless people, illustrating that even in the darkest moments, God's grace can bring about abundance in the form of resilience, faith, and the capacity to forgive.

Corrie ten Boom's narrative encapsulates the idea that, even in the most extreme scarcity, a person's faith and connection with the divine can lead to an abundance of inner strength, hope, and a profound impact on the lives of others.

e) Communal Sharing and Unity

The act of sharing the five loaves with the multitude emphasizes the importance of communal sharing and unity. It encourages a sense of community where resources are shared for the benefit of all. This aligns with the broader spiritual principle of love and compassion for one another.

The early Christian community, as described in the Book of Acts, practiced communal sharing. Believers shared their possessions to ensure that no one was in need. This unity and communal spirit became a testament to Christian fellowship.

f) Eucharistic Symbolism

Some interpretations connect the five barley loaves with the Eucharist or Holy Communion. The breaking of the bread by Jesus and its distribution to the people mirrors the Last Supper, where Jesus instituted the sacrament of the Eucharist, emphasizing spiritual sustenance through Christ.

Dietrich Bonhoeffer, a German Lutheran pastor, theologian, and resolute anti-Nazi dissident, lived during one of the darkest periods in human history. His life and eventual martyrdom exemplify the principles of Eucharistic symbolism, emphasizing sacrifice and spiritual sustenance.

Bonhoeffer vehemently opposed the Nazi regime's atrocities, particularly their persecution of Jews and suppression of religious freedoms. His stance against injustice and his commitment to Christ led him to actively resist the Nazi regime.

Bonhoeffer's theological reflections emphasized the transformative power of Christ's teachings and the necessity of living out one's faith in the midst of societal turmoil. He believed in the active, sacrificial following of Christ's example.

Bonhoeffer's decision to return to Germany from the safety of the United States during World War II demonstrated his commitment to his people and his refusal to be a passive bystander. He chose to face the dangers of Nazi persecution, aligning with the sacrificial nature of the Eucharist.

Bonhoeffer's arrest and subsequent imprisonment marked the culmination of his resistance. He continued his ministry within the confines of prison, providing spiritual guidance to fellow inmates. His steadfast commitment to his principles ultimately led to his execution just days before the end of World War II.

The Eucharist, or Holy Communion, is a sacrament in Christianity symbolizing the body and blood of Christ given for the redemption of sins. Bonhoeffer's sacrificial life and eventual martyrdom parallel the spiritual sustenance symbolized in the Eucharist. His actions mirrored the selfless giving and sacrifice central to the Christian faith.

Dietrich Bonhoeffer's life and writings, including works like "The Cost of Discipleship," continue to inspire Christians worldwide. His example challenges believers to live out their faith authentically, even in the face of adversity, echoing the transformative power and sacrificial essence of the Eucharist.

Dietrich Bonhoeffer's life echoes the Eucharistic symbolism of sacrifice, commitment to Christ, and spiritual sustenance. His legacy serves as a poignant reminder of the transformative impact of living out one's faith with unwavering dedication, even in the most challenging circumstances.

"The happiest people I know are those who lose

themselves in the service of others."

Gordon B. Hinckley

g) Teaching on Generosity

The account serves as a teaching on generosity, encouraging individuals to be generous with what they have, no matter how little. It challenges the perception that one's contribution is insignificant, highlighting that God can use even the smallest offerings for His glory.

The philanthropic work of Bill and Melinda Gates illustrates generosity. Through their foundation, they have contributed significant resources to address global health issues and poverty. Their commitment to giving demonstrates the impact of generosity on a large scale.

7. TWO SMALL FISH

The master fisherman called two brothers on the shores of the Sea of Galilee and bid them to follow him- Matthew 4:19. They were no longer going to hunt for edible fish but "fishers of men". In other words, they were going to do business directly with PEOPLE and not fish. Their network of relationships and contacts were enlarged.

In the transformative journey from fishing for edible fish to becoming "fishers of men," the narrative invites us to rethink the concept of abundance. It's not about the sheer quantity but the inherent power within the few. Similarly, in the realm of human connections, quality often surpasses quantity.

Just like the little lad's meager offering carried the potential to satisfy many when blessed, the value of our connections lies not in their vastness but in their strategic significance. In the digital age, where social networks abound, the emphasis should shift from accumulating connections to nurturing meaningful relationships.

In the modern world, networking has become a powerful tool for personal and professional growth. Your circle of influence plays a pivotal role in shaping your opportunities and experiences. Just as the master fisherman strategically chose two brothers for a specific purpose, our connections should align with our goals and aspirations.

The phrase "Your network determines your net worth" resonates profoundly in the era of networking platforms and social media. Building a network of strategic associations can open doors to opportunities, mentorship, and collaborative ventures. It's not about knowing everyone but about knowing the right people who can contribute to your journey.

In a society where everyone is connected, cultivating genuine, impactful relationships is a skill worth mastering. Like the two small fish that played a crucial role in the miraculous feast, our connections, no matter how limited, can have a significant impact when strategically aligned with our goals and aspirations.

"Surround yourself with only people

who are going to lift you higher."

Oprah Winfrey

In the professional realm, individuals often find that their career growth is closely tied to the quality of their professional network. Attending industry events, connecting on platforms like LinkedIn, and fostering relationships with colleagues can open doors to new opportunities, collaborations, and insights.

Entrepreneurs understand the value of networking in building successful businesses. Engaging with mentors, investors, and other entrepreneurs can provide valuable guidance, funding, and collaborative opportunities. The startup ecosystem thrives on strategic connections that can propel ventures to new heights.

In the realm of social impact and community engagement, having a network of like-minded individuals and organizations amplifies the potential for positive change. Activists, volunteers, and advocates often collaborate to address shared goals and make a meaningful impact on society.

As you navigate the intricate tapestry of relationships in your life, recognize that the power of your network extends far beyond sheer numbers. It lies in the strategic and purposeful connections that align with your aspirations and contribute to the realization of your miracles.

Like the little lad, the fish was few but carried the power to satisfy people when blessed. You always need a good network of strategic people in your life. Though you are to respect everyone and relate well with people, you cannot associate with everybody and anybody all the time. Some people are meant to be just acquaintances while others are supposed to be strategic associations to lead you to your miracle.

"Your network is your net worth."

Porter Gale

8. MAKE THE PEOPLE SIT DOWN

This seemingly ordinary act holds deeper significance, offering timeless lessons that extend beyond the shores of the Sea of Galilee.

Order and Organization:

Making the multitude sit down was an act of order and organization. In the chaos of a large crowd, establishing order creates a conducive environment for miracles to unfold.

It emphasizes the importance of structured approaches in managing challenges and creating space for divine interventions. In the modern context, this can be likened to the need for structured planning and organization in various aspects of life.

Equality and Inclusivity:

The act of instructing everyone to sit down reflects a commitment to equality and inclusivity. Regardless of social status, background, or any other distinguishing factor, all were invited to participate in the miracle. In our diverse and interconnected world, promoting equality and inclusivity remains a crucial principle for fostering harmony and collaboration.

Preparation for Abundance:

Making people sit down was not only about creating order but also about preparing for the abundance that was about to unfold. It set the stage for the miraculous multiplication of the loaves and fishes. Similarly, in our lives, moments of preparation and intentional positioning pave the way for unexpected blessings and abundance.

Building Anticipation and Faith:

The act of sitting down could be seen as a moment of anticipation and faith-building. As the multitude followed Jesus' instruction, there was an implicit trust in the possibility of something extraordinary happening. This echoes the significance of faith and anticipation in our personal journeys, encouraging us to believe in the potential for miracles even in seemingly ordinary moments.

Community and Togetherness:

Having the people sit down fostered a sense of community and togetherness. It created a shared experience as individuals collectively witnessed the unfolding miracle. In today's fast-paced and individualistic society, the importance of fostering genuine community bonds cannot be overstated. It reminds us of the strength found in unity and shared purpose.

Team Collaboration in a Professional Setting

In the corporate world, the concept of making people "sit down" translates to fostering team collaboration. Imagine a scenario where a leader encourages team members to gather, share ideas, and collectively strategize.

This collaborative approach often results in innovative solutions and heightened team performance. Just as the multitude witnessed a miraculous event together, a cohesive team working in harmony can achieve extraordinary results.

Family Gatherings

In the context of family gatherings, the directive to make people sit down emphasizes creating a space for shared experiences and strengthening familial bonds.

Picture a family reunion where everyone is encouraged to sit down, engage in conversations, and partake in activities together. This intentional togetherness fosters a sense of unity and contributes to the overall well-being of the family unit.

Community Events

Organizing community events with the instruction for people to sit down mirrors the importance of creating spaces for unity and collaboration. Whether it's a town hall meeting, a neighborhood initiative, or a local event, the act of gathering individuals fosters a sense of community spirit. People coming together, sharing ideas, and working towards common goals can lead to positive transformations within the community.

These examples highlight the versatility of the concept—applicable not only in spiritual contexts but also in various aspects of our daily lives. Whether in the workplace, family settings, or community initiatives, the principle of making people "sit down" underscores the power of unity, collaboration, and shared experiences in achieving remarkable outcomes.

It encourages us to recognize the strength found in collective efforts and the potential for extraordinary results when people come together with a shared purpose.

9.   GAVE THANKS

A heart of appreciation and gratitude for all the goodness showered on you. It is not by might nor by power. You need to always give thanks for all that you have enjoyed in life, what you have and even for what will be coming in future.

You also need to appreciate the people in your life for the positive contributions they make in your life. No man is an island in this world. You definitely need people to support and push you to the height you are desiring.

In the bustling city of ancient Rome, a painter and his son embarked on a monumental task – painting a colossal building that reached for the sky. The contract promised a reward of fifty thousand dollars upon completion, a tantalizing prospect that could transform their lives.

Little did they know that the true colors of their journey would be painted not on the walls but in the canvas of their relationship.

As the sun cast its golden glow on the cityscape, the painter's son, a silent hero in their duo, tirelessly held the ladder for his father. Day after day, week after week, the young boy stood firm, providing the support that allowed his father to ascend to the heights of the towering structure. Yet, the painter, consumed by greed and callousness, failed to recognize the silent symphony of his son's contribution.

The rhythm of ungratefulness played on until the final day of their monumental project. Frustrated by his father's dismissive attitude, the son decided it was time for the melody to change. With a heavy heart, he abandoned the ladder, leaving the painter to face the ascent alone.

As the painter reached the pinnacle, an abrupt and heart-wrenching note resounded. In his haste to descend, he missed a crucial step, leading to a catastrophic fall. The once vibrant hues of their shared endeavor turned into somber shades of tragedy. The fifty thousand dollar dream shattered, the building incomplete, and the contract canceled – all consequences of ungratefulness.

Let this tale be a passionate plea echoing through the corridors of life. Don't let the walls of your achievements be painted with the brush of ingratitude. Be like the brilliant sun, casting its warm rays on every contribution, no matter how small. Gratitude, like a vibrant color palette, enriches the canvas of our existence.

In your journey through the city of life, remember the tale of the ungrateful painter. Appreciate the people who stand beside you, for their contributions, no matter how seemingly insignificant, add depth and beauty to your masterpiece.

As the story unfolds, let gratitude be the melody that orchestrates your ascent, ensuring that the symphony of your life reaches the highest notes of fulfillment and shared success.

Friend, you don't want to be like this ungrateful man and ended up suffering such a demise. Be grateful for all the good things in your life. Thank God for the people who are in your life even if their contribution seem minimal in your eyes. Everybody who has made a contribution in your life needs appreciation and not dismissal.

"Your gratitude will determine your altitude"

10. HE DISTRIBUTED THEM

In life, each individual possesses a unique set of endowments. Whether it's a talent, a skill, a material possession, or the privilege of knowledge, everyone holds something valuable. The key lies not in hoarding these gifts but in sharing them generously with others for transformation.

The powerful act of distribution, as demonstrated by Jesus unveils a profound principle – the art of sharing. It was not merely about the abundance but, more importantly, about extending generosity to those in need. This lesson echoes through the corridors of time, resonating with the very essence of our humanity.

Here, the disciples played a pivotal role, embodying the spirit of collaboration and service. They actively participated in the process of distribution, ensuring that the abundance reached every hungry soul on that mountainside. Their role signifies the importance of communal effort in the act of sharing.

Imagine a world where every individual, like the master fisherman sharing his loaves and fishes, and the disciples, embraces the spirit of sharing. It goes beyond material wealth; it encompasses the sharing of ideas, experiences, and opportunities. The disciples, in their collaborative efforts, showcase the transformative power of working together for a common purpose.

Consider the impact of sharing knowledge. If you, like the disciples, hold the key to understanding a complex concept or have access to influential connections, imagine the transformative effect it could have on someone's life. The disciples' collective efforts ensured that the teachings and blessings of Jesus reached everyone present, reinforcing the idea that shared knowledge leads to shared empowerment.

The act of distribution, facilitated by the disciples, also dismantles the walls of selfishness and opens the door to collective growth. It's an acknowledgment that our individual strengths are enhanced when woven together in the fabric of shared experiences.

The disciples' role emphasizes that the joy of giving and the satisfaction of contributing to the well-being of others are shared experiences that bind us in a common purpose.

In the realm of ideas, the generosity of sharing becomes a beacon of innovation. The disciples, by actively participating in the distribution process, demonstrated that shared efforts lead to amplified impact. A single idea, when shared, can spark a chain reaction of creativity, leading to solutions for challenges that affect us all.

So, as you navigate the landscapes of your life, consider the masterful art of distribution, as exemplified by Jesus and enacted by the disciples. Be it a simple act of kindness, the sharing of your time, or the dissemination of knowledge, let your life be a testament to the profound impact of generosity.

For in sharing, with the disciples as companions in your journey, you not only enrich the lives of others but also weave a legacy that transcends the confines of individual success.

> "We make a living by what we get,
>
> but we make a life by what we give."
>
> Winston S. Churchill

11. GATHER THE FRAGMENTS THAT REMAIN

One important attitude of a successful individual is one who has learnt to save and preserve his or her inheritance. No matter how blessed you are today, if you fail to save and invest intelligently, you will soon run out of resources.

"Gather the fragments that remain" is not just a call to collect leftovers; it's a profound life lesson that transcends the immediate context of the biblical narrative. It's a call to stewardship, investment, and the relentless pursuit of knowledge and growth.

It beckons us to a deeply personal journey of stewardship, resilience, and the relentless pursuit of our own miracles. In the modern context, this principle translates into a commitment to preserving and multiplying the resources at your disposal.

Imagine your skills, knowledge, and ideas as precious fragments – they should not be wasted but carefully gathered and utilized for maximum impact. Here are more insights we can draw from the phrase above:

Preserving Your Inheritance:

Financial success and stability hinge on intelligent saving and investing. Even if you're currently blessed, without strategic planning, resources can dwindle. The lesson here is clear: save, invest, and ensure that your assets grow rather than diminish over time.

Imagine your skills, your unique gifts, and the beautiful mosaic of your ideas as fragments of a precious tapestry. These are not meant to be scattered and lost but carefully gathered, preserved, and woven into the fabric of your legacy. Much like a family heirloom, your talents deserve to be nurtured, passed down, and expanded upon for generations to come.

Consider the struggling artist who, despite facing financial challenges, decides to preserve their craft by taking small steps – creating a website, sharing on social media, and connecting with a community. Over time, this dedication transforms their passion into a sustainable livelihood.

"Your legacy is the influence you leave,

the investment you make, and the

imprint you engrave on the hearts of others."

Rob Liano

Continuous Learning:

The phrase "The more you learn, the more you lead" encapsulates the essence of continuous learning. In a rapidly evolving world, staying ahead requires a commitment to acquiring new knowledge. Invest your time in reading, researching, and staying updated on trends and advancements in your field.

In the symphony of life, the more notes you learn, the richer your melody becomes. Continuous learning is not just a pursuit of knowledge; it's a tune to personal growth and self-discovery. Your journey to leadership begins with the commitment to learn, adapt, and harmonize with the evolving rhythms of the world.

Picture a middle-aged professional, once content in their role, who decides to embrace the challenge of learning a new skill. Through online courses, networking events, and mentorship, he not only reinvigorate his career but becomes a source of inspiration for others contemplating a similar path

Financial Intelligence:

Your financial story is a narrative of choices – choices that can either diminish or multiply your resources. Seek not just monetary wealth but the wisdom to discern where to invest your time, energy, and money. Financial intelligence is the compass guiding you toward choices that resonate with your aspirations.

One major area of boom is the real estate sector which requires the relevant knowledge and skill to invest in. Meet the young entrepreneur who, armed with a small savings, delves into the world of forex and commodity trading. Through careful research, strategic investments, and learning from setbacks, they turn a modest sum into a thriving venture.

Invest wisely. Seek financial intelligence to make informed decisions about where to put your resources. There are strategic investments that can work for you even while you sleep. However, wise counsel is crucial; seek advice before making significant financial decisions.

Strategic Investments:

Expand your horizons through strategic investments in books, educational materials, seminars, workshops, and relationships. Your resources should be allocated in a way that ensures growth and value appreciation.

The fragments of your life include not just possessions but experiences, relationships, and wisdom. Invest strategically in areas that amplify your journey – books that enlighten, conferences that inspire, and relationships that nurture.

Envision an individual who, despite initial skepticism, invests in a life-changing seminar. The insights gained and the connections formed propel them forward, opening unexpected doors and transforming their trajectory. Your portfolio is not just financial; it's a composite of meaningful investments.

The Gradual Climb to Success:

Success is a series of steps, each one taking you higher. It's not an escalator but a winding staircase that demands effort, persistence, and a touch of faith. Embrace the climb, for with each step, you ascend closer to the panoramic view awaiting you at the summit.

As an aspiring writer who, amidst rejections and self-doubt, continues to write. Each word, each rejection, is a step toward the success I dream of. The climb is challenging, but the view from the top is unparalleled.

Success is rarely an overnight feat.

Climbing the ladder of success demands perseverance, determination, and a gradual ascent. Whether in faith, social life, finances, academics, or family, each step brings you closer to the pinnacle.

Optimism and Determination:

The journey might be challenging, but the key is to press on with determination. Your attitude, the can-do spirit, and the efficient use of even limited resources can bring about the miracles you desire.

The journey is not for the faint of heart. It requires optimism – a belief that your efforts matter and that each fragment you gather is a crucial piece of the mosaic. Determination fuels your climb, reminding you that the summit is not just a destination but a testament to your unwavering spirit.

Reflect on the individual who, faced with setbacks, chooses to see them as setups for future victories. Through optimism and determination, they turn challenges into stepping stones, inching closer to their dreams.

A Hand Away from Miracles:

Miracles aren't distant impossibilities; they're within reach. By wisely managing your resources, investing in personal growth, and maintaining a resilient spirit, you position yourself just a step away from the miracles awaiting you.

Dreams are not distant galaxies but collections within reach. They are born from your resilience, your choices, and your ability to see possibilities in the fragments of life.

Envision the single parent who, against all odds, manages finances, pursues education, and builds a supportive network. The miracle isn't a grand event but the accumulation of triumphs against adversity.

"Gathering the fragments" is not just a concept; it's a melody that resonates with the chords of our lives. It invites us to reflect on our journey, cherish our unique fragments, and compose a symphony that echoes with the resonance of miracles.

In practical terms, this philosophy guides individuals to make intentional choices in their finances, education, and personal development. The little resources available must be put to good use for profit and not allowed to waste away. Through determination and a can do spirit, the miracle you desire is just a hand away.

It's a call to action, urging everyone to gather the fragments, invest wisely, and persist in the climb toward their goals.

"Miracles come in moments.

Be ready and willing."

Wayne Dyer

CHAPTER TWO

MOVING STRATEGICALLY TOWARDS YOUR MIRACLE

"Who may ASCEND into the hill of the LORD?

or who may STAND in His holy place?

He who has clean hands and a pure heart,

Who has not lifted up his soul to an idol,

Nor sworn deceitfully"

Psalm 24:3-4

The greatest miracle you must desire and strife for is to ASCEND into the hill of the LORD. This is the PRESENCE OF GOD. All you need in life can be found and drawn from the Presence of God. He has all that we need and will ever want in this life, and without Him we are short-changed.

It is this that will make you different from the competition. It will set you apart in business, marriage, career, academics, ministry, politics, etc.

After all the miracles and wonders that the meekest man on earth, Moses performed he was still unsatisfied. He lacked something which silver and gold could not buy. It was something that could not be campaigned for on political platforms nor bargained for on the stock exchange.

You could not bribe for it. In fact, it is priceless! Nonetheless, it is what we need to get to the top. In my humble opinion, the miracle you are desiring is not possible without the presence of God or the backing of divinity.

"The most powerful position you can be in

is having God's presence in your life."

Germany Kent

Now the big question is, how do you ASCEND (climb up in order to possess) into the hill (miracle, victory, breakthrough, success) that you desire. How do you STAND (maintain, preserve, protect, develop and enhance) upon it?

It is not enough to reach the "hill" but one must move higher and "stand" in the "holy" place. We must ascend and stand!!

So I believe the "hill" and the "holy" place is not a physical geographical location, it is a sacred atmosphere where one carries the presence or glory of God. It is an *'engracing'* or an 'embalming' of the aura or glory of God which one carries with him or her in their daily engagements on earth.

It is a higher revelation of your identity, purpose and place in divinity which gives you authority, faith and confidence in your pursuits on earth. This mindset drives you and also attracts to you the forces of nature both the seen and unseen to effect changes. It empowers you to achieve your goals in life by drawing to your domain all the resources you need to reach the pinnacle of your goals.

'Ascending the hill' means striving to achieve all that we desire in life. This requires effort and determination. The base is full of average or below average achievements.

'Standing' here means you must maintain your successes in life. No matter how far you go or how high you climb on the mountain of life, you cannot afford to relax nor sit idle without doing what it takes to maintain (preserve, protect, promote or develop) your achievements.

To stand also means to protect and preserve your miracle before you lose it. It is a point of developing the necessary techniques and expertise to maintain or grow your resources. It is realizing our dependence on divinity for support and help in keeping what you achieve in life.

Now let us examine some steps to take in moving strategically towards the miracle you so much desire. I draw inferences from the journey between Elijah and Elisha from Gilgal to Jordan which led to a double portion of Elijah's anointing coming upon Elisha to demonstrate these strategic steps.

ELIJAH TAKEN UP TO HEAVEN (Reference: 2 Kings 2: 1-14 KJV)

1 And it came to pass, when the Lord would take up Elijah into heaven by a whirlwind, that Elijah went with Elisha from Gilgal.

2 And Elijah said unto Elisha, Tarry here, I pray thee; for the Lord hath sent me to Bethel. And Elisha said unto him, As the Lord liveth, and as thy soul liveth, I will not leave thee. So they went down to Bethel.

3 And the sons of the prophets that were at Bethel came forth to Elisha, and said unto him, Knowest thou that the Lord will take away thy master from thy head to day? And he said, Yea, I know it; hold ye your peace.

4 And Elijah said unto him, Elisha, tarry here, I pray thee; for the Lord hath sent me to Jericho. And he said, As the Lord liveth, and as thy soul liveth, I will not leave thee. So they came to Jericho.

5 And the sons of the prophets that were at Jericho came to Elisha, and said unto him, Knowest thou that the Lord will take away thy master from thy head to day? And he answered, Yea, I know it; hold ye your peace.

6 And Elijah said unto him, Tarry, I pray thee, here; for the Lord hath sent me to Jordan. And he said, As the Lord liveth, and as thy soul liveth, I will not leave thee. And they two went on.

7 And fifty men of the sons of the prophets went, and stood to view afar off: and they two stood by Jordan.

8 And Elijah took his mantle, and wrapped it together, and smote the waters, and they were divided hither and thither, so that they two went over on dry ground.

9 And it came to pass, when they were gone over, that Elijah said unto Elisha, Ask what I shall do for thee, before I be taken away from thee. And Elisha said, I pray thee, let a double portion of thy spirit be upon me.

10 And he said, Thou hast asked a hard thing: nevertheless, if thou see me when I am taken from thee, it shall be so unto thee; but if not, it shall not be so.

11 And it came to pass, as they still went on, and talked, that, behold, there appeared a chariot of fire, and horses of fire, and parted them both asunder; and Elijah went up by a whirlwind into heaven.

12 And Elisha saw it, and he cried, my father, my father, the chariot of Israel, and the horsemen thereof. And he saw him no more: and he took hold of his own clothes, and rent them in two pieces.

13 He took up also the mantle of Elijah that fell from him, and went back, and stood by the bank of Jordan;

14 And he took the mantle of Elijah that fell from him, and smote the waters, and said, where is the Lord God of Elijah? And when he also had smitten the waters, they parted hither and thither: and Elisha went over.

1. STRATEGIC ASSOCIATION

"...that Elijah WENT WITH Elisha..."

Your association will determine your destination. I believe the connection or cordial relationship which existed between the two made it possible for Elisha to come along with his master to the mount Gilgal in the first place.

As an assistant to the point man, he had related well with him and could discern that the master, Elijah was about to depart the earth. He understood his moods and moves at different points in time. By virtue of his close association, he had the rare privilege of coming along with the point man of the nation.

Imagine a college student seeking career guidance from a successful professional in their desired field. The mentorship and insights gained during this association can shape the student's future, offering a strategic advantage in their career path.

Elisha's decision to forsake his previous life and follow Elijah showcased a deep commitment to the mentor-disciple relationship. In our daily lives, the people we choose to walk with, talk to, and share experiences with can shape our perspectives, values, and ambitions

Elisha had forsaken his family, friends and profession to follow the man of God and learnt a lot from him. His line of thought and ministry patterns had been impacted due to his close association with the prophet.

Are the people around you inspiring growth and positive change, or are they hindering your progress? Just as Elisha's connection with Elijah influenced his journey, your relationships can impact your destination. Be intentional about fostering associations that contribute to your personal and professional development.

The kind of people you walk with, talk to and mingle will have a great influence on your life. If you walk with the wise you will be wise. In as much as you must help or pull those below you along, you need to be careful you are not drawn or brought down beyond expectation. You cannot associate with stagnant people and expect to climb to higher heights in life.

Strategic associations involve a mutual exchange of knowledge, experiences, and support. Elisha's journey with Elijah teaches us that the right companions can provide guidance, mentorship, and opportunities that lead to personal and professional growth.

"Coming together is a beginning,

staying together is progress,

and working together is success."

Henry Ford

2. STRATEGIC POSITIONING

"...that Elijah went with Elisha FROM GILGAL."

Your strategic position or location will determine your destination. Elisha was available and located in Gilgal at the time that Elijah was making the journey from Gilgal. Despite the picking of signals ahead and discerning the departure of his master earlier, he had to be readily available at the time the journey begun in Gilgal.

The area you find yourself will have great influence on the people you meet and the outcomes in your life. I have seen people who have lived in the ghettos and have never had the edge to move out because all that they see is the low life. While others have defied all odds and moved out to better places and make better meaning of their lives.

People who live in very civilized or affluent environments usually raise their children with that of other families of the same neighborhood. They attend special schools usually private and are given extra tuition beyond the classroom.

They are provided with all the support they need by virtue of the environment they live in. Parents and children of such communities grow up with a certain mindset that they are meant to be rich or influential in society. Chances are that, they will pass on the baton to the next generation.

Just as Elisha positioned himself in Gilgal, individuals aspiring for success must carefully select environments that foster growth. Whether it's a city with a thriving industry, an educational institution known for excellence, or a community that encourages innovation, the impact of location on one's journey cannot be underestimated.

Gilgal is a place of rolling away of reproach. Rolling away negativity and shaping mindsets.

Gilgal whispers of a mindset shift—a rolling away of negativity and the cultivation of a positive mental outlook. Beyond physical location, strategic positioning involves consciously shedding limiting beliefs and embracing a mindset aligned with one's goals.

You need to position your mental faculties on positive things. Roll away every negative thoughts and position your mind for greater works in life. It also means, you cannot just go anywhere at all as someone who is going to bring a great transformation in society.

If you want to be a very successful politician, you need to be at certain strategic places which will enhance your chances in future. You must be seen to be interacting well with people in the society if you are going to be a very likeable and victorious politician

Whatever you desire to become in future, you need to position yourself well by being at the right places where you meet the right people or receive the right information for transformation.

Elisha's journey teaches us that success is not only about the destination but the deliberate choices we make regarding where we are. Like a compass pointing north, strategic positioning aligns us with the magnetic forces that lead to positive outcomes, emphasizing the profound truth that sometimes, success begins with the simple act of being in the right place.

"Your beliefs don't make you a better person,

your behavior does."

Sukhraj S. Dhillon

3. STRATEGIC NEGOTIATIONS

...But Elisha said, "As the LORD lives ...I will not leave you!"

Your negotiations will determine your appropriation. Your ability to bargain for what you desire and crave for in life will go a long way to determine what will be served you or given back to you. Life does not give you what you deserve or wish for but, life gives you what you bargain or negotiate for. In some cases you may even have to fight for what you desire for.

People are prepared to present anything at all of less value to you so long as you do not talk about it. Circumstances and the environment which we find ourselves present issues and opportunities to you.

Some may be helpful while others may not, but the onus lies on you to decide which outcomes you want and how you are going to approach each situation. You must negotiate well in order to make good gains from the issues life offers you.

It is one thing knowing or seeing what you think may be good for you, but it's a totally different thing to take the needed steps to achieve or acquire them for your profit. Elijah, by failing to mention directly to the sons of the prophets or even his personal assistant of his final moments on earth, was expecting that they will pick the signals and take the necessary steps and actions to achieve what they desired.

Elijah gave them the opportunity to decide to be mediocre or remain as they were or to challenge themselves and bargain for something better that will transform their ministries. Some of the sons of the prophet picked the signals and knew almost every detail about the departure of Elijah but were not determined enough to do all it took to get the reward.

They could not pay the full price nor could they negotiate to go along with Elijah. They gave up without even trying to push further for what they desired in the point man.

Life's circumstances present a choice—to accept the status quo or to challenge oneself and bargain for transformation. Elisha's bold stance exemplifies the latter—an inspirational call to negotiate for a better, more transformative outcome.

Elijah's indirect cues to the sons of the prophets presented an opportunity. Life's challenges and circumstances can be viewed either as obstacles or as gateways to negotiation. Those who grasp the art of negotiation see potential where others see hindrances.

"Your life does not get better by chance,

it gets better by change."

Jim Rohn

Life, at times, demands a fight. Elisha's refusal to leave Elijah, despite discouragement, reflects the determination to fight for what one desires. Negotiations may require perseverance, resilience, and a willingness to confront challenges. In life's arena, the victory often goes to those who are willing to fight for their aspirations.

Elijah sought to discourage the young Elisha from following after him, but he did not give up. His answer to every proposal from the point man was, "... I will not leave you".

He knew exactly what he wanted and he bargained for it. When negative circumstances present themselves to you, don't accept them. Go for the best, because you deserve the best on the table of life.

In essence, the narrative of Elijah and Elisha's strategic negotiations reminds us that life's banquet offers a variety of dishes, but the ones we savor are often the result of assertive negotiations and the refusal to settle for less.

As you navigate life's marketplace, remember, it's not just about what you desire; it's about what you negotiate for.

4. STRATEGIC VISION

"And it came to pass, when they were gone over, that Elijah said unto Elisha, Ask what I shall do for thee, before I be taken away from thee. And

Elisha said, I pray thee, let a DOUBLE PORTION OF THY SPIRIT be upon me."
2 Kings 2:9

In the realm of strategic vision, the scripture from 2 Kings 2:9 serves as a beacon, illuminating the profound importance of visionary thinking and spiritual inheritance.

As Elijah prepares to depart, Elisha's request for a double portion of his spirit resonates with the essence of strategic vision — a divine yearning for a heightened awareness, purpose, and impact.

"Cherish your visions and your dreams

as they are the children of your soul,

the blueprints of your ultimate achievements."

Napoleon Hill

The Depth of the Vision:

Elisha's plea for a double portion is symbolic of a depth of vision that transcends the ordinary. It's an aspiration for spiritual insight and divine wisdom that goes beyond the surface, mirroring the desire for a strategic vision that pierces through the complexities of life. The narrative challenges you reader to seek a depth of vision that surpasses the mundane and reaches into the profound.

Spiritual Inheritance:

The exchange between Elijah and Elisha underscores the concept of spiritual inheritance. Elijah, as a mentor and guide, represents the wisdom and experiences that one generation passes on to the next.

Elisha's request for a double portion is a recognition of the transformative power embedded in spiritual legacy. This book invites you to consider your own spiritual inheritances and how they contribute to a strategic vision for the future.

The Quest for Impact:

Elisha's request is more than a personal desire; it's a quest for impact. It signifies a yearning to make a significant difference, to be a vessel of positive change in the world. The scripture prompts readers to ponder their own quests for impact — how their visions, driven by a sense of purpose, can ripple through time and generations.

Strategic Thinking:

At its core, the scripture underscores the concept of strategic thinking. Elisha's request is not a random wish but a calculated plea for a double portion — a strategic measure for enhanced spiritual insight and influence.

This mirrors the strategic thinking required in various aspects of life, encouraging you my precious reader to approach your goals, relationships, and endeavors with a thoughtful and purposeful mindset.

Leadership and Succession:

The exchange between Elijah and Elisha carries elements of leadership and succession planning. It raises questions about how leaders groom successors and how the spirit of vision and purpose is passed down. The scripture prompts readers to reflect on their roles as leaders, mentors, and successors, emphasizing the strategic nature of leadership transitions.

Elevation of Purpose:

Elisha's request for a double portion amplifies the elevation of purpose. It transcends personal ambitions and aligns with a higher calling. The scripture challenges readers to elevate their own purposes, seeking visions that are not only personally fulfilling but also contribute to the greater good. It calls for a strategic alignment of personal aspirations with a sense of divine purpose.

Jeff Bezos founded Amazon with a strategic vision to build the world's most customer-centric company. His focus on long-term growth and innovation led to the expansion of Amazon from an online bookstore to a global e-commerce giant. Bezos' vision also extended to areas like cloud computing (Amazon Web Services) and streaming services.

Greta Thunberg, a teenage climate activist, exemplifies strategic vision in addressing climate change. Her vision involves mobilizing global youth to demand urgent action on climate issues. Through initiatives like the Fridays for Future movement, Thunberg strategically amplifies the voices of young activists to influence policy and raise awareness.

These examples showcase how individuals with strategic vision can shape industries, redefine success, and create positive change on a global scale. Each leader's ability to envision a future different from the status quo propelled their respective organizations and movements toward significant accomplishments.

"You are today where your thoughts have brought you;

you will be tomorrow where your thoughts take you."

James Allen

5. STRATEGIC MISSION

"...and he said, YES I KNOW; keep silent!"

Your mission will determine your destination. You must have a clear-cut idea of what exactly you want in life and what to do to get there. Where exactly are you headed for in the short to medium term? It is popularly said that. "If you do not know where you are going, any road is right for you"

In the vast landscape of life, having a clear-cut mission is akin to possessing a detailed map guiding your journey. Elisha's resolute acknowledgment of his mission—going along to the last point of departure of his master—illustrates the importance of knowing where you are headed. Life's journey becomes purposeful when you can clearly articulate your destination.

How do you see yourself and where do you see yourself in a few years or months to come? What is your vision, mission and what steps are you taking to get there?

Goals are the small to medium term plans or targets that you set out to achieve. These help you to achieve the long-term vision or purpose in life. These shape your mission and the steps to take in accomplishing them.

Elisha knew exactly what he wanted to receive from Elijah the point man of the land. He knew exactly what to do and how long he had to endure on the journey till he accomplished his mission.

He therefore was not disheartened nor lose focus on his assignment. He wanted to see to it that he followed his master to the very final point of departure. His mission was to journey along till the end with Elijah. Thus, he was not going to be distracted nor discouraged by the negative propaganda of his peers.

"Your mission in life is not merely to survive,

but to thrive; and to do so with some passion,

some compassion, some humor, and some style."

Maya Angelou

In essence, Elisha's strategic mission serves as a compelling reminder: your life's journey gains purpose and direction when guided by a clear mission. Like Elisha, embrace the clarity of your destination, set meaningful goals, and stay resolute in the face of distractions. Your mission is not just a destination; it's a compass pointing the way to your extraordinary future.

Elon Musk, the visionary entrepreneur and CEO of Tesla and SpaceX, embodies modern strategic mission. Musk's ambitious goals extend beyond conventional expectations, encompassing sustainable energy, interplanetary colonization, and advanced transportation.

His strategic mission involves transforming industries, reducing global reliance on fossil fuels, and making humanity a multi-planetary species. Musk's ability to set audacious goals, such as creating a self-sustaining city on Mars, reflects the power of a clear and ambitious mission to drive innovation and shape the future.

Consider the life of Mahatma Gandhi, the leader of the Indian independence movement against British rule. Gandhi had a clear and compelling vision of a free and independent India.

His mission of nonviolent civil disobedience as a means to achieve this vision guided the entire nation's struggle for independence. Despite facing immense challenges and opposition, Gandhi's unwavering mission paved the way for India's eventual freedom in 1947.

6. STRATEGIC RESOLUTION/DETERMINATION

"Yes I know; KEEP SILENT"

In a world full of distractions and naysayers, maintaining focus on your vision is paramount. Elisha's resilience against negative propaganda from his peers mirrors the steadfastness required to navigate the often challenging journey towards your goals. Knowing your destination shields you from the detours of doubt and external influences.

Elisha's response, "Yes, I know; KEEP SILENT!" echoes the sentiment that a strong vision can withstand external pressures. It's a call to silence the noise of doubt and criticism, allowing your inner vision to guide you. Be resolute in your knowledge of where you are headed.

The sons of the prophet tried to discourage and dampen his spirit but Elisha was too much for them. He was resolute to receive something extraordinary from his mentor.

On the occasion when his mentor, teacher, provider, counsellor, commander, shepherd, comforter, friend, father and leader was leaving the earth forever, he needed to do something that will enable him tap into or inherit something that will keep him going for the rest of his life.

Detractors may attempt to hinder your progress—mocking your aspirations, pretending loyalty while engaging in gossip, or underestimating your capabilities.

However, your resilience and unwavering determination serve as a shield against the disparaging remarks and skepticism.

"When everything seems to be going against you,

remember that the airplane takes off

against the wind, not with it."

Henry Ford

In times of adversity, turn a deaf ear to the laughter and ridicule, and let determination drown out the naysayers. The path to success demands a resolute spirit, capable of weathering storms, dismissing discouragement, and persisting even when others attempt to undermine your journey.

Walt Disney, the legendary animator and entertainment entrepreneur, encountered numerous failures and rejections in his early career. He faced bankruptcy, criticism, and setbacks in the animation industry.

Despite the challenges, Disney's hunger for success, coupled with a clear vision of creating a magical world of entertainment, drove him to establish one of the most iconic and influential entertainment companies globally.

Remember, the journey to success is not a smooth one, but with your hunger for achievement and a steadfast focus, you can silence the doubts and criticisms, emerging stronger and closer to your goals.

7. STRATEGIC UNCTION

"...he took the mantle of Elijah that had fallen off him, struck the waters and said, "Where is *Adonai, the God of Elijah*?" As he indeed struck the waters, they parted here then there. Then Elisha crossed over." 2 Kings 2:14

"Your unction will make a way for your function"

When all is set and done, you will still face higher oppositions and challenges beyond human abilities and will need something more than the classroom or money can afford. Some problems in life defy medical solutions and science. Some go beyond lecturers, professors, politicians and human experts.

While some problems are physical and require physical solutions, others are spiritual and require divine solutions. Some 'mountains' don't respond to our intellectual abilities and will need divinity to intervene. Without God and the power of the Holy Spirit, certain problems cannot be overcome or surmounted.

It doesn't diminish the value of human knowledge but highlights that there are dimensions of life and challenges that can only be addressed through a connection with the divine.

The bible says, we wrestle not against flesh and blood but against principalities, powers and wicked forces in the heavenly realms. These seek to hinder us from reaching our targets in life and as much we need special grace, glory and unction of God to confront them head-on.

"I can do all things through Christ who strengthens me."

Philippians 4:13 (Bible)

Consider an individual struggling with addiction, going through numerous rehabilitation programs without sustained success. Strategic unction in this context might involve a spiritual awakening, a connection with a higher power, leading to a transformative change.

The person experiences a divine intervention that breaks the chains of addiction, providing a solution beyond conventional approaches.

In the narrative of Elijah passing his mantle to Elisha, we witness a transfer of spiritual authority and power. The mantle symbolizes more than just a physical garment; it carries the anointing and divine authority that Elijah possessed. When Elisha takes up the mantle, he is not merely inheriting a piece of cloth; he is stepping into a realm of spiritual empowerment.

Believe that you are more than a conqueror and that divinity resides in you. You have the power of God at work in and through you to overcome all challenges if you do not give up.

Call on the name of the Lord in times of difficulties and He will answer you. Move forward in faith and watch the impossibilities becoming possible before you by the power of divinity inside you.

"Your unction will make you function"

Imagine a person facing a severe and incurable medical condition despite the best efforts of medical science. In this scenario, strategic unction could manifest as a deep reliance on prayer, faith, and spiritual healing.

Miraculous recoveries or unexplained remissions may occur, transcending the limitations of scientific understanding.

Picture someone facing repeated setbacks and challenges in their career despite their qualifications and efforts. Strategic unction in this instance could involve seeking divine guidance, perhaps through prayer or meditation.

The person, infused with spiritual insight, makes strategic decisions guided by a higher purpose. This leads to unexpected opportunities, breakthroughs, and career advancements that surpass human expectations.

"There is no problem outside of you that

is superior to the power within you."

Bob Proctor

8. STRATEGIC CONDITION

"And he said, Thou hast asked a hard thing: nevertheless, IF THOU SEE ME WHEN I AM TAKEN from thee, it shall be so unto thee; but if not, it shall not be so." 2 Kings 2:10

Every major blessing and breakthrough has a price tag or condition attached to it. Once the condition is met or price is paid, you enjoy the blessing. Abraham had to sacrifice his son in the heart, Samson had to avoid razor on his hair and alcohol, Elisha had to SEE...TAKEN AWAY!

Conditions are not arbitrary; they are strategic elements that filter those truly committed from the casually interested. In Elisha's case, the condition was not arbitrary but central to the process. It demanded his unwavering attention and perseverance.

Elisha's ability to "SEE" the moment of Elijah's departure was a critical aspect of the condition. It signified attentiveness, focus, and a steadfast commitment to the process. Meeting the condition required more than physical sight; it demanded spiritual perception and understanding.

The condition set by Elijah was a prerequisite for the inheritance of the double portion. It wasn't a mere formality; it was a defining moment in Elisha's life. Meeting this condition was the key to unlocking a new level of power and authority.

This was the most important condition he had to fulfill before inheriting the double portion of his master's powers. Though all his efforts from the beginning of the journey were good and well recognized, had he failed to see the taking away of his master he would have lost the blessing, if he had given up at the last end, he would have lost the blessing. It was a condition that was clearly given by his master and he had to meet it before inheriting his power.

In contemporary life, this biblical lesson remains relevant. Goals, aspirations, and ambitions come with conditions. Whether in education, career, or personal growth, individuals must recognize and fulfill the conditions attached to their desired outcomes.

Elisha's persistence in the face of challenges symbolizes the resilience required to overcome obstacles on the path to achieving one's goals. Conditions are often accompanied by difficulties, and success demands an unwavering spirit.

The concept of strategic conditions extends beyond biblical narratives. It underscores the importance of careful decision-making, understanding the terms and requirements before embarking on a journey or pursuit.

Thomas Edison, one of history's greatest inventors, sought to illuminate the world with his invention of the electric light bulb. The strategic condition attached to this monumental achievement was unwavering persistence.

Edison faced countless failures and setbacks in his quest, but he set a condition for himself—to keep trying until he succeeded. His famous quote, "I have not failed. I've just found 10,000 ways that won't work," reflects his commitment to meeting the condition of persistence. In the end, his dogged determination led to the successful invention of the electric light bulb, transforming the world.

In essence, the story of Elisha teaches that blessings are not haphazardly distributed; they follow a strategic pattern. Recognizing, accepting, and meeting the conditions attached to our goals can be the decisive factor in the realization of our deepest desires.

It prompts individuals to approach their pursuits with a strategic mindset, understanding that every condition met brings them a step closer to their desired blessings.

"The price of success is hard work,

dedication to the job at hand,

and the determination that whether we win or lose,

we have applied the best of ourselves to the task at hand."

Vince Lombardi

9. STRATEGIC ACTION

"And Elisha saw it, and he cried, My father, my father, the chariot of Israel, and the horsemen thereof. And he saw him no more: AND HE TOOK HOLD OF HIS OWN CLOTHES, AND RENT THEM IN TWO PIECES." 2 Kings 2:14

There are many things you do every day but there are some things you don't do often. Some actions are considered crucial if you are really going to make a difference in life. While all actions are important and the processes to success are vital, certain strategic actions are crucial to your next level.

"Your action will determine your destination"

The things you do and say at a particular point in time will go a long way to affect the next stage of your life. Some people make strategic decisions and act in an extraordinary way and this shoots them into the limelight of our society.

Though others can do similar deeds, the great feat achieved by some people are remarkable and worthy of recognition by society. That is why there are all kinds of award schemes:- Noble Prizes, Guinness Book Of Records (GBR), Grammy Awards, American Idol, British Got Talent, Miss Universe, Tourism Ambassadors, Brand Awards, etc.

Your present state, is as a result of the past actions taken or not taken. What you said or did not say at a point in time has a bearing on your outcomes today. When pushed to the wall in life, what do you do or say to yourself or environment?

When opportunities come your way, what actions do your take? As long as you live on earth, you will have different opportunities to make great impact or change the course of your life at a point in time and there will be the need for the requisite actions to be taken.

"The best way to predict the future is to create it."

Peter Drucker

At the crucial moment when Elijah was whisked into the skies, Elisha had to do the unexpected. He shouted and tore his garment while keeping his eyes focused on his mentor levitating into the clouds. These actions were a fulfillment of the requirement to him receiving the double portion of the anointing or mantle upon his master.

Despite the fact that he knew exactly what he wanted from his mentor, if he had not followed relentlessly from Gilgal to Bethel, then to Jericho and from Jericho to Jordan, he would have missed his desire for a major transformation. The steps he took brought him ultimately to the point where Elijah gave him the secret to receiving a double portion of his mantle.

Furthermore, the fact that he had followed throughout the journey from Gilgal to Jordan was commendable but his cry aloud and constant gazing at his master while he was whisked into the atmosphere was the final action required to harness the master's mantle and power!

If you don't take the right decisions and actions to change your life, you may never be able to make any meaningful impact in life. Its fine to be ordinary in society but it takes extraordinary action to standout and make a mark.

"Your visions and unction without the

needed action will remain an illusion"

Asare Richmond

Actions make dreams a reality. When the going becomes tough and your desires seem to be delaying, you need to take the right actions to restore any lost times or opportunities till your desires come to pass.

When Elisha saw that his desire was almost whittling away at the sight of his master ascending into the skies, he shouted and rent his clothes.

So what do you do when all odds are against you in life? When life is beating you to it, what strategic actions do you take? Sometimes it requires that you do something beyond human comprehension if you are going to break forth into greatness.

"Actions bring visions to fruition"

Nelson Mandela's fight against apartheid in South Africa involved both resilience and strategic action. His decision to embrace reconciliation rather than revenge after his release from prison demonstrated a deliberate choice for national unity.

Mandela's strategic actions contributed to dismantling institutionalized racism and establishing a democratic South Africa.

Winston Churchill's strategic leadership during World War II included key actions such as his speeches that inspired the British people and strengthened international alliances. His decision-making during critical moments, like the Battle of Britain, showcased strategic thinking that played a pivotal role in the Allied victory.

Malala Yousafzai, an advocate for girls' education, demonstrated strategic action in the face of adversity. Surviving a Taliban assassination attempt, Malala continued her advocacy globally. Her actions, including speaking at the United Nations and co-authoring the memoir "I Am Malala," strategically amplified the importance of education for all.

Ordinary actions may maintain the status quo, but extraordinary actions become catalysts for change. Making a mark in society often requires going beyond the ordinary. Strategic action is the force that turns visions and unction into tangible reality, transforming dreams into achievements.

In essence, strategic action is the force that turns aspirations into accomplishments, pushing individuals to overcome challenges, seize opportunities, and make a lasting impact on their journey through life.

"The way to get started is to quit talking and begin doing."

Walt Disney

CHAPTER THREE

MEETING MIRACLE MONSTERS

"Every breakthrough encounters challenges and obstacles.

Every miracle has monsters!"

Asare Richmond

Every crown has a 'cross' attached. Behind every victory there is a story. Before every fame there is shame. Before you get there you must start from somewhere. Every King started as a kid. If you want to be great you must be ready to fight the monsters.

These come at different stages of the journey, from the beginning, along the line or just when you are about to hit the climax. There are even monsters after you have achieved your miracle. Every aspect of your life can be a target of attack by monsters as such you must be ready to deal with them.

Selena Gomez has been open about her struggles with mental health, which she attributes in part to the pressures of living in the spotlight, amplified by social media.

In numerous interviews, Selena Gomez has spoken about the impact of constant scrutiny and comparison on her well-being. The digital realm, with its unrealistic beauty standards and constant connectivity, created a challenging environment for her to navigate.

The pressure to conform to societal expectations and the fear of judgment from online interactions became formidable monsters in her personal journey.

Despite these challenges, Selena Gomez has used her platform to advocate for mental health awareness. By sharing her own experiences, she encourages others to confront similar monsters in their lives. Her story exemplifies the resilience needed to face modern challenges, particularly those intensified by the digital age and the constant gaze of social media.

"Monsters are real, and ghosts are real too.

They live inside us, and sometimes, they win."

Stephen King

In the grand tapestry of dreams and aspirations, where every step toward greatness is a brushstroke of determination, lie the shadows of monsters—formidable adversaries that test the mettle of the dreamer.

Embedded within the very fabric of extraordinary feats are the challenges that dance like shadows on the periphery of triumph. It's a journey where every crown earned is weighed down by the cross of trials, where victories are etched with stories of shame, and where the path to greatness starts from the humble ground of beginnings.

To be great is to engage in an epic battle against monsters that emerge at every twist and turn of the journey. These adversaries, like silent sentinels, appear at the inception, along the winding road, and sometimes just when the crescendo of success echoes in the distance. Astonishingly, even after miracles are achieved, monsters linger, threatening every facet of life.

Winston Churchill, who, after leading Britain through the tumultuous years of World War II, faced political challenges and criticism even in the aftermath of victory. Just as Elijah's triumph on Mount Carmel was met with a daunting threat from Jezebel, Churchill, having guided his nation through the darkness of war, found himself confronting the monsters of post-war reconstruction and shifting political landscapes.

"Then Jezebel SENT A MESSENGER unto Elijah,

SAYING, so let the GODS DO TO ME,

and more also, if I make not THY LIFE AS THE LIFE OF ONE of them

By TOMORROW ABOUT THIS TIME.

And when he SAW that, HE AROSE, AND WENT FOR HIS LIFE,

and CAME TO BEERSHEBA, which belongeth to JUDAH,

and LEFT HIS SERVANT there."

1 Kings 19: 2-3

After Elijah's extraordinary feat on Mount Carmel, where he called fire from above to consume his sacrifice, he faced a mighty monster named Jezebel. This biblical narrative encapsulates the essence of encountering monsters after performing a great miracle, a theme that resonates with our contemporary struggles.

As we draw inspiration from the timeless story of Elijah facing the menace of Jezebel, let's uncover the parallels between ancient struggles and the challenges we encounter today. Join me in decoding the tactics employed in this narrative.

By understanding how Elijah navigated this perilous situation, we empower ourselves to decipher and thwart similar attempts, safeguarding our miracles in the process. This narrative serves as a powerful reminder that in facing contemporary challenges, the wisdom gained from the past can illuminate the path to resilience and triumph

JEZ'S MENACING MESSAGE: A TALE OF THREATS AND FLIGHT

1. *"Then Jezebel SENT A MESSENGER unto Elijah,...*

The encounter between Elijah and Jezebel unfolds as a tale woven with threads of fear and cunning communication. The particular moment encapsulated in the phrase "Then Jezebel SENT A MESSENGER unto Elijah" serves as a poignant entry point into the strategic and calculated nature of Jezebel's threat.

Jezebel, a model of assertiveness and cunning, strategically opts for a MESSENGER to deliver her ominous message to Elijah. This choice is anything but arbitrary; it is a calculated act, a deliberate infliction of psychological torment. In a time when subtlety might have softened the blow, Jezebel opts for a method that amplifies the cruelty of her threat.

The message isn't merely a proclamation; it's a malevolent memo sent with the precision of an archer's arrow, aimed at the heart of Elijah's courage.

This act of sending a messenger underscores Jezebel's desire to instill fear in Elijah, to cast a looming shadow over his sense of security and peace of mind. In choosing a messenger, she adds a layer of ominous theatricality to her threat, heightening the emotional impact on Elijah. The messenger becomes the harbinger of impending doom, a dark herald bearing tidings of a fate crafted by Jezebel's disdain.

"The thing about fear is that it only works if you let it."

Maureen Johnson

In the modern context, the echoes of Jezebel's cunning communication reverberate through the myriad CHANNELS of our interconnected world. Threats, challenges, and messages of malevolence are not confined to ancient scrolls but manifest through letters, phone calls, and the digital corridors of our time.

A menacing email, a sinister text, or a chilling voicemail can be the modern equivalents of Jezebel's MESSENGER, delivering psychological blows with calculated precision.

Just as Jezebel's messenger served as a conduit for her calculated cruelty, modern mediums become the conduits for individuals to communicate their intentions, be they benevolent or malevolent.

An example that involves threats or intimidation through communication is the case of Kenyan journalist and human rights defender John Githongo. Githongo played a key role in exposing corruption within the Kenyan government.

As the Permanent Secretary for Ethics and Governance in Kenya, Githongo uncovered widespread corruption involving high-ranking officials, including the Anglo-Leasing scandal. Faced with the magnitude of the corruption he had unveiled, Githongo became a whistleblower, exposing the corrupt practices and the involvement of powerful individuals.

In response to his revelations, Githongo received threats and intimidation. While there might not be a single specific letter of threat, the intimidation tactics included veiled warnings and pressure to cease his anti-corruption efforts. Githongo, however, chose to go public with the information, facing personal risk for the sake of transparency and accountability.

This reflects the challenges faced by individuals who expose corruption and misconduct, with threats and intimidation employed as tools to deter them from continuing their efforts. It showcases the complexities and dangers associated with speaking out against powerful figures, even in the pursuit of justice and transparency.

"Challenges are what make life interesting.

Overcoming them is what makes life meaningful."

Joshua J. Marine

In 2008, Jestina Mukoko the Zimbabwean human rights activist was abducted from her home by state security agents. During her abduction, she was held incommunicado and faced physical and psychological abuse.

Following her release, Mukoko revealed that she had been threatened and intimidated during her captivity. While the threats may not have been conveyed through a traditional letter, the use of intimidation tactics aimed at silencing her activism is a stark parallel to the theme we've been discussing.

Jestina Mukoko's experience highlights the challenges faced by activists who speak out against perceived injustices. Intimidation, lies, threats, and physical harm are employed as methods to suppress opposition and discourage individuals from advocating for human rights and political reform.

"Never be afraid to raise your voice
for honesty and truth and compassion;

against injustice and lying and greed.

If people all over the world would do this,

it would change the earth." –

William Faulkner

In a world where communication shapes our perceptions and influences our emotional landscapes, the art of threat transcends the ages, finding new forms of expression in the evolving tapestry of human interaction.

Just as Jezebel's messenger served as a conduit for her calculated intent, modern messengers become vehicles for individuals to communicate their intentions, whether benevolent or malevolent.

In a world where communication shapes our perceptions and influences our emotional landscapes, the strategic use of a messenger transcends ages, finding new forms of expression in the evolving tapestry of human interaction.

As we navigate the complexities of communication in our contemporary lives, the ancient tale of Jezebel's messenger prompts us to scrutinize the nuances of human interaction.

It encourages us to discern the motives behind the messages we receive, especially when delivered through messengers, and to recognize that, across ages, the art of threat persists as a dark undercurrent in the human narrative.

2.   ...SAYING, so let the GODS DO TO ME..."

Queen Jezebel utters the chilling words, "...SAYING, so let the GODS DO TO ME..."

This emphasizes the invocation of the divine, as Jezebel swears by higher powers to underpin the severity of her curse upon Elijah. This act, embedded with spiritual weight, mirrors the timeless human tendency to amplify declarations through the invocation of higher authorities.

Jezebel's choice to swear by the gods isn't a mere linguistic flourish; it is a deliberate strategy to lend an air of solemnity and irrevocability to her threat. This serves as pillars supporting the gravity of her words, elevating them to the realm of irreversible decrees.

Her choice to swear by the gods transcends the mere use of strong language; it delves into the realm of the sacred, infusing her words with cosmic significance. This ancient practice aligns with the modern inclination to invoke deeply held beliefs, moral principles, or spiritual tenets in moments of intense expression.

In both contexts, the act of swearing by the divine becomes a potent rhetorical device, elevating the spoken words to a level beyond the ordinary.

Consider the modern executive issuing a stern directive in a corporate setting. In a boardroom, the gravitas of a decision might be intensified with phrases like "I swear by the company's mission" or "May our business suffer if this fails." The parallel lies not in the divine, but in the shared human instinct to infuse declarations with a sense of authority that transcends the individual.

In legal spheres, the use of strong language invoking justice or constitutional principles serves as a modern echo of Jezebel's oath. Lawyers may declare, "As the law is my witness" or "May justice prevail." The use of these concepts mirrors the ancient technique of emphasizing through uppercase letters, adding weight to their legal pronouncements.

Even in everyday conversations, people leverage strong language and invoke overarching principles to emphasize their resolve. Statements like "I swear on my family's name" or "May karma come back to me" carry echoes of Jezebel's oath, as individuals draw on higher ideals to accentuate their commitment or threat.

The ancient art of invoking the divine to lend weight to declarations transcends time and cultural boundaries. Whether in the biblical narrative of Elijah and Jezebel or in the intricacies of modern discourse, the act of infusing words with divine authority remains a potent means of conveying unwavering determination and consequence.

In deciphering these linguistic nuances, we glimpse the threads that weave the ancient and the contemporary into a shared tapestry of human expression.

"Silence becomes cowardice when

occasion demands speaking out

the whole truth and acting accordingly."

Mahatma Gandhi

One historical example of an individual invoking the divine in a significant and impactful manner is Mahatma Gandhi. Gandhi, a leader of the Indian independence movement against British colonial rule, was known for his commitment to nonviolent resistance and his emphasis on moral and spiritual principles.

In August 1942, during World War II, Gandhi initiated the "Quit India" movement, calling for the immediate end of British rule in India. In a speech delivered on August 8, 1942, Gandhi used powerful language infused with moral and spiritual conviction, invoking the divine to emphasize the righteousness of the cause. While not a curse, his words carried immense weight as he said:

"I wish to reaffirm the truth that I have been preaching to the world. I want to save time and paper. I merely want to give you a mantra to repeat. That mantra is: 'Do or Die.' We shall either free India or die in the attempt; we shall not live to see the perpetuation of our slavery."

Gandhi's invocation of the phrase "Do or Die" was not merely a call to action; it was a spiritual commitment, a moral imperative rooted in the profound belief that the cause of India's independence was just and worthy. The use of such language, coupled with the invocation of the idea of sacrifice and divine principles, resonated deeply with his followers and had a profound impact on the movement.

While Gandhi's approach was nonviolent and rooted in spiritual principles, his use of language and the invocation of higher ideals to underscore the gravity of the cause shares a thematic similarity with Jezebel's invocation of the divine in the biblical narrative. Both instances reflect the profound influence that the sacred can have in inspiring and rallying people around a cause.

The famous Russian writer Fyodor Dostoevsky, known for his profound exploration of existential and moral themes in his works, faced a critical moment in his life where he invoked the divine in a profound way.

In 1849, Dostoevsky was arrested for his involvement in a literary group that discussed banned books and ideas critical of the government. He, along with other members of the *Petrashevsky Circle*, was sentenced to death by firing squad. The night before the execution, Dostoevsky and the others were led to the scaffold, where they awaited their fate.

In a dramatic turn of events, the firing squad was halted, and their sentences were commuted to hard labor in Siberia. Dostoevsky, already grappling with the prospect of imminent death, described this moment as a profound turning point in his life.

He later wrote about the experience, stating that it was at that moment, facing the certainty of death, that he truly embraced his faith and turned to God. The sense of divine intervention in sparing his life became a transformative experience for Dostoevsky.

This historical example aligns with the theme of invoking the divine in critical moments. While it doesn't involve a curse or threat, it illustrates how individuals, even in the face of dire circumstances, may turn to the divine to emphasize the gravity of their intent or to seek meaning and purpose in profound moments of crisis.

Dostoevsky's experience adds a layer of complexity to the intertwining of human fate with spiritual convictions, echoing the timeless practice of invoking the sacred in moments of profound significance.

Jezebel's curse was a direct threat to Elijah's life, framed within the context of divine retribution. By invoking the gods and swearing by them, she positioned herself as the channel through which divine punishment would be meted out. This not only posed a physical threat but also carried a profound psychological weight.

Beyond the immediate physical threat, Jezebel's curse likely took a toll on Elijah's spiritual and emotional well-being. The idea of divine retribution would have carried significant weight for a prophet like Elijah, who had experienced powerful manifestations of God's presence. The sudden shift from triumph to the threat of divine punishment would have been emotionally jarring.

In such moments of profound vulnerability, Elijah's journey invites us to reflect on the resilience required in navigating the complexities of faith and the human experience, even amidst the shadows of doubt and fear.

3. … if I make not THY LIFE AS THE LIFE OF ONE of them

Imagine Elijah, who once stood tall on Mount Carmel, now confronted with the idea that his own life might become a mirror image of those he judged. The threat isn't just about harm; it's a chilling mental image, a way of saying, "You might become what you fought against."

It isn't a mere vow of vengeance; it's a calculated taunt, meticulously crafted to pierce Elijah's conscience, invoking the specter of those prophets of Baal he had executed with righteous fervor. It's a mind game, and Jezebel plays it masterfully.

"Every man's memory is his private literature."

Aldous Huxley

Imagine the emotional storm inside Elijah. He had wrestled with prophets of Baal, but now he grapples with fear and guilt. It's a gut-wrenching feeling, the realization that the tables have turned, and the hunter might become the hunted. The threat isn't just on his life; it's on his very sense of self, his identity shaken to the core.

This isn't just a threat on paper. Elijah feels it deep in his bones, so much so that he doesn't stick around. The fear pushes him to run, to escape the shadows of what Jezebel's words paint for him. It's not just about physical escape; it's about running from the haunting specter of a fate he once dealt to others.

Embedded within Jezebel's words is a pictorial threat, a cruel reminder to Elijah of the lives he extinguished on Mount Carmel. The taunt lies not just in the promise of harm but in the vivid imagery of Elijah's life being made akin to those he had dispatched. It's a psychological warfare, a calculated effort to etch in his mind the haunting image of his fate mirroring that of his adversaries.

Think about history– leaders, judges, those who dished out judgments. There's a haunting theme where they, at some point, faced the specter of their own decisions. It's like a script flipping, and they become characters in their own moral drama. Elijah, in Jezebel's threat, steps into that storyline.

During the oppressive regime of Nicolae Ceaușescu in Romania, dissent was met with brutal force. Fast forward to the Romanian Revolution of 1989, and Ceaușescu himself faced the wrath of the people. The leader who silenced opposition with an iron fist found himself tried and executed by the very populace he had suppressed, providing a stark example of the tables turning on a once-mighty ruler.

In our world, where judgments can be swift and public, the threat Jezebel throws at Elijah has echoes. It's like a social media storm turning against the one who once held the gavel. The emotional punch goes beyond the screen, hitting where it hurts the most – the heart and the soul.

In the realm of modern Russia, Alexei Navalny, a vocal critic of the Kremlin, faced numerous arrests and accusations. However, the script took a turn when Navalny's alleged poisoning became an international incident, drawing attention to the methods used against him. The critic, once silenced, turned the spotlight on those who sought to silence him.

In the corporate world, leaders who wielded immense power have faced public reckonings. Executives who were once at the pinnacle of success found themselves ousted from their positions due to revelations of misconduct, financial impropriety, or ethical lapses.

The same mechanisms that facilitated their rise became the instruments of their fall, echoing the theme of facing consequences in a different guise.

These real-life examples illustrate the global resonance of a theme where the architects of judgment find themselves entangled in the web of their own decisions.

Whether in political arenas, revolutions, or corporate boardrooms, the echoes of Jezebel's taunt reverberate across different parts of the world, reminding us of the complex dance between power, consequences, and the twists of fate.

"Memory is the diary that we all carry about with us."

Oscar Wilde

In the complex tapestry of our lives, family challenges can cast long shadows, creating a haunting picture when we find ourselves facing similar struggles. It's not just a matter of shared circumstances; it's an emotional journey through the echoes of our past, a story that unfolds when the challenges we encounter mirror those of our family and loved ones.

Imagine growing up in a family that faced financial hardships. The echoes of budget constraints, the stress of making ends meet – these become vivid memories in the canvas of your childhood.

When, later in life, you encounter your own financial challenges, it's not just a matter of balancing the books; it's an intuitive connection to the past. The shadows of your family's financial struggles paint a backdrop to your own financial narrative, influencing your decisions and emotional responses.

Picture a family where relationships were marked by turbulence. The echoes of arguments, silent struggles, or broken bonds leave imprints on your understanding of love and connection. When your own relationships face storms, the shadows of your family's relational challenges loom large.

It's not merely a matter of weathering the present storm; it's an emotional journey through the echoes of generational dynamics, forcing you to grapple with patterns that might have originated long before your time.

Furthermore, consider a family where mental health challenges were veiled in silence or misunderstood. The shadows of unspoken pain, the weight of stigma – these become part of your emotional DNA.

When you confront your own mental health battles, it's not just a personal struggle; it's an intimate dance with the shadows of your family's unaddressed pain. The echoes of generational mental health challenges paint a complex background to your own journey toward healing.

95

"Memory is the treasure house

of the mind wherein the monuments

thereof are kept and preserved."

Thomas Fuller

Envision another family where educational opportunities were limited. The echoes of missed chances, the pursuit of knowledge against odds – these form the backdrop of your upbringing.

When you face educational challenges, it's not just about grades or degrees; it's a narrative entwined with the shadows of your family's educational journey. The echoes of perseverance and hurdles become part of your own academic story.

When the shadows of hospital visits and resilience in the face of illness compose the emotional landscape of your early years. As soon as health challenges knock at your door, it's not just about medical treatments; it's a journey through the echoes of your family's health struggles. The shadows of strength and vulnerability paint a nuanced backdrop to your own health narrative.

In facing challenges reminiscent of our family's past, we become characters in a story that spans generations. The shadows cast by our family's triumphs and tribulations not only shape our responses but also add layers of depth to our own narratives.

It's a delicate dance with the echoes of our past, a journey where the challenges we encounter serve as emotional bridges connecting us to the stories etched in the very fabric of our familial history.

In the twisted dance of words, Jezebel's threat isn't just a threat; it's a psychological punch that makes Elijah feel the weight of his own past. It's emotional, it's raw, and it sends shivers down the spine.

"Every man's memory is his private literature."

Aldous Huxley

4.   ...By TOMORROW ABOUT THIS TIME.

The heartbeat of time, encapsulated in four words, "By TOMORROW ABOUT THIS TIME," reverberates through the narrative, setting the stage for a symphony of urgency. Like the insistent beat of a drum, these words propel us into a realm where time transforms from a passive observer into an active force, shaping destinies and dictating the cadence of fate.

The world held its breath during the Cuban Missile Crisis when the United States and the Soviet Union stood on the brink of nuclear war. The intense negotiations and back-and-forth communications between leaders were marked by a palpable urgency. The phrase "within the next 24 hours" became a chilling reminder of the imminent danger, forcing leaders to act swiftly to avert catastrophe.

Jezebel's ominous proclamation to Elijah injects the storyline with a palpable tension, creating a suspenseful pause that holds the audience in breathless anticipation. The stakes rise, and the emotional tempo accelerates as the impending deadline looms large, casting shadows over the protagonist's path.

The urgency encapsulated in these four words is more than a mere ticking clock; it is a relentless drumbeat that underscores the gravity of the situation. Each syllable echoes with the weight of consequences, pushing Elijah to confront not only the external threat but also the inevitable passage of time itself.

During the tragic events of September 11, 2001, emergency responders faced an urgent and unprecedented situation. The ticking clock represented the race to save lives and minimize further destruction. First responders, firefighters, and medical personnel worked tirelessly in an environment where every passing minute was critical.

97

As the arbiter of fate, time becomes an adversary that Elijah must contend with. The narrative unfolds within the tight confines of a ticking clock, heightening the drama and adding a layer of complexity to the protagonist's journey. Every moment becomes charged with significance, and the urgency becomes a driving force, urging Elijah to navigate the impending storm with swiftness and determination.

"By TOMORROW ABOUT THIS TIME" is not merely a deadline; it's a photographic frame where the narrative's climax converges with the relentless march of the clock. The urgency injected into these words serves as a catalyst, transforming a mere threat into a race against time, adding a layer of emotional complexity to Elijah's predicament.

The phrase conjures images of a ticking clock, each second resonating with the weight of impending doom. It's a cinematic close-up on Elijah, his every heartbeat synchronized with the countdown echoing in his ears. The urgency becomes a character in itself, pressing against Elijah's shoulders and guiding his every move.

"Time is the scarcest resource and unless it is managed,

nothing else can be managed."

Peter Drucker

In healthcare, the ticking clock is a constant presence. Emergency rooms, trauma units, and ambulances operate under intense time pressure to provide timely care. For example, the "golden hour" is crucial in trauma cases, emphasizing the importance of swift medical intervention to improve outcomes.

The concept of the "golden hour" is a stark illustration of time as a critical factor. The first 60 minutes after a traumatic injury often determine the chances of survival and recovery. Emergency responders and medical professionals operate under immense time pressure, highlighting the decisive role time plays in life-or-death situations.

When individuals go missing in remote or perilous environments, search and rescue teams operate under tight time constraints. The longer the search takes, the higher the risks for those in distress. The ticking clock in such situations underscores the need for efficient coordination and rapid response.

Moreover, "By TOMORROW ABOUT THIS TIME" is a psychological device that not only accelerates the pacing of the narrative but also deepens the emotional impact. It confronts Elijah not just with the threat of harm but with the limited nature of time itself.

The looming deadline forces him to grapple not only with the external danger posed by Jezebel but with the internal struggle against the ruthless march of time.

In the grand theater of storytelling, "By TOMORROW ABOUT THIS TIME" becomes a narrative pivot, a turning point where the tension is tuned to its highest frequency. It's a reminder that, in the world of words and emotions, time is not just a passive observer but an active participant, shaping destinies and intensifying the emotional crescendo of the story.

"Time is really the only capital that any human being has,

and the only thing he can't afford to lose."

Thomas Edison

5.   ... And when he SAW THAT...

There are monsters who will only surface when you are just about to grab your miracle. Others appear after you have successfully grabbed your miracle. What you SEE and how you SEE it determines the effect it will have on you. This will also inform you on how to handle and react to the situation.

In the complex dance between destiny and perception, the phrase "... And when he SAW THAT..." serves as a poignant reminder of the pivotal role our perception plays in navigating the web of life. It unveils a profound truth: monsters, symbolic of challenges and adversities, often reveal themselves at the most critical junctures of our journey.

The monsters Elijah faced were not merely physical adversaries but embodied the trials that emerge precisely when one is on the verge of a breakthrough. The message sent by the messenger carried a weight that transcended its words; it had the power to unsettle Elijah's resolve and cast shadows on the miracle he had just witnessed.

Elijah's reaction to what he SAW is a testament to the delicate balance between faith and perception. The text suggests that he allowed the message to penetrate his core, to the extent that it moved him and cast doubt on what he knew from the Lord. His perception, influenced by external negativity, momentarily overshadowed the divine assurance he had received.

"Change the way you look at things,

and the things you look at will change."

Wayne Dyer

When the prophet Elijah SAW the message from the messenger, it sent shivers down his spine. He paid attention to it, he accepted it, and he was moved. It also means that, he literally believed the bad new or message that was sent to him.

In your quest to greatness, refuse to SEE or pay ATTENTION to the message of the monsters on your way. Sometimes you need to close your eyes to the negative things around you. Refuse to accept the negative thing around you.

The lesson embedded in this narrative extends beyond Elijah's story. It delves into the universal truth that what we perceive, how we see the challenges around us, significantly influences our reactions and decisions.

The monsters that surface on our journey may aim to distract, instill fear, or cast doubt on our capabilities.

"What you refuse to see,

will reduce in the sea of life"

Asare Richmond

It advocates for a selective focus, a deliberate choice to close our eyes to the pessimistic messages that may surround us. In doing so, we safeguard the purity of our vision, preventing external influences from clouding our faith and determination.

The metaphorical quote, "What you REFUSE TO SEE, will REDUCE in the SEA of life," encapsulates the transformative potential of our selective vision. By refusing to acknowledge and internalize the negative, we diminish its impact, allowing positivity and faith to prevail in the vast sea of life's challenges.

Elijah's moment of vulnerability teaches us that, while challenges may be inevitable, our response to what we see can determine whether we are swayed by the monsters or steadfast in our pursuit of greatness.

THE GREAT DEPRESSION

The Great Depression, spanning from 1929 to 1939, stands as one of the most challenging periods in global economic history. Triggered by the stock market crash of 1929, it ushered in a profound economic downturn characterized by widespread unemployment, bank failures, and a severe contraction of industrial production.

This period brought immense financial hardship to individuals, families, and nations, leaving an indelible mark on the socio-economic landscape.

At the heart of the Great Depression's enduring impact lies the intricate interplay between the challenging economic conditions and the way people perceived and reacted to them.

The perception of scarcity and economic despair became a dominant force shaping individuals' behavior and societal dynamics.

1. Fear and Uncertainty as Catalysts:

The prevailing perception of economic scarcity engendered fear and uncertainty on a massive scale. As news of job losses, business closures, and financial collapse permeated society, a collective sense of insecurity took hold.

This fear became a catalyst for a range of behaviors that, collectively, deepened the economic crisis.

2. Reluctance to Spend and Invest:

The perception of economic hardship prompted a widespread reluctance among individuals to spend money or invest in various endeavors.

The fear of further financial losses led people to adopt conservative financial strategies, such as hoarding cash and avoiding non-essential expenditures. This collective belt-tightening had a cascading effect on demand, exacerbating the economic downturn.

The pervasive atmosphere of financial apprehension not only shaped individual spending habits but also fostered an environment where businesses hesitated to invest and expand, perpetuating a cycle of economic constriction that underscored the delicate interplay between individual choices and systemic economic health.

3. Economic Inactivity and Contraction:

Fueled by fear and uncertainty, the populace exhibited a reluctance to engage in economic activities. Businesses, uncertain about future market conditions, curtailed production and investment. Consumers, gripped by financial anxiety, withdrew from the market. This simultaneous pullback in both demand and supply contributed to a prolonged economic contraction, deepening the depression.

4. Prolonged Duration of the Depression:

The cyclical nature of the economic downturn, intertwined with the perceptions and behaviors it elicited, played a significant role in extending the duration of the Great Depression. The collective response to economic challenges, marked by fear-driven inactivity, created a self-perpetuating cycle that reinforced and prolonged the economic hardships faced by individuals and communities.

In essence, the Great Depression illustrates the profound impact that perceptions, shaped by economic conditions, can have on human behavior. The intertwining of fear, uncertainty, and a collective reluctance to engage in economic activities contributed to a challenging cycle that prolonged and deepened the crisis.

The lessons learned from this historic period continue to inform economic policies and responses to crises, emphasizing the critical role of perception in shaping the trajectory of complex socio-economic challenges.

PERCEPTION'S INFLUENCE ON DIPLOMACY

The Cuban Missile Crisis showcased the pivotal role of perception in shaping the course of events during a geopolitical crisis with the potential for nuclear Armageddon.

The Cuban Missile Crisis of 1962 stands as one of the most perilous moments in modern history, characterized by heightened geopolitical tension between the United States and the Soviet Union.

The discovery of Soviet ballistic missiles in Cuba brought the world to the brink of nuclear war. The challenge was not only the physical presence of missiles but the looming specter of global catastrophe, making it a paramount test of diplomatic finesse and strategic acumen.

The perception of imminent danger from the presence of nuclear missiles in Cuba created an urgent need for delicate diplomacy. Leaders on both sides, most notably U.S. President John F. Kennedy and Soviet Premier Nikita Khrushchev, understood the profound implications of public perception. The gravity of the situation demanded careful communication to avoid public panic.

"What you think, you become.

What you feel, you attract.

What you imagine, you create."

Buddha

Leaders had to manage public perception skillfully to prevent panic and maintain stability. President Kennedy, in a televised address, communicated the seriousness of the situation without inciting fear.

This strategic communication aimed to assure the public while conveying the severity of the crisis, highlighting the delicate balance required in managing perception during a high-stakes confrontation.

The perception of imminent nuclear war influenced diplomatic decisions and strategic resolutions. Leaders recognized that public perception could sway the course of events. Behind closed doors, negotiations and backchannel communications took place, driven by a shared awareness of the need to navigate the crisis without succumbing to public pressure or triggering irreversible actions.

The eventual resolution of the crisis was marked by strategic decisions influenced by the perceived consequences of various courses of action. A delicate agreement, involving the removal of U.S. missiles from Turkey and a public commitment by the U.S. not to invade Cuba, allowed both superpowers to step back from the brink.

In summary, the Cuban Missile Crisis underscores how managing public perception is an integral component of crisis resolution. The delicate diplomacy, strategic communication, and decisions shaped by the perceived consequences of actions highlight the intricate dance between global events and the perceptions that define them.

The crisis remains a testament to the critical role perception plays in navigating the complexities of international relations during moments of extreme tension.

"The only thing we have to fear is fear itself."

Franklin D. Roosevelt

6.   ...He AROSE and RAN...

In other words, he abandoned his post. Elijah's response to the threat from Jezebel, encapsulated in the words "He AROSE and RUN," unveils a heartbreaking incident in the life of a revered prophet.

It provides a profound insight into the dynamics of faith, emotional turmoil, and the consequences of momentarily forsaking one's divine calling.

Here are some insights to consider:

1. Abandoning the Prophetic Post:

Elijah, in the face of Jezebel's menacing message, chose to abandon his post as a prophet and messenger of God. This act wasn't merely a physical retreat; it symbolized a spiritual crisis wherein he momentarily relinquished his position and calling. The weight of what he heard and saw overwhelmed him, prompting a hasty decision devoid of divine consultation.

2. Emotional Decision-Making:

The text suggests that Elijah's decision was rooted in personal and emotional experiences rather than seeking the face of God. His response lacked the seasoned word of encouragement or faith that had characterized his previous actions. In this moment of vulnerability, he allowed the external threat to eclipse the internal assurance that had fueled his previous triumphs.

3. Dependence on Previous Anointing:

Elijah, having experienced victory over the prophets of Baal, might have relied on his previous anointing and power. However, this narrative unveils a crucial truth – past victories do not necessarily equip one for every battle. Elijah failed to consider the multi-dimensional nature of challenges – physical, psychological, and spiritual – and, as a result, found himself on the brink of defeat.

4. Forgetting the Source of Power:

The core lesson emerges from Elijah's failure to recognize that his position and power were products of divine grace. In times of adversity, he needed to depend on and consult the Lord, acknowledging the Almighty as the ultimate source of his strength. By abandoning his post, he momentarily forgot that his authority and influence were grounded in God's calling.

5. The Call to Recognize Unique Position:

The exhortation to recognize one's unique position in various spheres – family, school, workplace, community, nation, or globally – echoes through this narrative. Elijah's lapse serves as a cautionary tale for individuals facing challenges in their appointed roles. Neglecting one's calling or position in times of difficulty has implications not only for the present but for generations tied to that destiny.

6. Aborting Dreams of Unborn Generations:

The profound message resonates with the idea that abandoning one's post can have generational consequences. Dreams and visions tied to the destiny of unborn generations may be jeopardized by the actions or inactions of today. The narrative implores individuals to consider the broader impact of their decisions on the unfolding tapestry of destinies yet to come.

In navigating life's challenges, the lesson from Elijah's moment of vulnerability is clear: recognition of the divine source of strength and a steadfast commitment to one's calling can anchor individuals through tumultuous times.

Abandoning the post, whether physical or spiritual, risks not only personal defeat but the potential derailment of destinies intertwined with one's own. The narrative serves as a timeless reminder of the enduring significance of faith, dependence on God, and unwavering commitment to the unique purpose for which individuals are positioned in the grand narrative of existence.

Beloved as we go through the challenges of life, recognize that God has positioned you in a unique position be it in your family, school, workplace, community, nation or the globe for a special and specific purpose.

You don't have to neglect your calling or position in times of difficulty. If you run away or desert your position, what will be the fate of the many generations that are tied to your destiny. You can't abort dreams and visions of unborn generations by your actions or inactions today.

"Every great work,

every great accomplishment,

has been brought into manifestation

through holding on to the vision,

and often just before the big achievement,

comes apparent failure and discouragement."

Florence Scovel Shinn

The emergence of the COVID-19 pandemic in 2020 presented an unprecedented global health crisis. The virus's rapid spread, coupled with its high transmission rate, posed an immediate and severe challenge to public health worldwide.

As the virus began its global journey, there were instances where governments and health organizations faced criticism for what was perceived as a lack of preparedness and a delayed response.

This delay in recognizing and addressing the severity of the threat can be characterized as a temporary abandonment of the post of safeguarding public health.

In the early stages, some authorities downplayed the potential impact of the virus, viewing it as a localized issue that might not escalate. This underestimation contributed to delays in implementing necessary measures.

Understanding the virus's transmission dynamics was a key challenge. The delayed recognition of the extent of human-to-human transmission hindered the implementation of effective containment measures.

Some regions faced criticism for insufficient pandemic preparedness. The lack of stockpiles of medical supplies, testing infrastructure, and coordinated response plans contributed to a slower and less effective initial response.

Political, economic, or social considerations led to hesitancy in implementing stringent public health measures. Lockdowns, travel restrictions, and mass testing were not universally and promptly adopted, allowing the virus to spread more widely.

CONSEQUENCES OF THE DELAY:

1. Increased Transmission and Mortality:

The delayed response contributed to a higher rate of virus transmission, leading to increased cases and, consequently, a higher mortality rate in some regions.

2. Overwhelmed Healthcare Systems:

The delayed recognition and response strained healthcare systems, leading to overwhelmed hospitals, shortages of medical resources, and challenges in providing adequate care.

3. Prolonged Economic Impact:

The economic fallout was exacerbated by delays in implementing effective public health measures. Prolonged periods of lockdown and uncertainty contributed to deeper economic recessions in some areas.

LESSONS LEARNED:

1. The Importance of Swift Action:

The early stages of the pandemic highlighted the critical importance of swift and decisive action in the face of a novel and highly transmissible virus.

2. Global Collaboration and Preparedness:

The pandemic underscored the necessity for enhanced global collaboration and preparedness, emphasizing the need for coordinated responses and shared resources.

3. Continuous Monitoring and Learning:

Continuous monitoring, learning from experiences, and adapting strategies in real-time are crucial aspects of effectively responding to dynamic public health challenges.

While acknowledging the challenges faced during the early stages of the COVID-19 pandemic, it's important to recognize subsequent efforts to adapt, improve responses, and implement lessons learned. The experience serves as a pivotal moment in reshaping global health strategies, emphasizing the ongoing need for preparedness, collaboration, and proactive public health measures.

"Success is not final, failure is not fatal:

It is the courage to continue that counts."

Winston S. Churchill

FINANCIAL CRISIS 2008: NEGLECTING THE GUARDIANSHIP OF ECONOMIC STABILITY

The Challenge:

The Financial Crisis of 2008 marked a pivotal moment in global economic history, characterized by the collapse of major financial institutions and the ensuing recession. The challenge stemmed from a complex interplay of factors, including risky financial practices, subprime mortgage lending, and a lack of regulatory oversight.

Abandoning the Post: Neglecting Stewardship of Economic Health

In the lead-up to the crisis, some financial institutions neglected their roles as guardians of financial stability, engaging in practices that ultimately contributed to the systemic breakdown. The failure to uphold responsible financial practices can be viewed as an abandonment of their posts as stewards of economic health.

Risky Mortgage Practices:

One of the key contributors to the crisis was the proliferation of risky mortgage practices. Financial institutions, driven by the pursuit of short-term profits, engaged in subprime mortgage lending without adequate assessment of borrowers' creditworthiness.

Securitization and Complexity:

Financial products became increasingly complex, and the bundling of mortgages into securities made it challenging to assess the true risk associated with these assets. The complexity of financial instruments contributed to a lack of transparency and understanding.

Lack of Due Diligence:

Financial institutions neglected due diligence in assessing the risks associated with the assets they held. The widespread assumption that housing prices would continually rise led to a dangerous underestimation of potential risks.

Inadequate Regulatory Oversight:

Regulatory bodies, in some instances, failed to provide adequate oversight. There were gaps in the regulatory framework, allowing certain financial activities to proceed without sufficient scrutiny.

CONSEQUENCES OF THE NEGLECT:

1. Collapse of Financial Institutions:

Major financial institutions faced insolvency or collapse due to their exposure to toxic assets. Lehman Brothers' bankruptcy in 2008 marked a critical point in the crisis.

2. Global Recession:

The financial crisis triggered a severe global recession, leading to a contraction of economic activity, rising unemployment, and a decline in consumer and investor confidence.

3. Bailouts and Economic Interventions:

Governments around the world had to intervene with massive bailouts to stabilize financial institutions and prevent a complete economic collapse. The consequences extended to taxpayers who bore the financial burden of these interventions.

4. Long-Term Economic Impact:

The 2008 financial crisis had long-term economic repercussions, with some economies taking years to recover fully. The crisis highlighted the interconnectedness of global financial markets and the need for systemic reforms.

LESSONS LEARNED:

1. Importance of Risk Management:

The crisis underscored the critical importance of robust risk management practices within financial institutions, emphasizing the need for prudent lending and investment strategies.

2. Regulatory Reforms:

The financial crisis led to widespread calls for regulatory reforms to enhance oversight and prevent the recurrence of risky practices. Initiatives such as the Dodd-Frank Wall Street Reform and Consumer Protection Act aimed to address these concerns.

3. Global Cooperation:

The crisis emphasized the need for enhanced global cooperation and coordination in financial regulation to address systemic risks that transcend national borders.

The Financial Crisis of 2008 serves as a stark reminder of the consequences that can arise when financial institutions neglect their responsibilities as stewards of economic health. The aftermath prompted significant introspection, reforms, and a renewed commitment to sound financial practices and regulatory oversight.

7. ...FOR HIS LIFE

"...and you are not your own..." 1 Corinthians 6:19b (Bible)

In the wake of Elijah's flight for his life, the narrative takes a profound turn, delving into the sacred understanding that our lives are not our own. Drawing parallels to biblical teachings and contemporary wisdom, the text urges readers to recognize their existence as custodians of a divine gift, emphasizing the privilege of surrendering one's life for the greater good.

In the first place, the life he lived was not his own. We are all custodians of the life we have received from God. We are caretakers of this life we have from above. If for some reason, we are called upon to surrender for the sake of the gospel or for the betterment of the Kingdom of God and humanity, we should understand that it's a privilege.

Paul was absolutely right when he said, "I have been crucified with Christ; it is no longer I who live, but Christ lives in me; and the *life* which I now live in the flesh I live by faith in the Son of God, who loved me and gave Himself for me." Galatians 2:20

You must recognize that you are not your own as a child of God. Your gifting, talents, blessings, breath, are really not yours but a divine gift from above. Are you thus prepared to lay down your life and blessings for the Kingdom and other humans to benefit?

If the visions and aspirations we desire are not deep enough to deserve our lives, then they are not really transformational. You must be prepared to lay down your life or sacrifice something precious for the sake of the dreams we carry in our hearts. You must be a living sacrifice for others to see and emulate even if it causes you some discomfort.

"Verily, verily, I say unto you, except a corn of wheat fall into the ground and die, it abideth alone: but if it dies, it bringeth forth much fruit." John 12:24 KJV. Our lives must be a worthy investment for future generations.

The text emphasizes that, like a seed sown in the ground, our lives must be a worthy investment for future generations. It advocates for a legacy of impact that transcends individual existence, bringing forth much fruit in the lives of those who follow.

"The purpose of life is not to be happy.

It is to be useful, to be honorable,

to be compassionate, to have it make some difference

that you have lived and lived well."

Ralph Waldo Emerson

ELIJAH'S UNANTICIPATED DILEMMA

In modern times, it is worth it to consider having life insurance policy and other strategic investments and security so as to support us in case of sudden disaster or emergencies.

I believe that, with all the miracles and mighty works that Elijah had performed in Israel, he was not secured enough physically or not made enough economic investment for his family and ministry at the time that he was threatened by this monster of a queen.

The narrative below digs deep into the complexities faced by Elijah, a revered prophet, at a critical juncture. The absence of clarity regarding his succession plan, coupled with uncertainties about the fate of his family, presents a compelling story that resonates with the importance of considering both spiritual and practical aspects in our engagements in life.

1. Lack of Succession Planning:

Elijah's predicament shines a light on the absence of a clear succession plan. The text suggests that he did not have a designated successor, raising questions about the continuity of his ministry. This lack of foresight adds a layer of vulnerability to his situation.

2. Unanticipated Family Concerns:

The text highlights Elijah's apparent oversight regarding the future well-being of his family. The narrative suggests that he did not contemplate the aftermath of his potential demise on his loved ones. This oversight contributes to the urgency in his decision to flee for his life.

3. Survival Alternatives:

Elijah's lack of alternatives for survival in the face of a threat reveals the depth of his vulnerability. The narrative paints a picture of a prophet who, despite his powerful demonstrations of faith, grapples with the harsh reality of mortality. This vulnerability propels him to seek refuge.

4. The Urgency to Flee:

The desire to run for his life becomes a palpable response to the uncertainties surrounding Elijah's future. The absence of a concrete plan or assurance of protection compels him to prioritize immediate safety over potential long-term consequences.

5. The Call for Holistic Preparedness:

The text extends beyond Elijah's story to advocate for a holistic approach to life's uncertainties. It introduces the idea that engaging in spiritual activities should be complemented by consideration of practical matters. This includes contemplating the physical well-being and financial stability of oneself and one's family.

6. Importance of Investments:

Encouraging the reader to think about investments, the narrative implies financial prudence. While spiritual pursuits are essential, the text underscores the practical wisdom of securing one's financial future, ensuring a measure of stability for loved ones in the event of unforeseen circumstances.

7. Will and Insurance:

The text explicitly suggests the importance of having a will or some form of insurance in place. This acknowledgment reflects an understanding that spiritual preparedness should be accompanied by tangible arrangements to ease the burden on family and ensure a smooth transition in the face of unexpected departures.

8. Modern Relevance:

The narrative's exploration of Elijah's dilemma serves as a timeless lesson. It encourages individuals engaged in spiritual activities today to consider the practical implications of their commitments, emphasizing that preparedness extends beyond the spiritual realm.

In essence, the text urges a comprehensive perspective, recognizing that a well-rounded approach to life encompasses both spiritual and practical considerations. Elijah's unanticipated dilemma becomes a metaphor for the broader human experience, prompting reflection on the importance of holistic preparedness for the uncertainties that life may present.

THE NOBLE CALL TO SACRIFICE FOR DIVINITY AND HUMANITY

In the striking arena of life, there exists a sacred call, a profound beckoning that transcends personal ambitions and self-interest. It is the call to sacrifice, to willingly offer one's life for the greater good of humanity, in service to God, and for the advancement of society at large.

At the heart of this noble endeavor is the recognition that our lives are not solitary entities but interconnected threads in the intricate fabric of the human experience.

It is an acknowledgment that our existence carries a purpose far beyond individual pursuits and temporal desires. The call to sacrifice is a testament to the profound responsibility we bear as custodians of the life bestowed upon us.

Sacrifice for humanity signifies a selfless dedication to the well-being of others, an embodiment of empathy and compassion that extends beyond the boundaries of personal comfort. In embracing this call, we contribute to the collective betterment of our global family, fostering a world where kindness, justice, and love prevail.

The call to sacrifice for the Kingdom reflects a deep spiritual commitment— an acknowledgment of divine sovereignty and a surrender of personal will in alignment with a higher purpose. It is an expression of faith that transcends mortal boundaries, seeking to fulfill a sacred duty in service to the Creator and His divine plan.

Sacrifice for society recognizes the symbiotic relationship we share with the communities we inhabit. It involves placing the needs of others before our own, working towards the common good, and actively participating in the progress and advancement of our shared social tapestry.

History bears witness to the transformative power of individuals who heeded the call to sacrifice. From the selfless acts of humanitarian leaders

117

to the martyrs who laid down their lives for causes greater than themselves, each sacrifice has left an indelible mark on the annals of time.

In the face of this noble call, we find not only a duty but an opportunity—a chance to elevate our existence from the mundane to the sublime, from the temporal to the eternal.

The willingness to sacrifice for humanity, God, and society is a profound act of love—a demonstration that our lives are vessels capable of carrying the light of positive change to every corner of the world.

As we contemplate this call to sacrifice, let us remember that in giving of ourselves, we receive the immeasurable richness of a life well-lived—a life marked by purpose, compassion, and an enduring legacy of love for the greater good of all.

CESAR CHAVEZ: MERGING FAITH AND SOCIAL JUSTICE IN THE UNITED FARM WORKERS MOVEMENT

Cesar Chavez's journey as a labor leader and civil rights activist was deeply influenced by his spiritual foundation within the Catholic Church. Growing up in a Mexican-American family, Chavez's faith played a pivotal role in shaping his worldview and instilling values of compassion, justice, and solidarity with the marginalized.

Motivated by his Catholic teachings and inspired by the principles of nonviolence advocated by figures like Mahatma Gandhi and Martin Luther King Jr., Chavez embarked on a mission to improve the working conditions of farmworkers.

In 1962, he co-founded the National Farm Workers Association, later merging with the Agricultural Workers Organizing Committee to become the United Farm Workers (UFW) union in 1966.

Combining Spiritual Values with Practical Strategies:

Chavez's approach was a unique blend of spirituality and practical activism. His spiritual values, rooted in the Catholic social teachings emphasizing the dignity of labor and the rights of workers, became the moral compass for the UFW.

This alignment of faith and social justice laid the groundwork for a movement that sought not only better wages and working conditions but also human dignity for farmworkers.

Advocacy for Farmworkers' Rights:

Chavez's activism extended beyond traditional labor issues. He and the UFW fought against the exploitation of farmworkers, addressing concerns such as pesticide exposure, unsanitary living conditions, and discriminatory labor practices. The union organized strikes, marches, and boycotts, employing nonviolent tactics reminiscent of Chavez's spiritual influences.

Intersection of Faith and Social Justice:

The United Farm Workers Movement, under Chavez's leadership, became a powerful example of the intersection of faith and social justice. Chavez's Catholic faith infused the movement with a sense of moral obligation, framing the struggle for farmworkers' rights as a sacred duty.

This connection between spirituality and activism resonated with a diverse coalition of supporters, including clergy, students, and civil rights advocates.

Legacy and Impact:

Chavez's legacy extends beyond legislative victories and improved working conditions. His ability to unite people across religious, ethnic, and socioeconomic lines showcased the transformative potential of combining spiritual values with practical strategies for social change.

The UFW's motto, "La Causa" (The Cause), encapsulates the deeper purpose of the movement—a pursuit of justice rooted in a spiritual commitment to human dignity.

Cesar Chavez's life and work exemplify the profound impact that can arise when individuals fuse their spiritual convictions with tangible efforts to address social injustices.

His legacy serves as a testament to the enduring influence of a leader who navigated the complex terrain of labor rights and social justice through the lens of his deeply held faith.

AUNG SAN SUU KYI: A SPIRITUAL JOURNEY INTO POLITICAL ACTIVISM

Roots in Buddhist Principles:

Aung San Suu Kyi's transformative journey from a life centered on Buddhist principles to political activism reflects the profound impact of spirituality on her sense of duty and commitment.

Born into a family deeply involved in Burma's struggle for independence, Suu Kyi's upbringing was steeped in the teachings of Buddhism, a religion emphasizing compassion, nonviolence, and moral integrity.

Transition to Political Activism:

Suu Kyi's life took a dramatic turn when, in 1988, she returned to Burma to care for her ailing mother just as the country was undergoing a political upheaval.

The people's demand for democracy resonated with Suu Kyi's deep-seated convictions about justice and human rights. Embracing her sense of duty, she transitioned from a life focused on family and academia to a prominent role in Burma's political landscape.

Commitment to Democracy and Human Rights:

Aung San Suu Kyi's commitment to democracy and human rights was profoundly shaped by her Buddhist principles. The concept of "mettā" or loving-kindness in Buddhism, along with the belief in the inherent dignity of every individual, fueled her dedication to championing the rights of the Burmese people. Her advocacy extended beyond political freedoms to encompass broader human rights concerns.

Navigating Practical Challenges under Military Rule:

Suu Kyi's decision to engage in political activism meant confronting the practical challenges of operating under a military junta. Her commitment to nonviolence aligned with Buddhist principles, even in the face of brutal repression. The military regime imposed periods of house arrest, restricting her movements and communication, but Suu Kyi's resolve remained unbroken.

Global Symbol of Peaceful Resistance:

Aung San Suu Kyi's principled stand against the military regime turned her into a global symbol of peaceful resistance. Her approach to political activism, rooted in spirituality, garnered international support and led to her being awarded the Nobel Peace Prize in 1991.

Transition to Political Leadership:

As Burma transitioned to a more open political system, Aung San Suu Kyi faced the complexities of leading a country emerging from decades of military rule.

Her spiritual grounding continued to influence her leadership style, emphasizing reconciliation and dialogue as essential components of the democratic transition.

Challenges and Criticisms:

In her role as a political leader, Suu Kyi faced challenges and criticisms, particularly regarding the *Rohingya crisis*. The complexities of ethnic and religious tensions in Burma tested her commitment to human rights, showcasing the intricate interplay between spiritual principles and the pragmatic demands of governance.

Legacy and Ongoing Journey:

Aung San Suu Kyi's journey from a life shaped by Buddhist principles to political activism underscores the dynamic relationship between spirituality and social engagement.

Her enduring legacy lies not only in her role as a political leader but also in her ability to inspire individuals worldwide with the idea that one's spiritual values can guide a principled and impactful approach to governance.

"Great achievement is usually born of great sacrifice,

and is never the result of selfishness."

Napoleon Hill

CHAPTER FOUR

MANAGING MIRACLE MONSTERS

In the rollercoaster ride toward our dreams, we all face those daunting moments, those "Miracle Monsters," that make us question if the journey is worth it. If you followed keenly along from Chapter Three, you would remember when we explored the raw reality of "Meeting Miracle Monsters."

It was a recognition that challenges are not some abstract part of the journey; they're as real as the air we breathe.

We looked at ourselves and said, "Yes, I've faced monsters — doubts, setbacks, and the fear of the unknown." It was a moment of honesty, where we embraced the untidy, challenging, and imperfect path to our dreams.

Now, as we step into Chapter Four, "Managing Miracle Monsters," it's not just about acknowledging these challenges; it's about figuring out how to dance with them.

Imagine this as the part of the story where the central character doesn't just face the dragon but learns to ride it. We're moving from survival mode to taking the reins, steering through the storms, and turning challenges into allies.

Here, the story evolves from mere confrontation to a strategic dance with challenges. It's an acknowledgment that the journey doesn't end at the meeting; it transforms into a symphony where challenges are not just faced but orchestrated into opportunities.

In as much as you cannot avoid miracle monsters in your life, you will need to learn how to manage or deal with them. As mentioned, they can appear before, during or even after your desires are realized.

"Managing Miracle Monsters" is not about mere survival; it's about thriving in the face of adversity. We shift from reactive encounters to proactive engagement, exploring strategies that turn challenges into stepping stones and mindset shifts that redefine obstacles as conduits for growth.

Join me in this expedition through the corridors of resilience and the terrain of adaptability. Together, we will unravel the secrets of those who have not just faced *Miracle Monsters* but have masterfully managed them.

We will be exploring strategies not because we're desperate but because we're eager to thrive, to make the journey not just bearable but beautiful. So, as we dive into this chapter, think of it as a conversation over a cup of coffee.

It's me sharing my story with you and stories of folks who didn't just survive but soared through challenges. It's about navigating life's messiness, turning stumbling blocks into stepping stones, and finding strength in vulnerability.

At this juncture, we're not just flipping the script; we're rewriting it. It's a journey of growth, where trials transform from villains to mentors. So, grab a seat, and let's explore together — because in the mess of managing monsters, you might just discover the magic of making your dreams come true.

In the crucible of daunting challenges, the point man of the nation Elijah, despite being entrenched in a very difficult situation, demonstrated a resilience that went beyond mere survival.

His actions, guided by a profound wisdom, eventually became the compass that helped him navigate the hard times. Instead of succumbing to the weight of difficulties, he used his moments of weakness as opportunities to showcase his inner strength.

Every decision, every maneuver, was a testament to his ability to not just weather the storm but to steer through it with purpose. In the end, his strategic conduct in the face of adversity proved instrumental in not only overcoming challenges but in paving a way to triumph. In weakness, he found a reservoir of wisdom that propelled him through the storm.

"The strongest people are not those

who show strength in front of us

but those who win battles

we know nothing about."

Jonathan Harnisch

1. HE WENT TO BEERSHEBA

Beersheba is a place of oath or covenant. It is a place where we renew our vows or commitment to God. When we fall or lose our zeal and enthusiasm in life or failing to meet the goals we set, we need to go back to "Beersheba".

It is place where we first started the dream or journey to success and it's always a place of refreshing. As we remember and touch base with our "Beersheba" we ignite a fresh fire and passion to forge ahead despite the roadblocks that stand before us.

Consider the story of Jessica, a successful entrepreneur who faced a series of setbacks in her business. Pressures and challenges seemed insurmountable, leading her to question her initial passion. In her moment of despair, Jessica decided to go back to her "Beersheba" — the small café in her home town where she first conceived the idea of her business.

Sitting in the same corner where the dreams were born, she reconnected with the enthusiasm and commitment that fueled her entrepreneurial journey. This retreat to her entrepreneurial "Beersheba" became the turning point that reignited her determination, eventually leading to the resurgence and success of her business.

"You can't connect the dots looking forward;

you can only connect them looking backward.

So you have to trust that the dots

will somehow connect in your future."

Steve Jobs

Beersheba, in its essence, served as a symbolic retreat, a haven where one could reconnect with the initial fervor and enthusiasm that ignited the journey to success.

It was a hallmark, a place of refreshing, where the flames of passion were reignited despite the daunting roadblocks ahead. In times when goals seemed elusive, and the zeal waned, Beersheba beckoned as a place of rejuvenation.

Reflect on the life of Winston Churchill during World War II. As Britain faced the relentless pressure of war, Churchill, burdened by the weight of leadership, would retreat to his "Beersheba" — a small room in the underground war rooms in London.

It was here that he would reflect on his commitment to the nation, read historical accounts of British resilience, and renew his faith in the face of adversity.

This retreat to his wartime sanctuary allowed Churchill to emerge stronger, providing the leadership needed to navigate the challenging times and ultimately contribute to the Allied victory.

"Sometimes the best way to move

forward is to revisit where you started."

Anonymous

When you face a miracle monster along the journey of life, remember you always have a deep and personal secret place to go that can ignite or renew your strength to continue the journey.

It may be a physical place or a spiritual atmosphere that you may need to connect to, or probably a relation or beloved to talk to. Someone who is able to bring out the very best out of your life and motivate you to make the right decisions.

When attached by a monster of life, remember your first love of prayer, study of the holy scriptures, personal devotion, sharing the good news with others, giving to the poor and needy, volunteering in society, reading and writing, exercises, going back to do certain courses, etc.

Your visions and dreams could be under siege but never give up. If for some reason, you need to shed some tears, it's fine to do that. After a short while, quickly bounce back by re-connecting with your base or renewing your vows and the important decisions you made from the beginning. If it requires that you start all over again, do so and bounce back better and bigger.

In the realm of sports, consider the journey of Serena Williams, a tennis icon. After a series of setbacks and injuries that tested her passion for the game, Serena decided to revisit her "Beersheba" — the tennis court where she first discovered her love for tennis.

Practicing on the same court, surrounded by the echoes of her early victories, she tapped into the passion and joy that initially fueled her commitment to the sport. This return to her tennis "Beersheba" became a pivotal moment in her career, leading to subsequent triumphs and solidifying her legacy in tennis history.

Elijah by going to Beersheba after the threat was prepare to renew his mind and heart. He went to revive himself again as the point man of the land. He renewed his faith and fellowship with the Almighty.

Elijah's journey to Beersheba wasn't just a physical movement; it was a spiritual and emotional revival. As the point man of the land, he took deliberate steps to renew his mind and heart, rekindling his confidence and re-establishing fellowship with the Almighty.

Exploring the life of Mahatma Gandhi during India's struggle for independence. Faced with immense challenges and setbacks, Gandhi would retreat to his "Beersheba" — a simple *ashram* in Gujarat.

Here, he would reflect on the core principles of non-violence and *satyagraha*, renewing his commitment to the cause of independence. His retreat to the *ashram* became a source of strength, providing the clarity and resilience needed to lead a nation towards freedom.

Beersheba wasn't just a place on the map; it was a sanctuary of renewal and a testament to the strength found in reconnecting with one's foundational commitments.

In moments of adversity, the message is clear— go back to the first point of oath that initiated the journey before considering surrender. In these moments, tap into your subconscious mind and command it to respond positively, reigniting the same enthusiasm that marked the journey's beginning.

2.   LEFT HIS SERVANT THERE

"The first step in crafting the life you want

is to get rid of everything you don't."

Joshua Becker

Familiarity they say breeds contempt. For several years of ministry with this servant, Elijah could not get back what he had imparted in this particular servant. All the miracles, wonders and activities he had performed did not build in this servant enough strength, faith and motivation to give back to his master when he needed it most.

He was not a motivator or inspirer!

In order words, he had not maximized the opportunities that came his way. He was not profitable and helpful to his master's ministry at a crucial moment. In fact, he was a liability not an asset at the point in time. He was only an excess baggage with no advantage.

Thank God when Elijah realised this, he packed and 'stacked' him before any further bad fate. Anything that does not add more value to yourself and vision in life must be dropped. However, I must state that, Elijah might have left his servant there because, he felt he may be safer in that town than coming along in the face of the looming terror.

The narrative emphasizes the importance of shedding anything that doesn't add value. Just as Elijah had to leave his unprofitable servant, individuals must be willing to part ways with negative thoughts, unproductive attitudes, and any aspect of life that does not contribute to personal or collective advancement.

It serves as a call to introspection, urging individuals to evaluate relationships, thoughts, and behaviors that may hinder growth.

Any negative mindset and attitudes must be dropped. Anything that will not enhance your course in business, marriage, academics, ministry and economy must be left behind. You may have to lay behind certain relationships which do not add value or help you progress in life.

Unlike this servant, Elisha became a better steward and assistant to his master Elijah. The comparison between Elijah's two servants — the unprofitable one and Elisha, who became a better steward- underscores the significance of choosing associates wisely.

It implies that the right kinds of relationships contribute positively to personal and collective growth. Elisha's eventual success as a faithful assistant highlights the transformative power of positive associations.

I want to point out the four kinds of association we need as we move towards our miracle. This section serves as a poignant reminder that the people we surround ourselves with, the thoughts we entertain, and the attitudes we cultivate significantly impact our ability to progress and achieve our goals.

It calls for intentional choices in associations and a discerning attitude toward anything that hinders personal and collective advancement.

a) Gilgal Association

The concept of "Gilgal Association" is rooted in the biblical significance of Gilgal, a place symbolizing the rolling away of reproach and the breaking of bondages. This type of association is characterized by friendships and connections that play a pivotal role in helping individuals overcome limitations, servitude, and negative mentalities.

Harriet Tubman, a key figure in the abolitionist movement during the 19th century, can be seen as embodying the spirit of a Gilgal Association. Tubman, born into slavery, not only liberated herself but also dedicated her life to helping others escape the bonds of slavery.

She became a conductor on the Underground Railroad, a network of secret routes and safe houses that facilitated the escape of enslaved individuals to freedom.

Tubman's associations were characterized by a commitment to breaking the bondage of slavery and rolling away the reproach associated with it.

Her intentional choices in friendships and alliances reflected a discerning attitude toward anything that hindered personal and collective advancement. By leading others to freedom, she actively participated in the rolling away of the reproach that came with the institution of slavery.

"I freed a thousand slaves;

I could have freed a thousand more

if only they knew they were slaves."

Harriet Tubman

There are friends and associations that help us come out from any bondage or stronghold. We need people who will help us come out of any servitude or negative mentality and bondage of life. People who take us backward in life must be discarded.

Here are some characteristics of a Gilgal association:

Breaking Bondages:

Associations categorized under Gilgal play a crucial role in liberating individuals from various forms of bondage. These could include psychological strongholds, unhealthy habits, or any limiting factors that hinder personal growth. Friends within this category become catalysts for positive change, supporting each other in breaking free from the shackles that might otherwise impede progress.

Rolling Away Reproach:

Gilgal is synonymous with the rolling away of reproach. Friends in this category actively contribute to eliminating the stigma or shame associated with past mistakes or unfavorable circumstances.

They create an environment where individuals can shed the weight of reproach and move forward unburdened. Such associations provide encouragement, understanding, and a non-judgmental atmosphere for personal transformation.

Discarding Backward Influences:

The narrative emphasizes the need to discard individuals or associations that take us backward in life. This is a call for discernment in recognizing relationships that hinder progress. Gilgal associations require intentional choices to distance oneself from influences that hold one back, preventing personal growth and advancement.

Importance of Positive Influence:

In essence, Gilgal associations underscore the importance of surrounding oneself with positive influences that actively contribute to personal development. These friends become pillars of support, helping each other navigate challenges, overcome obstacles, and ultimately experience a rolling away of reproach.

Discerning Attitude:

The overarching message is the necessity of maintaining a discerning attitude toward associations. It's a call to intentionally choose relationships that align with the vision of personal and collective advancement. By actively seeking Gilgal associations, individuals create a supportive network that facilitates growth, liberation from bondage, and the rolling away of reproach.

In summary, you should evaluate your friendships and connections, ensuring that they contribute positively to your journey. Discarding backward influences and intentionally cultivating Gilgal associations become essential steps in the pursuit of personal and collective advancement.

Nelson Mandela, a prominent leader in the anti-apartheid movement in South Africa, exemplifies the principles of Gilgal Association in a modern context. Mandela's intentional choices in associations were centered on breaking the bondage of apartheid and rolling away the reproach associated with racial discrimination.

During his long imprisonment, Mandela forged connections with like-minded individuals who shared the vision of a liberated, non-racial South Africa.

His friendships and alliances within the anti-apartheid movement played a crucial role in dismantling the discriminatory system and ushering in a new era of freedom. Mandela's discerning attitude toward associations contributed significantly to the collective advancement of a nation.

b) Bethel Association

You need people who will draw you closer to God, the source of life and all its blessings. You need people who will inspire you unto good works. People who will bring out the best in you. These bring out the best talents and gifting deposited in you. Anyone who makes you feel down, weak and unaccepted must be dropped.

Gandhi's association with the works of Leo Tolstoy and John Ruskin played a significant role in shaping his philosophy of nonviolent resistance. These spiritual advisors influenced Mahatma Gandhi to connect his political activism with deeply rooted moral principles.

The concept of "Bethel Association" is reflected in Gandhi's intentional choices to be close to individuals who emphasized simplicity, truth, and moral integrity. His relationships with like-minded individuals cultivated an environment that brought out the best in his commitment to nonviolence and justice.

Gandhi surrounded himself with a community of supporters who shared his values and goals. This association not only strengthened his resolve during challenging times but also contributed to the collective advancement of the Indian independence movement.

Bethel Association underscores the significance of cultivating a relationship with the divine. Individuals seeking Bethel Associations prioritize connections with people who share a commitment to spiritual growth and understanding. This may involve shared religious beliefs, spiritual practices, and a mutual journey towards a deeper connection with God.

Here are some pointers to look out for:

Inspiring Good Works:

Those in Bethel Associations serve as sources of inspiration for good works. The emphasis is on positive character development, moral uprightness, and a commitment to making a positive impact on the world. This type of association encourages individuals to act ethically and contribute to the well-being of others.

Enhancing Skills and Values:

Beyond personal connections, Bethel Association extends to the places and environments one engages with. It involves choosing surroundings that enhance skills, values, and morals. This may include educational institutions, workplaces, and communities that align with one's personal and spiritual goals.

Inspiration for Achievements:

Bethel Associations provide a support system of people who inspire and motivate each other to achieve greatness. Whether in academic pursuits, career goals, or personal aspirations, the association encourages individuals to reach the highest heights in life.

Friendship Determines Outcome:

The phrase "Your friend will determine your end" encapsulates the essence of Bethel Association. It emphasizes the profound impact that friendships and associations have on the trajectory of one's life. Positive, uplifting friendships contribute to a positive and fulfilling life journey.

In essence, Bethel Association is about intentionally cultivating connections that lead to spiritual fulfillment, positive character development, and the realization of personal potential. It's a conscious choice to surround oneself with influences that inspire growth and contribute to a purposeful and impactful life journey.

Malala Yousafzai, a Pakistani education activist and Nobel laureate, exemplifies the principles of Bethel Association in a modern context. Malala's commitment to education for girls and her advocacy for human rights have been shaped by associations with individuals who draw her closer to noble causes.

Malala's association with her father, Ziauddin Yousafzai, who is an education activist himself, played a crucial role in shaping her values. Her close relationship with her father, who encouraged her education and activism, brought out the best in her dedication to educational rights.

Malala's interactions with other Nobel laureates, such as Kailash Satyarthi, further drew her closer to the global cause of education for all. These associations inspired and motivated her to amplify her voice for the rights of children and girls worldwide.

Malala's association with international organizations and activists who share her commitment to education has contributed to the advancement of her cause. These associations have provided her with a platform to inspire positive change globally.

Places that will not enhance your skills, values and morals must be discarded. Be closer to people who inspire and motivate you to achieve the best and reach the highest heights in life.

"Your friend will determine your end"

c) Jericho Association

In our journey through life, we often find ourselves navigating through battles – be it personal struggles, career challenges, or the complexities of relationships. Jericho Association, in the contemporary sense, is about recognizing the importance of companionship and shared efforts in the face of life's trials.

Jericho is a place of battle. You always need people to be by your side in times of difficulties. Others will make your battle worse unlike others who will ease the challenges in your life. Jericho Association symbolizes the importance of having the right allies during challenging times, acknowledging that life often presents battles and struggles.

Today's fast-paced and interconnected world brings its own set of challenges. From the pressure of career aspirations to the complexities of maintaining relationships, life's battles take on various forms in our day-to-day experiences.

There are battles all over us as such we need the right crop of people to support us navigate these difficult times. You need people who will stand with you. Those that make your life a hell must be avoided.

Here are more characteristics to consider:

Companionship Matters:

Jericho Association sheds light on the significance of having the right companions during life's struggles. In the modern social context, this translates into the value of companionship, understanding, and shared experiences with friends, family, and those who genuinely care.

Support Network:

In the modern era, a support network is crucial for navigating difficulties. Jericho Association encourages individuals to surround themselves with people who offer genuine support, encouragement, and practical assistance during tough times. This includes friends, family, mentors, and colleagues.

Identifying Positive Influencers:

Not everyone in our lives contributes positively during challenging moments. Jericho Association prompts individuals to identify and connect with those who uplift, inspire, and genuinely contribute to easing the challenges. This might involve seeking advice from mentors, sharing struggles with supportive friends, or collaborating with understanding colleagues.

Avoiding Negative Influences:

Modern life introduces various negative influences, ranging from toxic relationships to unsupportive environments. Jericho Association advises individuals to steer clear of people who exacerbate their challenges or create unnecessary hurdles. Recognizing and distancing yourself from such influences is crucial.

Digital Battlefields:

In the digital age, battles extend into virtual spaces. Social media, online interactions, and digital challenges are part of the modern landscape. Jericho Association urges individuals to be mindful of their online connections and to foster positive relationships in both physical and virtual realms.

Shared Struggles:

Individuals in Jericho Associations share their struggles and victories. In the modern context, this might involve participating in support groups, engaging in online communities, or connecting with like-minded individuals who understand the unique challenges one faces.

Your Battle Determines Your Allies:

The phrase "Your battle determines your allies" encapsulates the essence of the Jericho Association in the modern world. It highlights the idea that the challenges one faces will reveal the true nature of their allies. Positive allies will stand by and offer support, while negative influences will only make the battle more difficult.

At its core, the Jericho Association reminds us that the battles we face unveil the true nature of our allies. The phrase "Your battle determines your allies" resonates emotionally, emphasizing that those who stand by us during tough times are the ones worth keeping close to.

In summary, the Jericho Association encourages individuals to intentionally build a support system of allies who contribute positively during life's battles. The focus is on creating a network that helps navigate challenges, fosters resilience, and promotes collective victories in the face of adversity.

.

"Your battle determines your title"

The Civil Rights Movement was a pivotal era in the United States marked by the tireless efforts of activists striving for racial equality. Martin Luther King Jr., often regarded as the movement's leader, Rosa Parks, and numerous others united against the deeply entrenched racial segregation and systemic injustice present in American society.

Their collective determination formed a formidable force, creating a unified front that resonated with millions. The movement was characterized by nonviolent protests, marches, and impactful speeches, most notably King's iconic "I Have a Dream" speech.

This Jericho Association successfully challenged discriminatory laws, leading to landmark legislative changes such as the Civil Rights Act of 1964 and the Voting Rights Act of 1965.

#METOO MOVEMENT (2017-PRESENT):

The #MeToo movement is a contemporary Jericho Association that addresses the pervasive issues of sexual harassment and assault. It began with survivors bravely sharing their personal stories, highlighting the prevalence of such misconduct across various industries.

The movement gained momentum through the collective voices of individuals, predominantly women, who refused to remain silent about their experiences. The widespread use of social media provided a platform for survivors to share their narratives, fostering a sense of solidarity.

The movement transcended geographic boundaries, creating a global conversation about the need for cultural shifts, accountability, and the dismantling of power imbalances. The #MeToo movement has prompted increased awareness, legal reforms, and a reassessment of societal norms related to consent and harassment.

In both historical and modern contexts, these Jericho Associations illustrate the power of collective action. They showcase how individuals, united by a shared vision for justice and equality, can bring about transformative change on a societal scale.

The strength derived from unity, resilience in the face of adversity, and the amplification of voices are common threads that bind these movements together.

d) Jordan Association

The Jordan Association represents a symbolic place of crossing over. In the biblical context, the crossing of the Jordan River was a significant event, symbolizing the Israelites' transition from the wilderness into the Promised Land.

Similarly, in our personal and professional lives, the Jordan Association signifies a critical juncture where we need individuals who play a pivotal role in propelling us toward our goals and aspirations.

The Women's Suffrage Movement, a pivotal moment in history, indeed exemplifies the characteristics of a Jordan Association, with leaders like Susan B. Anthony and Elizabeth Cady Stanton at the forefront.

Susan B. Anthony, Elizabeth Cady Stanton, and other leaders inspired women from diverse backgrounds to join a collective effort aimed at achieving a shared goal—women's right to vote. Their leadership spurred a transformative movement that crossed over societal norms and expectations.

The suffrage leaders provided guidance and direction to women navigating the complexities of advocating for their rights. Facing opposition and societal resistance, these leaders stood as beacons of encouragement, motivating women to persist in their collective journey toward securing voting rights.

The movement had a shared vision of crossing over gender-based discrimination. Women from different walks of life united under the banner of suffrage, illustrating the power of collective action in dismantling systemic barriers that denied them a fundamental right.

The suffrage leaders' efforts laid the foundation for future generations of women. Their work created a path for women to cross over legal and societal impediments, contributing to the eventual ratification of the 19th Amendment in 1920, granting women the right to vote in the United States.

The suffrage movement's influence extended beyond the United States, inspiring women's rights activists globally. The collective journey of suffragists catalyzed similar movements in other parts of the world, fostering a shared global aspiration for gender equality.

The suffrage movement not only secured voting rights but also catalyzed a broader transformation in societal norms. It challenged deeply rooted beliefs about women's roles and capabilities, paving the way for subsequent movements advocating for women's rights in various spheres.

The Women's Suffrage Movement, with its collective spirit and determination to cross over barriers, serves as a poignant example of a Jordan Association. The leaders and participants in this movement demonstrated that shared vision, perseverance, and unity can lead to transformative societal change.

You must cross over to possess your possession. You always need people who will help and inspire you to greater heights. These push you to go the extra mile in achieving your goals in life. They push you forward even beyond what you could imagine. They celebrate your victories and not your miseries.

Here are some characteristics of this association:

Crossing Over to Possess Your Possession:

The idea here is that reaching your goals often requires overcoming obstacles and making significant strides. The individuals associated with the Jordan moment are those who guide and support you as you make critical leaps in your journey.

Inspiration to Greater Heights:

The people in your Jordan Association are not content with the status quo; they encourage and inspire you to reach higher. Their presence elevates your aspirations and encourages you to aim for goals beyond your initial expectations.

Pushing Beyond Imaginable Limits:

These individuals challenge you to go beyond what you thought was possible. They believe in your potential and motivate you to stretch your limits, unlocking capabilities and talents you might not have realized were within you.

Celebrating Victories, Not Miseries:

A distinguishing feature of the Jordan Association is that the people within it are genuinely happy about your successes. They celebrate your victories, providing positive reinforcement and creating an environment where accomplishments are acknowledged and applauded.

Application to Personal Growth:

In our personal growth journeys, the Jordan Association becomes crucial. These are the mentors, friends, or colleagues who guide us through pivotal moments, encouraging us to take risks, embrace challenges, and celebrate achievements.

They contribute to the crossing over from one phase of life to the next, ensuring that we not only reach our goals but exceed them.

By surrounding ourselves with individuals who embody the spirit of the Jordan Association, we enhance our ability to navigate challenges, set ambitious goals, and experience personal and professional fulfillment. This association becomes a catalyst for transformative moments and a source of strength during critical junctures in our journey.

APOLLO 11 MISSION (1969)

The Apollo 11 mission stands as an unparalleled testament to the spirit of the Jordan Association. The team, comprised of astronauts Neil Armstrong, Buzz Aldrin, and Michael Collins, along with a multitude of engineers, scientists, and support staff, embarked on a journey that transcended the boundaries of human achievement.

Astronauts Pushing Limits:

Armstrong and Aldrin, the first humans to set foot on the moon, exemplified the courage and determination needed to cross over into uncharted territory. Their steps on the lunar surface marked a momentous leap for humanity, inspiring individuals to dream beyond the confines of Earth.

Engineering Innovations:

The engineers and scientists at NASA pioneered groundbreaking technologies to ensure the success of the mission. From developing the

Saturn V rocket to creating the lunar module, their collaborative efforts pushed the boundaries of aerospace engineering, setting new standards for exploration.

Collective Vision and Celebration:

The collective vision of landing on the moon rallied the entire team. The successful mission wasn't just a triumph for NASA; it was a shared victory for humanity. The celebrations that followed reflected a global acknowledgment of what could be achieved when diverse minds come together for a common goal.

Inspiration for Generations:

Apollo 11's success left an indelible mark on history, inspiring generations to pursue careers in science, technology, engineering, and mathematics (STEM). The mission's legacy continues to serve as a beacon, encouraging individuals to reach for the stars and explore the unknown.

ONGOING GLOBAL EFFORTS IN CLIMATE CHANGE:

In the face of the existential threat posed by climate change, the collective response from activists, scientists, and policymakers worldwide mirrors the characteristics of the Jordan Association.

Environmental activists, such as Greta Thunberg and numerous grassroots movements, embody the spirit of pushing boundaries. Their advocacy for climate action goes beyond individual interests, aiming to cross over the challenges of environmental degradation through widespread awareness and mobilization.

Scientific Collaboration:

Scientists globally collaborate to understand and address the complexities of climate change. Collaborative research, data sharing, and interdisciplinary efforts aim to cross over the challenges posed by climate-related issues, fostering innovative solutions for a sustainable future.

Policy Initiatives and Global Cooperation:

Policymakers and leaders from different nations engage in global forums to collectively address climate change. Initiatives like the Paris Agreement represent a shared commitment to cross over the challenges of reducing greenhouse gas emissions and mitigating the impacts of climate change on a global scale.

Inspiring Transformative Actions:

The collective push for climate action inspires transformative changes in various sectors. From renewable energy initiatives to sustainable practices in industries, the global effort to combat climate change reflects a shared vision of crossing over environmental challenges for the well-being of the planet.

In these ongoing efforts, the Jordan Association dynamic propels humanity toward a shared goal of addressing climate change, demonstrating that collaborative action is essential to navigate the challenges posed by environmental degradation.

3.   WENT A DAY'S JOURNEY AHEAD

"Today, do just a little bit more.

Turn going the extra mile into a habit

- it is what lifts most successful people above the crowd."

Bob Proctor

One of the sure ways of dealing with miracle monsters and challenges is to go the extra mile. You have to go the extra mile in acquiring the needed skills, knowledge and capacity to handle the monsters that confront you.

In the pursuit of success, one often encounters obstacles and adversaries, the so-called "miracle monsters" that challenge the very fabric of one's being. How do you confront these formidable foes? By going beyond the customary, by embarking on a journey of continuous self-improvement and unwavering commitment.

Financial challenges often present formidable monsters, but going the extra mile involves more than seeking quick fixes. It means adopting prudent financial habits, budgeting meticulously, and making informed investment decisions.

The world may present shortcuts and quick fixes, tempting you with fleeting gains, but the real triumph lies in traversing the extra mile. This journey is not just about the distance covered but the depth of knowledge, skills, and capacity gained along the way.

It's a commitment to acquiring the tools needed to confront and conquer the monsters that stand in the way of your aspirations.

Warren Buffett, the legendary investor and philanthropist, is a testament to going the extra mile in financial life. His disciplined approach to investing, continuous learning, and long-term vision set him apart in the world of finance.

Buffett's commitment to prudent financial habits and his ability to navigate market complexities showcase the transformative impact of going beyond conventional strategies. His life teaches us that financial success is achievable through patience, knowledge, and a commitment to lifelong learning.

When faced with the monster of economic uncertainties, going the extra mile ensures building a financial fortress that withstands the tests of unforeseen circumstances.

"One of the most important principles of success

is developing the habit of going the extra mile."

Napoleon Hill

In a world often enticed by the allure of instant gratification, the extra mile demands patience and a relentless work ethic. While others may resort to dubious means to amass wealth, you choose the path of hard work and integrity, building a foundation for enduring prosperity. This commitment sets you apart, creating a legacy of sustainable success that withstands the test of time.

The academic journey is fraught with challenges, and going the extra mile here means pushing beyond the boundaries of conventional study habits. It involves late-night sessions, embracing the joy of learning, and seeking knowledge beyond the classroom.

When facing the monster of academic obstacles, going the extra mile means persistently pursuing excellence, understanding that each effort contributes to a foundation of wisdom that lasts a lifetime.

Education, a cornerstone of personal and professional growth, requires venturing beyond the common grounds. Late-night study sessions, dedication to continuous learning, and a thirst for knowledge propel you ahead, ensuring that you're not merely seeking academic achievements but acquiring wisdom that transcends the ordinary.

Marie Curie, the pioneering physicist and chemist, went the extra mile in her academic pursuits, breaking gender barriers in the male-dominated scientific community. Despite facing adversity, Curie's dedication to groundbreaking research in radioactivity earned her two Nobel Prizes.

Her relentless pursuit of knowledge and excellence serves as an inspiration for those aspiring to excel in academic life, demonstrating the transformative power of passion and dedication.

In the realm of relationships, going the extra mile means investing time and effort into meaningful connections. It's about valuing authentic bonds over superficial interactions, recognizing that true satisfaction comes from providing exceptional products and services to those you serve.

In the realm of family and relationships, going the extra mile takes the form of sacrificial love and unwavering commitment. It's about investing time, understanding, and patience into building connections that withstand the tests of time.

When faced with the monster of misunderstandings or conflicts, going the extra mile means choosing empathy over ego, forgiveness over resentment, and creating a haven of love that shields against the storms of life.

The path to greatness is not paved with mediocrity; it demands uniqueness and a commitment to solving distinctive problems in society. To be extraordinary in a world moving at an accelerating pace, you must embrace the challenge of offering something unparalleled. Going the extra mile becomes the bridge between the ordinary and the exceptional, propelling you towards a future where your impact resonates profoundly.

Arnold Schwarzenegger, the bodybuilder turned actor and politician, exemplifies going the extra mile in health and fitness. His disciplined approach to bodybuilding, even in the face of skepticism, propelled him to become a seven-time Mr. Olympia.

Schwarzenegger's commitment to health extended to his advocacy for fitness and wellness, showcasing the transformative power of prioritizing physical well-being. His life teaches us that dedication to health can lead to personal fulfillment and inspire positive change in others.

Navigating a career path demands more than fulfilling job responsibilities. Going the extra mile means continuously upgrading skills, seeking innovation, and contributing beyond the expected. Confronting the monster of professional stagnation, it involves stepping into leadership roles, mentoring others, and leaving an indelible mark on the workplace.

As you navigate the complexities of life, remember that the extra mile is not just a route; it's a mindset, a philosophy that propels you forward when the journey becomes arduous. It's the secret weapon against the monsters that threaten your dreams – a relentless pursuit of excellence, an unwavering commitment to surpassing expectations, and a refusal to settle for anything less than greatness.

Navigating the complexities of morality requires more than adhering to societal norms. Going the extra mile in moral life involves making choices aligned with values, even when it seems easier to compromise.

When confronted with the monster of moral dilemmas, it means taking the higher ground, standing firm in integrity, and ensuring that every decision contributes to a life of purpose and virtue.

There is a way that seems right to man but in the end, it is destruction. You must go the extra mile in prayer, love for fellow humans, worship and the study of the word if you are going to excel in your ministry, family or organization.

Despite enduring 27 years of imprisonment, Mandela emerged with a commitment to forgiveness and reconciliation. His ability to reconcile with former oppressors, promote unity, and build a nation founded on forgiveness showcases a remarkable dedication to going beyond the expected in family and relationships.

Mandela's legacy teaches us that transformative change can begin with the individual choices we make in our personal lives.

The rapid pace of modern trends can be overwhelming, but going the extra mile means adapting with agility. It involves staying abreast of technological advancements, embracing change, and innovating in the face of evolving landscapes. When confronted with the monster of obsolescence, going the extra mile ensures relevance and resilience in an ever-changing world.

You must go the extra mile to provide the necessary products and services your customers need for maximum satisfaction. To be a distinct youth or individual, you can't do the ordinary things and expect to be extra-ordinary or very significant in life.

The world is moving so fast that it will take more than the ordinary to make a great impact in it. You need something very unique and solves a unique problem in society to be great.

"There are no traffic jams when you go the extra mile."

Zig Ziglar

Steve Jobs, the co-founder of Apple Inc., revolutionized industries through his commitment to going the extra mile in his career. Jobs's relentless pursuit of innovation, attention to design detail, and commitment to creating products that transformed the tech landscape exemplify the transformative power of passion and dedication in one's profession.

His life teaches us that pushing boundaries and embracing creativity can lead to unparalleled success.

Elon Musk, the entrepreneur and visionary, consistently goes the extra mile in navigating modern trends. From revolutionizing the electric car industry with Tesla to spearheading space exploration with SpaceX, Musk's ability to anticipate and shape modern trends showcases a commitment beyond the ordinary.

His transformative impact on multiple industries teaches us that embracing innovation and pushing the boundaries of what is possible can redefine entire sectors.

In each aspect of life, going the extra mile is not just a choice; it's a pledge to confront and conquer the monsters that threaten the essence of our existence. It's an emotional and relatable commitment to a life that transcends the ordinary, where every effort contributes to a legacy of resilience, fulfillment, and enduring success.

"You will smile at the end when you go the extra mile"

Asare Richmond

4. WENT INTO THE WILDERNESS

Your wilderness determines your greatness. The wilderness is a place of preparation. It is a place of silent schooling. It is a place where God trains and builds your character and attitudes. All negative behaviours and characters must be dealt with in the wilderness.

All fears, worry and anxiety must be burnt here. You are taught to build enough faith and strength to deal with the giants that are ahead. When you overcome the lions and bears in the wilderness you kill every monster that appears before you in any area of your life.

"Into the forest I go, to lose my mind and find my soul."

John Muir

Entering the wilderness is not merely a physical journey; it's a plunge into the depths of your emotional and spiritual landscape. It's a sacred pilgrimage where the terrain is not just external but echoes the intricate passages of your soul.

This wilderness, during challenging times, becomes the crucible where emotions are distilled and the divine hand prepares you for the battles ahead.

As you step into this sacred sanctuary, the emotional baggage you carry becomes a tangible weight. The divine guide within beckons you to lay down these burdens—fears, doubts, anxieties—before proceeding further. Here, amidst the quiet rustle of leaves and the distant whispers of the wind, emotional preparation unfolds.

In the wilderness, emotions are not suppressed; they are acknowledged and embraced. Like a therapeutic rainfall, tears cleanse the soul. Every drop is a prayer, a conversation with the divine, expressing vulnerability and surrender. The divine preparation in the wilderness involves navigating the tumultuous rivers of emotion, emerging on the other side cleansed and renewed.

This emotional odyssey is intertwined with the spiritual unfolding. It's a journey where silence is a sacred language, and solitude becomes the canvas upon which the divine paints its masterpiece. The wilderness is not just a physical space; it's an inner sanctum where the divine prepares your spirit for the battles that lie ahead.

The wilderness becomes not just a place but a state of being—an internal landscape where you confront and conquer your personal Goliaths.

The foundation laid in the wilderness is not just for personal edification; it's a gift to the world. Like a lighthouse standing firm amidst the storm, your well-built foundation becomes a beacon of hope and inspiration to others navigating their tumultuous seas.

In times of challenge, the wilderness becomes a cocoon, a place of divine metamorphosis. The emotional storms that rage within are not stifled but are allowed to dance, unraveling the intricacies of the human experience. The divine, in this silent classroom, teaches the alchemy of turning emotional vulnerabilities into strengths.

As you navigate the labyrinth of your emotions, you uncover the divine within—the unwavering anchor amidst the storm. It's a sacred encounter, a communion where the divine breathes life into your spirit. Here, prayers are not just words; they are the echoes of the heart reaching out to the unseen hands that guide and prepare.

The wilderness becomes a sanctuary where emotional and divine preparations intertwine, creating a harmonious symphony. The challenges faced, the tears shed, and the prayers whispered become the notes that compose a melody of resilience and grace.

In this divine preparation, the wilderness transforms from a place of solitude into a sacred inner temple, where the spirit is fortified for the journey ahead.

"Keep close to Nature's heart... and break clear away,

once in a while, and climb a mountain or spend a week

in the woods. Wash your spirit clean."

John Muir

So, in the wilderness of challenging times, let the emotional storms cleanse, and the divine whispers prepare. For in this sacred space, the soul is not just readied for battles but is cradled in the arms of the divine, emerging stronger, wiser, and more attuned to the symphony of life.

Therefore it's vital that you build a solid foundation to withstand the trials of life. When the foundations is deep and well built in secret it's able to stand the storms of life. When the foundation is weak, no matter the super structure on it, it will still fall in the storms of life.

So, in the wilderness, embrace the challenges, overcome the fears, and let the storms refine you. For in the crucible of solitude, you emerge not just as a conqueror of monsters but as a beacon that illuminates the path for others to follow. Smile, for every extra mile you tread in the wilderness is a step towards greatness.

In the depths of human suffering during the Holocaust, Viktor Frankl's journey stands as a testament to the power of divine and emotional preparation in facing unimaginable challenges.

Frankl, a psychiatrist and Holocaust survivor, traversed the emotional wilderness of concentration camps, enduring profound hardships. Despite the physical and emotional torment, he found a higher purpose and meaning that sustained him through the darkest times.

The emotional wilderness, in Frankl's experience, became a crucible for refining his character and strengthening his resolve. It was in this desolate landscape that he confronted and conquered fears, worries, and anxieties. The storms of life that raged around him became the backdrop for building an unshakable foundation of faith and resilience.

Frankl's approach to his own suffering and that of his fellow prisoners was a form of divine preparation—a connection to a higher purpose that transcended the immediate horrors. He discovered that, even in the face of the monstrous challenges posed by the Holocaust, one could find meaning and purpose.

This divine preparation provided a guiding light through the darkest hours, enabling him to maintain a sense of humanity and dignity.

Post-liberation, Viktor Frankl channeled his experiences into the development of *logotherapy*, a psychotherapeutic approach that emphasizes finding purpose and meaning in all forms of existence.

His legacy serves as a beacon for those navigating their own emotional wilderness, reminding us that even in the bleakest moments, there's a potential for growth, transformation, and the discovery of profound meaning.

Frankl's story illustrates that the emotional wilderness is not just a place of suffering but also a realm where individuals can tap into inner strength, resilience, and spiritual fortitude. The journey through this wilderness, when embraced with a divine and emotional perspective, can lead to profound personal transformation and a renewed sense of purpose.

HARRIET TUBMAN - GUIDED BY FAITH IN THE WILDERNESS OF SLAVERY

Harriet Tubman, an African American abolitionist and political activist, endured the brutalities of slavery in the 19th century. Her life's journey serves as a compelling example of navigating the emotional wilderness through faith and divine connection.

Harriet Tubman, born into slavery, escaped to freedom and then made numerous perilous journeys back into slave territory to rescue around 70 enslaved individuals through the Underground Railroad. Her endeavors were fraught with dangers, including the risk of capture and severe punishment.

In the emotional wilderness of slavery and the fight for freedom, Tubman leaned heavily on her deep faith and connection to a higher purpose. She often spoke of having vivid dreams and visions that she interpreted as messages from God, guiding her on the path to liberation. Tubman's conviction and trust in these divine communications fortified her spirit and determination.

The storms Tubman faced in her quest for freedom were both physical and emotional, but her unwavering faith provided a compass through the darkest moments. She believed that her actions were not only her own but divinely guided, instilling in her the strength to endure and lead others to freedom.

Harriet Tubman's story illustrates that, even in the most oppressive conditions, individuals can find resilience and purpose through a connection to something greater than themselves.

The emotional and divine preparation she underwent in the wilderness of slavery empowered her to stand against injustice and lead others to a brighter, liberated future.

CORRIE TEN BOOM - RESILIENCE AMIDST ADVERSITY:

Corrie Ten Boom, a Dutch Christian and Holocaust survivor, faced the horrors of World War II when she and her family provided refuge to Jews during the Nazi occupation. Eventually, they were discovered, arrested, and sent to concentration camps.

In the midst of the harrowing experiences in the concentration camps, Corrie's unwavering faith and resilience became a source of inspiration. She, too, traversed an emotional wilderness, grappling with the loss of family members and the brutality of the Holocaust.

Corrie's deep connection to her Christian faith served as a foundation for emotional and divine preparation. In the face of unimaginable suffering, she found solace and purpose in her beliefs. This divine preparation allowed her to endure the storms of life with remarkable courage and compassion.

After the war, Corrie ten Boom dedicated her life to spreading a message of forgiveness and reconciliation. Her story is a powerful testament to the transformative potential of facing adversity with a foundation of faith and emotional strength.

Corrie's experiences in the emotional wilderness became a crucible for developing a profound understanding of human suffering and the capacity for divine grace.

These examples collectively underscore the idea that navigating the emotional wilderness with a sense of purpose, faith, and emotional resilience can lead to extraordinary transformations, even in the face of the most challenging circumstances.

5. HE COMMUNICATED, POURING OUT HIS HEART

In the realm of adversity, Elijah's response teaches a profound lesson about the power of communication. Amidst challenges and monsters, how we articulate our thoughts can either exacerbate our struggles or pave the way for triumph. Elijah's communication strategy becomes a beacon, guiding us on how to navigate the storms of life.

In time of difficulties and challenges you need to be mindful of what you say. What you say in times like these will either magnify your problems or reduce them. When you talk negative, you experience negative. When you speak positive, you experience positive.

"The more you talk about negative things in your life,

the more you call them in. Speak victory not defeat."

Joel Osteen

Life and death are in the power of the tongue. In times of crisis, the words we choose become instruments that either breathe life into desolate situations or deepen the shadows. You have to make the right choice of speaking life into every situation around you. Speak life to the dry bones in your marriage, academics and business and it shall come to life again.

Elijah's counsel encourages a deliberate practice of positive affirmation. Speaking life into the dry bones of our circumstances implies an acknowledgment of our ability to influence outcomes through the spoken word.

In the face of adversity, self-encouragement becomes a powerful tool for fostering resilience and summoning the inner strength necessary for overcoming challenges.

Don't talk yourself down in times of difficulty. Never think you ca not overcome the monsters that are in your life. Encourage yourself and speak to the situation and believe that you will come out of the situation if you do not give up.

Talk to the right people in times of difficulties. Speak with the more experienced and more knowledgeable and can support and help you navigate the issues of life. Let them motivate and inspire you by their teachings and wise counsel. Let them share their mistakes and apply them in your life where necessary.

Never discuss anything with gossips and people who cannot help you overcome the challenges of life. You will be wasting your precious time. They will only listen and magnify your problems instead of encouraging you.

Discard people who do not give you good advice and contribute positively to your dreams and aspirations in life. The right communication will lead to the right destination.

Elijah's story warns against the pitfalls of sharing challenges with individuals who lack the capacity to offer constructive advice. The caution to discard interactions with gossips and unhelpful voices underscores the importance of protecting one's mental and emotional space during difficulties.

"Your communication will determine your destination"

In today's context, this principle echoes through various aspects of life. Whether in personal relationships, professional endeavors, or mental well-being, the power of communication remains a potent force.

From positive self-talk to seeking guidance from mentors and avoiding toxic influences, the relevance of Elijah's communication strategy extends to the complexities of the contemporary world.

Malala Yousafzai, a Nobel laureate and advocate for girls' education, utilized the power of communication to bring attention to the challenges faced by young girls seeking an education in Pakistan. Her eloquence and courage transformed her personal story into a global movement for change.

Winston Churchill's speeches during World War II exemplify the impact of positive communication in times of crisis. His ability to rally the British people through the darkest days of the war showcases the transformative influence of words on collective morale and resilience.

> "Words have the power to both destroy and heal.
>
> When words are both true and kind,
>
> they can change our world."
>
> Buddha

CHIMAMANDA NGOZI ADICHIE - COMMUNICATION FOR SOCIAL CHANGE:

Chimamanda Ngozi Adichie, a contemporary Nigerian author and feminist, has emerged as a powerful voice advocating for gender equality through her literary works and public discourse. Adichie's impact lies not only in her storytelling prowess but also in her ability to use communication as a catalyst for social change.

In her acclaimed TED Talk, "We Should All Be Feminists," Adichie skillfully dissects the complexities of gender roles, challenging stereotypes and advocating for a more inclusive society. Her ability to articulate the subtle ways gender biases manifest has resonated globally, sparking conversations and inspiring a new wave of feminism.

Her novels, such as "Half of a Yellow Sun" and "Americanah," delve into the intricacies of identity, race, and gender. Through her characters, she communicates the nuances of societal expectations, shedding light on the challenges faced by women navigating patriarchal systems. By intertwining storytelling with social commentary, Adichie employs communication as a tool to foster empathy and understanding.

Beyond literature, Adichie engages in public conversations that confront ingrained biases and encourage critical thinking. Her unwavering commitment to challenging societal norms through communication has positioned her as a key figure in the global discourse on gender equality.

In essence, Chimamanda Ngozi Adichie exemplifies the transformative potential of communication in effecting social change. Through her eloquence and fearless engagement with challenging topics, she empowers individuals to question prevailing norms and envision a more equitable world.

"Our lives begin to end the day we become silent

about things that matter."

Martin Luther King Jr.

GRETA THUNBERG - COMMUNICATION FOR ENVIRONMENTAL ACTION:

In the annals of environmental activism, Greta Thunberg stands out as a formidable force, using communication as a catalyst for urgent climate action. Born in 2003, Thunberg gained international recognition for her

Fridays for Future school strike, which evolved into a global youth movement demanding decisive measures against climate change.

At the heart of Thunberg's impact lies her unwavering commitment to communicate the gravity of the climate crisis. Armed with a conviction that transcends her age, she addresses world leaders, policymakers, and the global public with a simple yet powerful message: the Earth is in peril, and immediate action is imperative.

Thunberg's speeches, notably at international forums like the United Nations Climate Action Summit, showcase a masterful use of communication to cut through bureaucratic inertia.

She employs a direct and unapologetic style, emphasizing the moral responsibility of current generations to safeguard the planet for future ones. By framing climate change as an existential threat, she compels individuals and institutions to confront uncomfortable truths.

Beyond traditional platforms, Thunberg leverages social media to amplify her message. Her Twitter account, followed by millions, serves as a conduit for disseminating information, organizing events, and fostering a sense of global solidarity among climate activists.

The ripple effect of Thunberg's communication is evident in the millions of students worldwide participating in climate strikes and the growing momentum behind environmental policies. Her ability to galvanize action through communication illustrates the transformative power of a clear, resonant message, particularly in rallying younger generations to champion a sustainable future.

In essence, Greta Thunberg exemplifies how effective communication can serve as a rallying cry for urgent and collective responses to global challenges.

Her unwavering commitment to environmental advocacy underscores the profound impact that a determined voice, particularly from the younger generation, can have on shaping the discourse and action around critical monsters of globe.

6. ARISE AND EAT

When setbacks come your way, never give up. You should not remain in the mess. You may have backslidden in one area of your life but, this should not be the end of the world for you.

Setbacks are not signs of defeat but rather opportunities for a resilient rebound. The phrase "Arise and Eat" encapsulates the essence of standing tall after a fall and nourishing oneself for the journey ahead.

"When you slip, stand straight,

don't stick and stay else you will stink"

Richmond Asare

Life's journey is marked by inevitable stumbles and falls. Whether it's a failed business venture, an academic setback, or a personal struggle, the key lies not in the fall itself but in the subsequent rise. The ability to dust off the remnants of disappointment and stand upright defines true resilience.

The story of Steve Jobs, the visionary behind Apple Inc., unfolds as a poignant saga of resilience, innovation, and the undying human spirit. Jobs faced a profound fall from grace when he was ousted from the very company he co-founded, plunging into a wilderness of professional setbacks and personal turmoil.

Yet, within the depths of adversity, Jobs discovered a wellspring of determination that would redefine the tech landscape.

The man who had once been at the forefront of revolutionary tech innovation found himself in the wilderness of corporate rejection. Jobs, however, refused to be defined by his ousting. The emotional toll of being separated from the company he helped build could have been debilitating, but instead, it became the crucible in which his tenacity was forged.

Jobs's return to Apple in 1997 marked a resurgence that mirrored the mythical rise of a phoenix from its ashes. Determined to turn the tide, he orchestrated a remarkable turnaround for the company.

The visionary, once cast out, now led Apple to unprecedented success, introducing iconic products like the iPod, iPhone, and iPad. The emotional intensity of this resurgence reverberated not just in boardrooms but in the collective consciousness of an industry witnessing a transformative comeback.

"Quitters never win, and winners never quit" echoes the sentiment that enduring success is not bestowed upon those who surrender to adversity. Every fall is a call to rise again, armed with newfound strength and wisdom. In the face of failures, it is the persistent spirit that forges the path to victory.

The products that would redefine personal technology emerged from the ashes of Jobs's personal and professional challenges. The iPod, iPhone, and iPad weren't just technological marvels; they were emotional testaments to Jobs's ability to channel setbacks into innovative triumphs.

The emotional resonance of this journey extends beyond business success—it's a testament to the capacity for human creativity and innovation to thrive amidst adversity.

Steve Jobs's story is more than a tale of corporate success; it's an emotional odyssey of resilience and self-discovery. The weight of his fall was felt not.

"It's not whether you get knocked down;

it's whether you get up."

Vince Lombardi

When you trail a course in school, rise up and re-sit till you overcome. The call to "re-sit till you overcome" resonates with the pursuit of knowledge and excellence. Education is not solely about acing every test but about learning from failures, embracing growth, and emerging wiser and more determined.

The second facet of this concept underscores the significance of preparation. Life's challenges require more than just innate talent; they demand continuous self-improvement and preparation. Going the extra mile in preparing yourself adequately underscores the need to upgrade skills, acquire knowledge, and stay relevant in an ever-evolving world.

"Success depends upon previous preparation,

and without such preparation, there is sure to be failure."

Confucius

In today's competitive landscape, staying abreast of advancements is not a luxury but a necessity. The metaphorical significance of "EAT enough" goes beyond mere sustenance; it's a call to nourish one's mind, skills, and abilities. Adequate preparation becomes the armor that shields against the onslaught of life's monsters.

When your first business fails, never throw in the towel. Rise up and come back for the victory you deserve. Your place cannot be replaced in the Palace of life. As already mentioned above, 'Quitters never win and winners never quit.'

Go the extra mile in preparing yourself adequately for the challenges ahead. The competition now is very keen as such, you must up-grade yourself constantly else, you will become obsolete.

"Arise and Eat" is not just a rallying cry; it's a declaration of triumph over adversity. Each rise from a fall and every act of preparation serves as an echo, resonating the unwavering spirit of resilience. In the grand symphony of life, setbacks are mere pauses; the real melody lies in the triumphant notes of those who choose to rise and keep moving forward.

Abraham Lincoln's early life was marked by humble beginnings. Born into a log cabin in Hardin County, Kentucky, in 1809, Lincoln experienced the hardships of poverty.

His family's modest means required him to work various jobs, from farm laborer to rail-splitter, instilling in him the values of hard work, perseverance, and self-reliance. Largely self-educated, Lincoln's voracious appetite for reading and learning allowed him to transcend the limitations of his formal education.

In his early adulthood, Lincoln attempted several business ventures, including running a general store. Unfortunately, these enterprises faced financial difficulties, leading to significant debts and eventual bankruptcy. These setbacks highlighted the precarious nature of economic life on the frontier and the challenges Lincoln faced in securing financial stability.

Lincoln's incursion into politics started with an unsuccessful run for the Illinois State Legislature in 1832. Over the years, he faced multiple electoral defeats and setbacks, including failed bids for the U.S. House of Representatives and the U.S. Senate.

These political disappointments could have deterred a less determined individual, but Lincoln saw them as opportunities for growth and refinement.

He endured profound personal losses, notably the death of his beloved son, Willie, in 1862. This heartbreaking event, combined with the ongoing challenges of the Civil War, placed an immense emotional burden on Lincoln. The weight of grief and responsibility could have overwhelmed him, yet it became another crucible in which Lincoln's character was tested.

Abraham Lincoln's resilience in the face of adversity was a defining trait. Instead of succumbing to despair or letting defeats define him, he used each setback as a stepping stone to succeed.

Lincoln's story teaches us that setbacks need not define us; instead, they can serve as stepping stones toward ultimate success. His legacy remains a powerful reminder of the strength found in resilience, determination, and an unyielding spirit.

"Preparation is the key to success."

Alexander Graham Bell

TURNING REJECTION INTO TRIUMPH

J.K. Rowling's path to literary acclamation is a captivating tale of resilience, perseverance, and the transformative power of imagination. Her story sounds as a testimony to the indomitable spirit that can turn rejection into an extraordinary literary journey.

In the early '90s, Rowling found herself navigating the challenges of single motherhood while grappling with financial constraints. Her personal struggles could have easily become insurmountable obstacles, but Rowling's determination to provide a better life for her daughter fueled her pursuit of a dream that extended far beyond her immediate circumstances.

The inception of the wizarding world in Rowling's mind faced rejection after rejection from publishers. The initial manuscript for the first Harry Potter book encountered skepticism and dismissal from the industry.

Rowling's resilience in the face of repeated rejection is a testament to her unwavering belief in the magical universe she had crafted. The road to literary success was far from easy.

She encountered financial difficulties, at times relying on government assistance to make ends meet. The persistence required to continue refining her craft amidst such challenges speaks volumes about her dedication to the story she was determined to share with the world.

Rather than allowing rejection letters to define her narrative, Rowling used them as stepping stones. She embraced the opportunity to improve her writing and sought a publisher who recognized the brilliance within her stories.

The eventual acceptance of the Harry Potter series by Bloomsbury marked a turning point not just for Rowling but for the literary landscape as a whole.

The transformation from an unknown writer to a literary phenomenon underscores the triumph of creativity, determination, and the unwavering belief in the power of one's imagination.

Rowling's journey encourages aspiring writers and dreamers to persist in the pursuit of their visions, reminding us that within the realms of perseverance lies the potential for magical narratives to unfold.

"Perseverance is not just the willingness to work hard.

It's that plus the willingness to be stubborn

about your own belief in yourself."

Marilyn vos Savant

7. TRAVELED IN THE STRENGTH OF THAT FOOD

"Do not wait to strike till the iron is hot,

but make it hot by striking."

William Butler Yeats

In the journey towards manifesting your visions and dreams, action is the bridge between aspiration and actualization. It's not merely about acquiring knowledge or possessing natural talents; true transformation occurs when that acquired wisdom is translated into tangible actions. Your dreams remain ethereal until you step into the realm of action.

Actions give reality to your visions. No matter the amount of information and natural gifting you have; until you take concrete steps towards your dreams, they will remain dreams and not realities. After you have acquired the needed skills and training, you must go all out to put into practice what you know.

Imagine Elijah under the broom tree, having received nourishment but still languishing in the shadows of despair. It wasn't until he chose to embark on the journey to Horeb that he began to experience the strength of the food he had consumed. This narrative teaches us a vital lesson — information should pave the way for transformational action.

"Knowing is not enough; we must apply.

Willing is not enough; we must do."

Johann Wolfgang von Goethe

Information must lead to transformation. All that you need to succeed is embedded within you. Just go ahead and exercise your convictions. Take the initiative first and God will add His grace. If Elijah had not taken the first step towards Horeb, he would have remained under the broom tree. A place of sorrow and disappointment.

The strength of your vision lies in your ability to turn knowledge into action. All the skills, talents, and training you acquire serve as potential energy waiting to be unleashed.

Elijah's journey wasn't about waiting for perfect conditions or seeking other grand opportunities. It was about contentment with what he had and using it purposefully.

Your journey might begin with the seemingly modest resources you possess, but it's the initiative, passion, and unwavering determination that will set you on the path to success.

Much like Elijah, you may find yourself in situations where the road ahead seems challenging, but the strength lies in utilizing what you have at your disposal.

He traveled in the strength of what he had eaten. This also means he used the abilities and capabilities he acquired not waiting for perfect conditions. He was also not relishing other sumptuous meals or opportunities far away. He was content with that which he had and used it profitably.

Whatever situation you find yourself take the initiative to correct and overcome it. Pursue your goal and aspirations with deep passion. Don't look back, go forward in the strength you have. Yours may start with the little you have in hand but it can increase if you do not give up.

Don't let your dreams remain stagnant under the broom tree of hesitation. Take the first step towards your goals. The strength of the food you've consumed – the knowledge, skills, and capabilities – will manifest when you choose to traverse the path of action.

Progress might start small, but it's the consistent steps forward that lead to significant advancements.

"Inaction breeds doubt and fear.

Action breeds confidence and courage.

If you want to conquer fear, do not sit home and

think about it. Go out and get busy."

Dale Carnegie

In your pursuit, remember that waiting for perfect conditions is a mirage. The strength of your journey lies in the courage to move forward with what you have. Each step taken in the direction of your dreams is a testament to the power of initiative and the realization that, indeed, you can achieve greatness in the strength of the nourishment you have acquired.

JOAN OF ARC'S COURAGE IN THE HUNDRED YEARS' WAR

Joan of Arc was born around 1412 in Domrémy, a small village in northeastern France. She came from a humble background, the daughter of farmers, and grew up in a time when France was embroiled in the Hundred Years' War with England.

From an early age, Joan displayed a strong sense of faith and claimed to have visions and messages from saints, including a divine mission to support Charles VII, the Dauphin, and help him reclaim the French throne.

Joan's lack of formal education did not deter her from pursuing her divine calling. Driven by her unwavering conviction and deep faith, she approached Charles VII, urging him to allow her to accompany his forces. Despite skepticism from some quarters, Joan's conviction and charisma won her a place in the French army.

Joan faced numerous challenges, including doubt from within her own ranks and the inherent dangers of war. However, she played a crucial role in the lifting of the siege of Orléans in 1429, a turning point in the Hundred Years' War.

Unfortunately, Joan was eventually captured by the Burgundians, handed over to the English, and subjected to a politically motivated trial. In 1431, at the age of 19, she was unjustly condemned and burned at the stake.

Joan's fall, marked by her unjust execution, was followed by a remarkable rise. Twenty-five years after her death, a retrial declared her innocent of charges, and she was canonized as a saint by the Catholic Church in 1920.

Joan of Arc's journey, from a simple peasant girl to a symbol of courage and faith, illustrates the transformative power of acting on deeply held convictions.

OVERCOMING SETBACKS AND SHINING BRIGHT

Lionel Messi's journey from a young boy in Rosario, Argentina, to a global football icon was shaped profoundly by his education at FC Barcelona's La Masia academy.

Despite facing challenges such as a growth hormone deficiency that affected his physical stature, Messi's early years at La Masia became the crucible for his development.

The academy not only provided him with the necessary football education but also instilled values of resilience and perseverance.

Messi's time in the youth ranks showcased not only his talent but also his extraordinary skills on the pitch. His ability to dribble past opponents with unparalleled precision, coupled with his goal-scoring prowess, set him apart even at a young age.

Barcelona's coaching staff recognized his potential and unique style of play, laying the foundation for what would become an illustrious career.

The faith that Barcelona showed in Messi's abilities became evident when he made his debut for the first team at the age of 16 in 2003. The decision to include a relatively young and physically unassuming player in the senior squad reflected the belief in Messi's exceptional footballing acumen. His debut marked the beginning of a transformative era for both Messi and Barcelona.

Messi's journey to football superstardom was not without its challenges. Concerns about his size and adaptability to the demands of professional football emerged. These setbacks, however, fueled Messi's determination to prove himself on the grand stage.

In 2008, he faced injuries that temporarily interrupted his meteoric rise. Yet, his resilience and unwavering commitment to the sport allowed him to bounce back stronger.

Messi's resurgence post-injuries was nothing short of spectacular. He not only regained his form but elevated his game to new heights. His contributions were pivotal in Barcelona's success, winning numerous domestic and international titles. Messi's ability to turn setbacks into stepping stones demonstrated not just his footballing prowess but also his mental fortitude.

Messi's journey from La Masia to becoming a football legend encapsulates the theme of "TRAVELED IN THE STRENGTH OF THAT FOOD."

His education at the academy, coupled with setbacks and ultimate triumphs, illustrates the transformative power of determination, resilience, and unwavering self-belief in the face of challenges. Messi's story continues to inspire aspiring footballers worldwide.

CONFUCIUS (551–479 BCE):

Confucius, also known as Kong Fuzi or Kongzi, was a Chinese philosopher and teacher whose thoughts on ethics, morality, and social relationships have had a lasting impact on Chinese civilization.

In the ancient state of Lu, during the vibrant period of Chinese philosophy, there lived a sage named Confucius. His teachings, later compiled into "The Analects," would echo through the corridors of time, shaping the ethical framework of generations to come.

Confucius, a man of profound wisdom and humility, embarked on a journey to cultivate virtues and guide others toward a path of benevolence. His famous quote, "It does not matter how slowly you go as long as you do not stop," reflected his own life's journey.

Despite facing personal challenges and societal upheavals, Confucius remained steadfast in his commitment to moral education and ethical conduct.

Confucius was not merely a philosopher confined to scholarly pursuits; he actively engaged with the world around him.

He believed in the transformative power of education, emphasizing the importance of self-improvement and lifelong learning. In his role as a teacher, he imparted wisdom to his disciples, encouraging them to embrace the values of benevolence, righteousness, and filial piety.

One of Confucius' core teachings, encapsulated in the quote "When we see men of a contrary character, we should turn inwards and examine ourselves," underscored the introspective nature of his philosophy. He urged individuals to reflect on their own actions before passing judgment on others. This introspection, he believed, was crucial for personal growth and societal harmony.

Confucius' influence extended beyond the classroom. He sought to implement his ethical principles in governance, advocating for leaders to prioritize the welfare of the people and uphold moral integrity. While he faced resistance from political authorities of his time, his commitment to virtuous leadership left an indelible mark on the annals of Chinese political thought.

As Confucius traversed the landscapes of ancient China, his legacy grew, not through force or coercion but through the enduring power of his ideas. The slow and deliberate pace of his teachings, like a river carving its course through time, demonstrated the profound impact that patient and unwavering dedication could have on shaping the moral compass of a society.

Confucius, the unassuming sage, left behind a philosophical legacy that transcended centuries. His teachings continue to resonate, inspiring individuals to navigate the complexities of life with patience, introspection, and a commitment to the betterment of oneself and society.

In the quiet wisdom of his words, Confucius remains a beacon, guiding those who heed his timeless counsel toward a path of enduring virtue.

8. HOREB, THE MOUNTAIN OF GOD

Horeb, the Mountain of God, symbolizes a crucial phase in our journey—a place where the weary soul finds rest, where the flickering flame of inspiration is reignited, and where divine guidance flows abundantly. As you ascend this mountain, the air becomes crisper, carrying with it the whispers of your Maker, gently nudging you towards new vistas.

This sacred peak is not merely a geographical location but a spiritual realm where the anointing, strength, and gifts bestowed upon you are renewed. It's a place of spiritual rejuvenation, where you drink from the well of divine inspiration, fortifying yourself for the next leg of your odyssey.

"The key to continual and deeper

spiritual renewal and revival

is the continual re-discovery of the gospel."

Timothy Keller

In the solitude of Horeb, you commune with your Creator, receiving fresh instructions that illuminate your path. Here, the clutter of the world fades, allowing you to discern the still, small voice within, guiding you towards the next level of your purpose. The mountain serves as a canvas where the divine paints the blueprint of your destiny.

This is a place of renewing the anointing, strength and gifting within you. You are refreshed here. It is a place where you receive new instructions and inspiration from your maker. He guides and directs you in the next level. You must be able to buy into the mind of the Lord as without Him, you can do nothing.

In the fast-paced rhythm of modern life, Horeb, the Mountain of God, becomes a sanctuary for recalibration and renewal — a digital-age retreat for the soul. Here, amidst the constant buzz of notifications and the demands of a connected world, you find a virtual summit where the divine meets the digital.

Horeb in the contemporary context is not just a physical destination but a mental and spiritual space you create — a mindfulness app for the soul. It's where you intentionally unplug from the noise, seeking solace in meditation apps or reflective moments amidst the digital chatter.

In the virtual solitude of this modern Horeb, you connect with your inner self and the spiritual, receiving a WiFi signal from the divine.

Crucially, Horeb is a place of reflection and gratitude. As you stand on this hallowed ground, you're prompted to acknowledge and appreciate those who contributed to your ascent. The mentors, guides, and supporters who walked with you in the valleys, imparting wisdom and sharing experiences—Horeb is where you honor their influence.

Yet, the journey doesn't end on the mountain; it's a call to press on. It's a challenge to resist the allure of mediocrity, urging you to reach for the summit in every endeavor. This is not the time to settle for averages; it's a summons to sacrifice for excellence. Stand out, aspire for the best, and let your journey reflect the pursuit of the highest peaks in life.

This digital mountain is a place where you download fresh insights and updates, not from a celestial satellite but from the cloud of collective wisdom—TED Talks, podcasts, and online mentorship programs. It's a space where the algorithms of inspiration guide you toward your purpose, and the digital breadcrumbs left by mentors light your path.

In the serene hum of Horeb, you also engage in a virtual reflection, expressing gratitude not just through words but through the sharing and reposting of impactful content. Here, influencers and thought leaders become the modern-day prophets, contributing to your journey with their valuable bytes of wisdom.

"The time has come to turn to God and reassert our trust in Him

for the healing of America - our country is in need of

and ready for a spiritual renewal."

Ronald Reagan

In the shadow of Horeb, let the echoes of divine guidance and the wisdom of mentors propel you forward. The sacrifices made in this sacred space will be the building blocks of your legacy—a legacy that refuses to settle, reaching for the stars, and leaving an indelible mark on the tapestry of existence.

This is a place you appreciate the people who have helped you reach the heights you have attained. You must be redirected, corrected and motivated by their teachings and experiences. At this stage, you must also press on till you achieve the best or reach the highest peak in whatever endeavour.

Never settle for averages but go for the ultimate. You must sacrifice to obtain the best and standout among the crowd. You cannot settle for less. Reach for the best and highest in life.

But the digital Horeb is not a final destination; it's a Launchpad for action in the physical world. It's a call to leverage the insights gained in the digital realm and apply them in your daily life—a fusion of the virtual and the tangible.

It's a reminder that the modern journey doesn't end on the mountain; it's about translating the lessons learned in the digital sanctuary into real-world impact.

"Renewal is the ongoing process of discovery and

reinvention, a commitment to seeing the world

with fresh eyes and an open heart."

Oprah Winfrey

In the tumultuous milieu of 19th-century military hospitals during the Crimean War, Florence Nightingale faced a daunting reality. Witnessing the suffering of soldiers in unsanitary conditions, she retreated into her own mental sanctuary – her Horeb. This wasn't a physical mountain but a place of deep contemplation and reflection.

Born into a wealthy British family, Nightingale was expected to conform to societal norms for women of her status. However, driven by a passion for nursing, she defied conventions, pursuing education in the field against her family's wishes.

The Horeb moment for Nightingale wasn't just a serene escape; it was a crucible of transformation. Her early nursing efforts in Crimea faced immense challenges. The harsh conditions, lack of supplies, and resistance from military authorities could have been her breaking point. However, her retreat into the mental space of Horeb wasn't an escape from reality but a confrontation with it.

From the depths of this mental sanctuary, Nightingale emerged with a vision for change. She implemented rigorous hygiene practices, transforming the military hospitals. Her statistical analysis showcased the importance of sanitation, leading to significant improvements in healthcare practices. Nightingale's Horeb wasn't an ivory tower but a battleground where she fought for the well-being of those in her care.

The emotional toll of witnessing the suffering of soldiers, coupled with the resistance she faced, could have easily broken Nightingale. Yet, her retreat into Horeb became a source of strength. It was a place where she found resilience, determination, and a vision that transcended the challenges before her.

Florence Nightingale's Horeb wasn't just a personal retreat; it became the birthplace of modern nursing. Her legacy endures as a testament to the power of finding solace in challenging times, allowing one's mind to dream beyond the immediate struggles, and emerging with a vision that transforms lives.

CATHERINE HAMLIN - RESTORING DIGNITY IN OBSTETRIC FISTULA

Catherine Hamlin, born in Sydney, Australia, initially pursued a medical career. She and her husband, Reginald, went to Ethiopia in the 1950s for a short-term assignment. However, witnessing the severe childbirth injuries experienced by Ethiopian women ignited a lifelong commitment.

The Hamlins encountered women suffering from obstetric fistula, a devastating condition resulting from prolonged obstructed labor. This experience became their calling. After the death of her husband, Catherine faced the challenge of continuing their mission alone.

Catherine's emotional journey involved not only witnessing the physical suffering of countless women but also dealing with personal loss. The emotional toll of working in challenging conditions and facing the loss of her partner required resilience and determination.

Rather than succumbing to challenges, Catherine Hamlin established the Addis Ababa Fistula Hospital, providing free surgical repair for women with obstetric fistula. Her work extended to training medical professionals and raising awareness about maternal health issues.

Catherine Hamlin's resilience and dedication to restoring dignity to women suffering from obstetric fistula made a significant impact in Ethiopia and globally. Her legacy lives on through the hospital and foundation she co-founded, offering hope and healing to countless women.

The Horeb for Catherine Hamlin was Ethiopia, where she found her life's purpose in serving women facing unimaginable hardships. Her story illustrates the transf3ormative power of compassion, resilience, and the enduring impact one person can have on the lives of many.

"Passion is the bridge that

takes you from pain to change."

Frida Kahlo

NICK VUJICIC - INSPIRING MILLIONS WITH HOPE

Nick Vujicic, born in Melbourne, Australia, faced extraordinary challenges from birth. He was born without limbs, a condition known as tetra-amelia syndrome. Growing up, Nick experienced profound physical and emotional struggles due to his unique situation.

Nick's journey involved navigating the difficulties of acceptance and building resilience. His early years were marked by questioning his self-worth and purpose. However, he transformed his perceived limitations into sources of strength.

The emotional hurdles Nick faced included bullying, self-doubt, and the pervasive fear of not fitting in. Confronting societal expectations and overcoming internalized negativity were essential steps in his emotional healing.

Rather than allowing his physical condition to define him, Nick turned his life around. He became a motivational speaker, author, and advocate for people facing adversity. His organization, '*Life Without Limbs*', aims to inspire individuals worldwide to embrace their uniqueness.

Nick Vujicic's impact extends globally through his motivational speaking engagements, books, and online presence. His story of triumph over personal struggles resonates with diverse audiences, fostering a message of hope, resilience, and the power of a positive mindset.

Nick Vujicic found his Horeb in embracing his unique circumstances and using them as a platform to inspire others. His story exemplifies the strength that can arise from personal acceptance, determination, and a commitment to making a positive impact on the world.

"Inspiration comes from within yourself.

One has to be positive.

When you're positive, good things happen."

Deep Roy

CHAPTER FIVE

MAINTAINING YOUR MIRACLE: THE

MAJESTIC MILESTONE

"To maintain success is to embrace the responsibility that

accompanies triumph, knowing that sustained excellence

is a testament to enduring commitment."

Anthony Robbins

In the journey of pursuing dreams and overcoming life's challenges, the attainment of a miracle is a significant milestone. However, the real test lies not just in achieving the extraordinary but in sustaining it over time.

'Maintaining Your Miracle,' delves into the crucial phase where the initial euphoria of success transitions into a lifelong commitment to preserving the miraculous.

As we explore this chapter, we will embark on a reflective journey that goes beyond the moment of triumph. Maintaining a miracle demands a unique set of principles, mindset shifts, and intentional actions. This chapter aims to guide you through the intricacies of safeguarding the extraordinary gifts life bestows upon you.

We will unravel the secrets of those who have not only experienced miracles but have also cultivated the resilience and wisdom to keep them alive. From historical figures to modern examples, their stories will serve as beacons, illuminating the path towards sustainable success.

It is so much heartwarming and satisfying when you receive the miracle or breakthrough you desire. You are filled with songs of joy and ecstasy as you lay hold of your miracle after several days, weeks, months or years of waiting and working. Sometimes one cannot explain the feeling.

However, it is not enough to have a breakthrough today and not know how to maintain it or build upon it. A story is told of a man who had a big financial breakthrough and bought a very porch car. He was so excited that he decided to chill out with some friends. They went to the best resort out of town and really had a lot of fun.

At sunset, they decided to return but unfortunately due to the excitement and the fun they had, they drove the new car at top speed. Unfortunately, the car was involved in a fatal accident on their way. The man died on the spot.

His own breakthrough had led to his demise. The miracle murdered him because he was not smart enough to handle it well. He could not enjoy the blessings that were left. He lost his life. Friend, this should not be your story after you achieve great feats in life.

You should not allow your miracle or breakthrough lead to your destruction. You must be able to manage your achievements and successes. God is not handicapped to bless you but is more concerned about how you manage and develop what comes your way. It is the management or development of his resources in your hands the bigger issue here.

"Enduring setbacks while maintaining the ability to show others

the way to go forward is a true test of leadership."

Nitin Nohria

In the wake of this sobering reality, our journey through the delicate art of maintaining a miracle unfolds. The story of the man and his fatal fate serves as a beacon, illuminating the path our characters must tread with utmost care. The narrative pivots from the elation of achievement to the weighty responsibility of stewardship.

It beckons us to consider the following questions: How do we navigate the treacherous waters of success without losing sight of the shore? What strategies must be employed to ensure that our breakthroughs do not become the instruments of our downfall?

As we embark on this chapter, we unravel the profound truth that the reception of a miracle is only the prelude to a more intricate and demanding narrative. Just as a skilled gardener tends to the blossoming flowers with care and attention, we must nurture our miracles with wisdom and foresight.

For the journey of maintaining a miracle is not a passive stroll; it is an active engagement with the blessings bestowed upon us. It calls for the development of character, the refinement of habits, and the cultivation of a mindset that appreciates the fragility and preciousness of the extraordinary.

THE MAJESTIC MILESTONE

The exodus of the Israelites from the bondage of Egypt was undeniably a demonstration of God's power and providence. Yet, as they stood at the threshold of the Promised Land, a pivotal question lingered: Would they continue to acknowledge and serve the One who led them through the wilderness?

God's concern transcended the physical journey; it delved into the spiritual terrain of obedience and commitment. The blessings awaiting them in Canaan were not mere entitlements; they were promises conditioned upon the people's fidelity to the divine commandments.

"Faith is taking the first step even

when you don't see the whole staircase."

Martin Luther King Jr.

In the same vein, our personal journeys are marked by breakthroughs and miracles. The elation of achievement, the joy of answered prayers, and the thrill of newfound success are akin to the Israelites' arrival at Canaan. However, the narrative reminds us that the true test lies in whether we can navigate the land of abundance with a heart that still acknowledges the Source.

At the banks of the Jordan River, a set of commandments and instructions were imparted—a blueprint for the Israelites' conduct in their newfound land. Similarly, in the fabric of our lives, we encounter guiding principles and moral compasses, urging us to steer our miracles with wisdom and gratitude.

Let us, then, explore the commandments given at the Jordan River as timeless beacons lighting our path in maintaining the miracles we receive. Each commandment, a nugget of wisdom; each instruction, a roadmap for navigating the intricate landscapes of success.

Just like the Israelites, you and I stand on the precipice of our blessings, poised to enter our own Canaan. The question echoing through the ages is whether we can navigate the terrain of success while staying anchored to the principles that sustain it.

The commandments given at the Jordan River become our compass, pointing towards a path where obedience and gratitude coexist.

As we traverse the landscapes of maintaining miracles, let's take a moment to ponder the significance of obedience, gratitude, and faithfulness. The echoes of ancient wisdom will resonate through the pages, offering insights into how to nurture and protect the extraordinary in our lives.

So, as we delve deeper, envision yourself standing at the threshold of your own Promised Land. The lessons from the Israelites will be your lanterns, illuminating a path that not only leads to Canaan but ensures it's sustained, flourishing through unwavering commitment to divine principles.

Join me as we traverse the Jordan River of life, where the echoes of ancient commandments resonate in the contemporary pursuit of preserving and building upon the miracles bestowed upon us.

Reference: Numbers 33:50-55

50 On the plains of Moab by the Jordan across from Jericho the Lord said to Moses,

51 "Speak to the Israelites and say to them: 'When you cross the Jordan into Canaan,

52 drive out all the inhabitants of the land before you. Destroy all their carved images and their cast idols, and demolish all their high places.

53 Take possession of the land and settle in it, for I have given you the land to possess.

54 Distribute the land by lot, according to your clans. To a larger group give a larger inheritance, and to a smaller group a smaller one. Whatever falls to them by lot will be theirs. Distribute it according to your ancestral tribes.

55 "'But if you do not drive out the inhabitants of the land, those you allow to remain will become barbs in your eyes and thorns in your sides. They will give you trouble in the land where you will live."

The passage provides a rich foundation for exploring the themes of obedience, stewardship, and the challenges associated with maintaining blessings. The divine instructions given at the plains of Moab offered a blueprint for the Israelites as they prepared to enter the Promised Land.

In the shadows of history, on the plains of Moab, Moses stood as the conduit for divine instructions to the expectant Israelites. The Jordan River glistened on the horizon, its waters mirroring the aspirations of a people on the brink of a miraculous transition.

Here, amidst the whispers of winds and the ancient soil beneath their feet, the Lord spoke words that transcended time and found resonance in the tapestry of their lives.

"Speak to the Israelites and say to them: 'When you cross the Jordan into Canaan, drive out all the inhabitants of the land before you. Destroy all their carved images and their cast idols, and demolish all their high places. Take possession of the land and settle in it, for I have given you the land to possess.'"

The divine mandate echoed not just in the ears of a nomadic people but in the corridors of our contemporary existence. The Promised Land, a metaphor for our miracles and breakthroughs, demands more than passive ownership; it demands active stewardship.

"Distribute the land by lot, according to your clans. To a larger group, give a larger inheritance, and to a smaller group, a smaller one. Whatever falls to them by lot will be theirs. Distribute it according to your ancestral tribes." (Numbers 33:54)

The act of distribution underscores the wisdom that not all blessings are uniform, yet each is significant. In the allocation of their inheritance, the Israelites faced choices and responsibilities—much like the decisions we encounter in our quest to maintain the miracles we receive.

Yet, a solemn warning resonates through the ages, carried by the winds of ancient admonition:

"But if you do not drive out the inhabitants of the land, those you allow to remain will become barbs in your eyes and thorns in your sides. They will give you trouble in the land where you will live." (Numbers 33:55)

As we navigate the landscapes of our miracles, the commandments at the Jordan River become signposts, urging us to demolish the idols that threaten the sanctity of our blessings. The inhabitants of doubt, complacency, and disobedience must be driven out, lest they become thorns in the sides of our prosperity.

These instructions are invaluable stratagems, intricately linked to the principal theme of 'Maintaining Miracles.' They are designed to empower individuals to live, sustain, and relish their blessings in their Promised Land.

In alignment with this principle, I have enumerated some of these instructions and drawn inferences from them, illustrating their applicability as we seek to acquire and sustain the miracles or successes we achieve in our modern world. I have also shared very vivid and practical real life examples to nail these points home.

Now come along with me as we dissect these directives and make minced meat of them.

1. DRIVE OUT ALL THE INHABITANTS OF THE LAND

On the plains of Moab by the Jordan River, specific instructions were given to them as to what to do in the land. They were to drive out all the inhabitants of the land, destroy their high places, demolish every molded image and places of idol worship.

Instructing the Israelites to drive out all the inhabitants of the land, serves as a powerful metaphor for eliminating hindrances to blessings and miracles. It's a compelling foundation for exploring practical points to help maintain and develop breakthroughs.

These were going to be major hindrances if the blessings were to be enjoyed in the new land. In the same way, if we are to have the full benefit of the blessings or miracles we desire, we must drive out all negative mentality and attitudes.

These fight against the full potential of your miracle. Any relationship that can affect your breakthrough or goals this modern world must be driven out.

"Don't let negative and toxic people

rent space in your head.

Raise the rent and kick them out."

Robert Tew

1. Drive out Negative Mentality and Attitudes

On the plains of Moab, at the cusp of Canaan, the divine command rang clear: "Drive out all the inhabitants of the land." The call was not merely geographical conquest but a spiritual imperative.

In the same vein, to fully relish the blessings and miracles in our lives, we must embark on an internal expedition.

Negative mentalities and attitudes stand as formidable inhabitants that obstruct the path to our miracles. Just as the Israelites were directed to demolish high places and cast down molded images, we must dismantle the mental strongholds that hinder the realization of our full potential. Thoughts of doubt, fear, and unworthiness must be driven out, creating space for the blossoming of our miracles.

Additionally, any relationship that casts shadows on our breakthroughs and goals must be scrutinized. Whether it be toxic friendships, unsupportive associations, or relationships that drain our energy, we must be discerning in our choices. In the landscape of our miracles, surrounding ourselves with positive influences and supportive connections becomes paramount.

"Surround yourself with only people who are

going to lift you higher."

Oprah Winfrey

2. Cultivate a Mindset of Gratitude

To maintain and develop the breakthroughs we achieve, gratitude becomes the fertile soil in which our miracles flourish. The act of acknowledging and appreciating the blessings bestowed upon us opens the door to a continuous influx of positivity.

As the Israelites were instructed to take possession of the land, our possession is not just physical but encompasses a mental and emotional landscape. Gratitude becomes the cornerstone, transforming our perspective and fostering a mindset that attracts more blessings.

Regularly reflect on the journey, celebrating milestones and expressing gratitude for the miracles already present, creating a harmonious environment for further growth.

"Gratitude turns what we have into enough."

Aesop

3. Embrace Continuous Learning and Adaptability

Distributing the land by lot, as instructed in Numbers 33:54, implies a strategic and intentional approach to resource management. Similarly, in our pursuit of maintaining miracles, an openness to continuous learning and adaptability is paramount.

Just as a larger group was given a larger inheritance, we too must recognize the varying landscapes of our lives. This demands an eagerness to learn, grow, and adapt to the dynamic nature of our circumstances.

Seek knowledge, remain curious, and be willing to adjust strategies as needed, ensuring that you are equipped to effectively manage and develop your breakthroughs

4. Establish Clear Goals and Action Plans

In the divine instructions, the Israelites were directed to distribute the land according to their clans, considering the size of the group. This principle echoes the importance of setting clear goals and action plans in our lives.

Define your vision and aspirations clearly, considering the unique characteristics of your journey. Just as different clans received different inheritances, your goals may vary in scope and nature. Develop actionable plans that align with your objectives, allowing for a systematic approach to maintaining and building upon your breakthroughs.

5. Foster a Supportive Community

Finally, the cautionary account emphasizes the consequences of allowing inhabitants to remain in the land. In our pursuit of miracles, the support and understanding of a community become invaluable.

Surround yourself with individuals who uplift and encourage you. Build relationships that contribute positively to your journey. Just as the Israelites were cautioned about the troubles inhabitants could bring, be mindful of relationships that may become obstacles to your progress. A supportive community acts as a safeguard, helping you navigate challenges and celebrate successes.

I have further enumerated some keys which can help maintain and develop whatever breakthrough you achieve. These include:

a) Identification: Unveiling the Layers of Your Miracle

The essence of identification lies in peeling back the layers of your miracle—the blessings and challenges intertwined within every opportunity. In the mosaic of your breakthroughs, understanding what you have and who you are becomes the foundational step towards effective maintenance and development.

i. Unveiling Your Blessings:

Just as Moses led the Israelites through the wilderness, guiding them to the plains of Moab, you must embark on an introspective journey. Identify the blessings that have graced your life, recognizing their depth and significance.

What opportunities lie before you? What achievements have you garnered? Understanding the scope and nature of your blessings allows you to appreciate them and paves the way for intentional stewardship.

ii. Knowing Your Identity:

In the wilderness of life, your identity is your compass. If you don't recognize who you are, the opportunities that knock may go unnoticed. Take a moment to reflect on your values, passions, and purpose. Understand the unique qualities that define you.

In the shadow of the Jordan River, embrace the truth of your identity—the strengths that empower you and the weaknesses that demand growth.

iii. Identifying Challenges:

Every blessing carries its own set of challenges. Just as the Israelites were instructed to drive out the inhabitants of Canaan, you must identify the obstacles that may threaten your miracles.

What are the potential pitfalls? What challenges may arise in the pursuit of your goals? Identifying these challenges positions you to strategize effectively, ensuring that you navigate the terrain of your breakthroughs with clarity and purpose.

iv. Crafting a Course of Action:

Identification is not merely a passive exercise; it is a call to action. Armed with the knowledge of your blessings, understanding of your identity, and awareness of potential challenges, craft a course of action. Decide how you will steward your miracles.

What steps will you take to nurture and develop the opportunities before you? The plains of Moab beckon, and your journey begins with a purposeful stride towards intentional management and growth.

b) Information gathering: Navigating the Landscape of Knowledge

Having identified the blessings and challenges that accompany your breakthrough, the next crucial step is information gathering—a journey into the landscape of knowledge that empowers you to maximize your opportunities.

i. Maximizing Opportunities:

Recognition of an opportunity is the first glimmer of light in the dawn of progress. Yet, to stand out in the brilliance of that light, you must delve into the art of information gathering.

Just as the Israelites surveyed the land of Canaan, you must explore and gather insights that will enable you to harness and maximize your blessings. Information acts as the compass that guides you through the terrain of opportunities, ensuring that you make decisions rooted in wisdom and foresight.

ii. Seeking Guidance from Experience:

The wisdom of those who have walked similar paths is an invaluable resource. Engage with experienced individuals who can offer insights and advice. Seek guidance from mentors, elders, or experts who have navigated similar opportunities. Their experiences become beacons of light, illuminating the way forward and providing you with a richer perspective.

iii. Research and In-Depth Exploration:

In the vast expanse of the Internet and libraries, lies a treasure trove of knowledge waiting to be unearthed. Whether it's conducting research online, in books, or through other reputable sources, your commitment to in-depth exploration is paramount.

Equip yourself with a thorough understanding of the dynamics surrounding your blessings. The information you gather becomes the foundation upon which sound decisions are built.

iv. Informed Decision-Making:

Gathering information isn't a mere formality; it's a strategic move towards informed decision-making. As you stand at the crossroads of opportunities, ensure that you possess all the relevant data needed to make wise choices. Avoid the pitfalls of impulsive decisions by grounding your choices in a comprehensive understanding of the blessings and challenges that lay ahead.

In the unfolding chapters, our characters embark on a quest for information—a journey that takes them from the wisdom of mentors to the vast realms of research.

Join them as they navigate the landscape of knowledge, recognizing that the ability to maintain and develop their miracles rests on the bedrock of informed decision-making.

c) Investment in New Resources: Nurturing the Garden of Self-Growth

Having identified and gathered the necessary information, the journey towards maintaining and developing breakthroughs continues with a crucial step—investment in new resources. Just as a garden requires consistent care and nourishment to thrive, your inner landscape demands intentional investment for sustained growth.

i. Quality Time, Energy, and Money:

Investment begins with the allocation of your most precious assets —time, energy, and money. To maintain and develop your breakthrough, you must consciously dedicate these resources towards self-improvement.

Recognize that the more you invest in yourself, the richer your internal reservoir becomes. This wealth of personal development becomes the bedrock upon which your external successes rest.

"To invest in yourself is the best investment of all.

It will not only improve your life,

it will improve the lives of all those around you."

Robin S. Sharma

ii. Continuous Learning and Skill Enhancement:

The landscape of success is ever-evolving. In a world where competition intensifies, the need for continuous learning and skill enhancement becomes paramount. Attend conferences, seminars, and engage in online courses that align with your goals.

Read relevant books that broaden your perspectives and expose you to new ideas. This commitment to learning ensures that you not only keep pace with industry trends but also stay ahead of the competition.

iii. Awareness of Current Affairs:

In the fast-paced currents of the world, awareness is key. Stay informed about current affairs, technological advancements, and industry shifts. This awareness positions you to adapt to changing landscapes and seize emerging opportunities.

Just as the Israelites had to be aware of the challenges in the land of Canaan, your awareness of current trends arms you with the foresight needed to navigate the challenges and opportunities that arise.

iv. Consciously Investing in Yourself:

The journey of maintaining miracles is a personal odyssey. Consciously invest in yourself every day. This involves not only external endeavors but also inner reflections. Develop habits of mindfulness, self-reflection, and a positive mindset.

Nurture your mental and emotional well-being as passionately as you invest in external resources. The equilibrium between internal and external investment ensures a holistic approach to self-growth.

In the forthcoming pages, our characters embark on a path of self-investment—a commitment to continuous learning, skill enhancement, and the nurturing of their inner landscapes.

Join me as I follow them nurture the garden of self-growth, recognizing that the sustained development of their miracles begins with the conscious and intentional investment in new resources.

d) Support Base: Pillars of Strength on the Journey

In hustle and bustle of life, the significance of a robust support base cannot be overstated. As you navigate the twists and turns on the path to maintaining your breakthrough, having pillars of strength becomes essential.

Just as the Israelites relied on their leaders and mentors, your journey is enriched by those who inspire, guide, and challenge you.

i) Inspirational Guides:

Life is a perpetual journey, and challenges are inevitable companions. Amidst the trials and tribulations, having individuals to look up to for inspiration and direction becomes a beacon of light.

Seek out mentors with superlative experience and knowledge—individuals who have weathered storms and emerged triumphant. Their wisdom becomes a compass, guiding you through the intricacies of maintaining and developing your miracles.

ii) Solid Support in Adversity:

When all odds seem insurmountable, a solid support base acts as a propellant. Surround yourself with individuals who stand by you, offering unwavering support during challenging times.

These are the friends, family, and mentors who lend strength when your own falters. Their encouragement becomes the scaffolding that upholds you, ensuring you press on even when the journey seems arduous.

iii) Honest Critique and Guidance:

A support base goes beyond mere encouragement—it extends to honest critique and guidance. In moments of introspection, you need individuals who can candidly point out shortcomings and mistakes.

These mentors act as mirrors, reflecting areas for improvement. Their constructive feedback becomes the catalyst for growth, propelling you towards the pinnacle of your desires.

iv) Mentors for Continuous Improvement:

The journey to maintaining miracles is not static; it's a continuous evolution. Mentors play a pivotal role in bringing out the best in you. Their mentorship is a dynamic process, guiding you through challenges, celebrating victories, and fostering an environment of continuous improvement. With mentors by your side, the pursuit of excellence becomes a collaborative endeavor.

In the unfolding pages, our characters lean on their support base—a network of mentors, guides, and pillars of strength. Join me as we see how they draw inspiration, navigate challenges, and strive for continuous improvement. The lesson echoes through the narrative: a solid support base is not just a luxury; it is an indispensable companion on the journey of maintaining and developing miracles.

The lesson echoes through the narrative: a solid support base is not just a luxury; it is an indispensable companion on the journey of maintaining and developing miracles.

NURTURING MIRACLES IN THE EVERYDAY

Within the realms of faith and the pursuit of daring dreams, Sarah Toulouse emerges as our guiding light through the complex journey of everyday miracles. In the delicate weave of her narrative, I uncover the profound significance of a practice that forms the bedrock of our exploration- *Maintaining Your Miracles.*

In the soft glow of dawn, Toulouse, with a well-worn journal in hand, carves a moment of silence amidst the whirlwind of life. Her journey unfolds within the pages of gratitude, mindfulness, and a reverent acknowledgment of miracles nestled within the ordinary.

In the context of faith and daring dreams, daily reflections emerge not as mere reflections but as a transformative strategy—a compass that directs Sarah, and by extension our readers, toward the nurturing of miracles.

As we explore into this narrative, Sarah's reflections transcend the confines of ink and paper. They become echoes of resilience, gratitude, and an unwavering belief that miracles are not elusive phantoms but companions in the journey of faith.

This practice, seemingly modest, serves as a foundational piece in the puzzle of maintaining miracles, an art Sarah has mastered through the ebb and flow of her daring dreams.

Together, we will navigate the significance of the strategies that underpin her journey. Each strategy, seemingly unassuming, acts as a beacon, illuminating the path to catching and sustaining miracles against the backdrop of life's challenges.

In the soft hues of dawn, Sarah, armed with a weathered journal, takes a deliberate pause to embark on a ritual that transcends routine. Her journey unfolds within the pages of gratitude, mindfulness, and the sacred acknowledgment of miracles woven into the mundane.

Now, let's zoom in on the heart of our exploration—Sarah's daily reflections. Why this deliberate act of pausing in the rush of life? The answer resonates with the very essence of our chapter's subtitle, "Maintaining Your Miracle."

In the context of faith and daring dreams, daily reflections emerge not as mere considerations but as a transformative strategy—a compass that directs Sarah Toulouse, and consequently my precious reader, toward the nurturing of miracles.

As we dig into this chapter, her reflections become more than ink on paper. They become echoes of resilience, gratitude, and an unwavering belief that miracles are not elusive specters but companions in the journey of faith.

This practice, seemingly modest, serves as a foundational piece in the puzzle of maintaining miracles, an art Sarah has mastered through the ebb and flow of her daring dreams.

Join me in peeling back the layers of her world, where daily reflections illuminate a path sprinkled with the hues of gratitude and mindful awareness.

As the sun rises on this chapter, we embark on a collective exploration—a symphony of strategies that resonate with the beating heart of faith and the audacity of daring dreams.

Goal Setting And Planning: Charting A Course For Daring Dreams

In the symphony of maintaining miracles, Sarah's journey underscores the transformative power of goal setting and planning. With her daring dreams stretching before her like an unexplored horizon, she embraces a proactive approach, setting realistic goals as beacons guiding her path.

Picture Sarah, pen in hand, as she meticulously outlines her aspirations. Each goal becomes a roadmap—a series of achievable milestones that pave the way toward the fulfillment of her daring dreams. From the grandiose to the seemingly modest, each goal is a stepping stone in her quest for miracles.

But goal setting for Sarah is not merely an exercise in ambition; it is a deliberate act of staying focused. In a world brimming with distractions, she hones her gaze on the objectives at hand.

This focus becomes her shield against the storms of doubt and the allure of shortcuts, ensuring that each step taken is purposeful and aligned with the greater narrative of her faith-filled journey.

As she achieves each milestone, a sense of accomplishment fuels her momentum. Yet, it is the ongoing process of planning that propels her forward. She revisits her goals, refines her plans, and adapts to the evolving landscape of her daring dreams. In this dance between aspiration and adaptation, she discovers the transformation of maintaining miracles.

Community Engagement: A Tapestry of Support and Faith

In the medley of maintaining miracles, the narrative pivots to the significance of community engagement—a poignant chapter in Sarah's story. As she traverses the uncharted terrain of faith and daring dreams, the embrace of a supportive community becomes a cornerstone of her resilience.

Envision Sarah not as a solitary wanderer but as part of a textile of interlocked souls. The pursuit of daring dreams, fueled by faith, becomes a shared odyssey. In this community, each member contributes a thread—a story, a perspective, a nugget of wisdom. Together, they form a resilient fabric that fortifies Sarah in moments of uncertainty.

The supportive community serves as a sounding board for her daring dreams—a space where ideas are nurtured, doubts are dispelled, and victories are celebrated. In moments of adversity, it is the collective strength that sustains her spirit, reminding her that the journey is not solitary but a shared pilgrimage.

The storyline becomes a mirror, prompting introspection on the significance of shared experiences and shared faith in the pursuit of miracles. Through community engagement, the pages resonate with the chorus of interconnected hearts, underscoring that maintaining miracles is not a solitary endeavor but a harmonious collaboration with like-minded people.

Education and Continuous Learning: A Journey of Adaptable Resilience

Within the narrative of maintaining miracles, Sarah's odyssey takes a pivotal turn toward the transformative realm of education and continuous learning. As a superwoman fueled by faith and daring dreams, Sarah recognizes the dynamic nature of her journey—a journey that demands adaptability and resilience through an unending quest for knowledge.

Imagine Toulouse not as a static soul but as a seeker—a perpetual student in the grand academy of life. Education, for her, extends beyond the walls of traditional classrooms. It becomes a fluid, ever-evolving stream of learning experiences. Online courses, workshops, insightful conversations—each contributes to the mosaic of her knowledge, shaping her into a resilient force on her daring quest.

The importance of continuous learning reverberates through her life, emphasizing that maintaining miracles is not about standing still but about navigating the ever-shifting tides with an insatiable hunger for understanding. Sarah's story is an invitation for you to adopt a similar mindset—a mindset that embraces every twist and turn as an opportunity to learn, adapt, and grow.

As we see, education and continuous learning is not just strategies but companions on the journey of faith and daring dreams. Through Sarah's narrative, you are encouraged to see each challenge as a classroom, each setback as a lesson, and each triumph as a testament to the transformative power of a resilient, adaptable mind.

Physical Well-being: Nurturing the Vessel for Miracles

In the saga of maintaining miracles, the narrative delicately intertwines with the theme of physical well-being—a testament to the symbiotic relationship between the vessel and the journey. Sarah, in her pursuit of faith and daring dreams, becomes not just a protagonist but a steward of her physical health, recognizing that the body is both a temple and vehicle for the miraculous.

Picture Sarah, not as an indefatigable superhero, but as a mindful caretaker of her well-being. Regular exercise becomes not a chore but a celebration of vitality—a dance with the rhythms of life. A balanced diet transforms into more than sustenance; it becomes a banquet of nutrients that fuel her resilience and energy for the journey ahead.

Physical well-being, in Sarah's narrative, extends beyond the superficial. It becomes a commitment to sufficient rest—a sanctuary for rejuvenation and recovery. As she encounters the rigors of maintaining miracles, she embraces the importance of holistic well-being, understanding that a healthy vessel is better equipped to navigate the challenges that arise.

This becomes a mirror, prompting introspection on the intricate dance between the physical self and the miraculous journey. Through Sarah's mindful stewardship, the pages resonate with the notion that maintaining miracles is not just about the destination but about nurturing the vessel that carries the sacred cargo of faith and daring dreams.

Shared Goals and Values: Harmonizing the Symphony of a Collective Journey

In the grand symphony of maintaining miracles, Sarah's narrative echoes the harmonious chords of shared goals and values. As a protagonist entwined in a journey of faith and daring dreams, she discovers the transformative power that emerges when characters align their aspirations and principles for a shared purpose.

Visualize Sarah not as a lone voyager but as part of a collective—a band of souls journeying together. In this shared odyssey, characters synchronize their goals, weaving a tapestry of shared values. Each member contributes a unique thread, creating a resilient fabric that propels them forward in unity.

The story unfolds as a testament to the strength found in shared purpose. Sarah and her companions, driven by a common vision, find inspiration in each other's goals and draw strength from the collective pursuit of miracles.

You are invited to peer into this communal journey, recognizing that the road to maintaining miracles is not just about personal ambitions but about the symphony that emerges when individual goals harmonize with shared values.

Through Sarah's experiences, the narrative becomes a guiding light—a reminder that in the collective pursuit of daring dreams, shared goals, and values become the navigational stars, steering characters through the receding tide and flows of their miraculous journey.

Conflict Resolution: Navigating Turbulent Waters with Grace

As the chronicle of maintaining miracles unfolds, Sarah's journey introduces the inevitable—conflicts. Acknowledging that conflicts may arise becomes a poignant factor, aligning with the realities of any daring journey. Yet, Sarah's resilience lies not just in the absence of conflict but in the strategies employed for effective resolution.

Sarah is not someone shielded from disagreements but as a navigator steering her vessel through turbulent waters with grace. Conflict resolution becomes an art—a dance that strengthens relationships rather than tearing them asunder.

In moments of discord, Sarah and her companions lean into open communication, actively listening, and seeking understanding.

The narrative weaves conflict into the fabric of the journey, underscoring that maintaining miracles is not a placid lake but a dynamic river. Through the prism of Sarah's experiences, readers witness that conflicts, when approached with empathy and a commitment to resolution, become stepping stones, not stumbling blocks.

Conflict resolution, as depicted in Sarah's narrative, is a testament to the resilience of relationships—a recognition that maintaining miracles is not a solitary endeavor but a collective dance.

I encourage you my reader to embrace the wisdom embedded in the narrative, understanding that conflicts, when navigated with grace, can become catalysts for deeper understanding and, ultimately, strengthen the bonds within the community of faith and daring dreams.

Celebrate Milestones: A Joyful Pause Along the Journey

In the melodic cadence of maintaining miracles, the narrative takes a jubilant turn toward the celebration of milestones. Aligned with the overarching theme of the book, this strategy emphasizes the importance of not just striving toward the destination but reveling in the achievements and positive changes along the journey.

Sarah, our protagonist, becomes a joyful reveler, not just in the grand victories but in the small triumphs that sprinkle the path of her daring dreams. Each milestone, whether significant or subtle, becomes a cause for celebration—a moment to pause, reflect, and bask in the glow of progress.

Through Sarah's experiences, the storyline becomes a reflection, prompting one to embrace the practice of celebrating milestones in their own lives.

The pages resonate with the idea that each step forward, each positive change, is a note in the symphony of faith and daring dreams, and celebrating these moments adds a vibrant melody to the overarching narrative of maintaining miracles.

In the tapestry of Sarah's journey, maintaining miracles becomes a symphony of strategies, each note echoing with resilience, faith, and daring dreams. Daily reflections serve as the poignant prelude, inviting readers to join Sarah in the sacred ritual of gratitude and mindful awareness.

As the sun rises on her story, the pages unfold to reveal the transformative power of mindfulness and meditation—tools that illuminate the path through challenges with clarity.

The narrative then pivots toward goal setting and planning, where Sarah emerges not just as a dreamer but as a proactive architect of her destiny. Her goals, meticulously crafted, become milestones in a journey that demands focus and adaptation.

Education and continuous learning become the melody that resonates through her narrative, portraying the dynamic, ever-evolving nature of the path she treads.

Physical well-being is depicted as the dance partner in this journey—a companion that Sarah nurtures with care. The narrative intertwines the pursuit of miracles with mindful stewardship of the vessel that carries the sacred cargo of faith and daring dreams.

Sarah's journey extends beyond the singular, as shared goals and values become the harmonious chords in her symphony. The collective pursuit of miracles emerges as a testament to the strength found in unity, where characters align their aspirations for a shared purpose.

Conflict resolution, presented as an art in the narrative, becomes a powerful strategy, transforming conflicts into stepping stones that fortify relationships.

The jubilant notes of celebration resonate as Sarah pauses to acknowledge milestones—big and small—along the journey. This practice becomes a joyful affirmation, a recognition that maintaining miracles is not just about reaching the destination but savoring the vibrant notes along the way.

Sarah's Invitation to Maintaining Miracles

As the final chord of Sarah's symphony reverberates, readers are invited to step into the rhythm of maintaining miracles. Through her experiences, Sarah extends an invitation to a journey where daily reflections, mindfulness, goal setting, continuous learning, physical well-being, shared goals, conflict resolution, and celebration intertwine to form a vibrant narrative of faith and daring dreams.

In the cadence of Sarah's narrative, maintaining miracles is not a solitary endeavor but a collective dance—a symphony where individual notes harmonize with shared values, conflicts are resolved with grace, and every step forward is a celebration.

The pages become a mirror, reflecting the transformative power found in intentional practices and the resilience that arises from a community bound by faith.

Sarah's journey becomes more than a story; it becomes an anthem—an anthem that resonates with the very essence of maintaining miracles. As readers embrace the strategies woven into her narrative, they are beckoned to embark on their own odyssey—a journey where the pursuit of miracles is not just a destination but a continuous, joyful dance with the melodies of faith and daring dreams.

The Symphony of Maintaining Miracles

As we draw the curtains on this chapter, the echoes of wisdom and the resonance of experiences linger in the air. "Maintaining Your Miracle" is not merely a chapter; it is a symphony—an orchestration of principles, cautionary tales, and timeless truths that reverberate through the corridors of life.

In the pages preceding, we embarked on a journey with our characters, traversing the plains of Moab, navigating the Jordan River, and delving into the divine instructions that guide the preservation and development of miracles.

From the command to drive out hindrances to the strategic investment in self-growth, the narrative unfolded as a tapestry woven with threads of wisdom and practical insights.

Identification became the clarion call—a call to unveil the layers of our miracles, to understand the blessings, recognize our identity, and confront the challenges that lay in wait. Information gathering emerged as the bridge between knowledge and wisdom—a journey into the landscape of understanding that propels us towards informed decision-making.

Information gathering becomes the steady flow of water, nurturing the roots of our breakthroughs. Just as the Israelites sought guidance from the experienced, our commitment to continuous learning and exploration ensures that our decisions are rooted in a wellspring of knowledge. The landscape of success is dynamic, and armed with information, we navigate its contours with wisdom and foresight.

Investment in new resources became the melody—a commitment to nurturing the garden of self-growth through the allocation of time, energy, and money. Like diligent gardeners, we tended to the soil of our internal landscape, recognizing that the richness within is the bedrock upon which our external successes stand.

And then, the symphony climaxed with the harmonious notes of a robust support base—a network of mentors, guides, and pillars of strength. In the vast expanse of life's orchestra, their presence became the resonant chords that fortified our characters against the discordant notes of adversity.

The support base, our sturdy pillars, anchors us in the fertile soil of encouragement and constructive guidance. As we walk the path of maintaining miracles, the presence of mentors and a solid support network becomes not just a luxury but a fundamental necessity.

In moments of adversity, they are the pillars that prop us up, and in times of celebration, they amplify our joy.

"Be mindful of your self-talk.

It's a conversation with the universe."

David James Lees

2. DESTROY ALL THEIR CARVED IMAGES, THEIR CAST IDOLS, AND DEMOLISH ALL THEIR HIGH PLACES.

In the pursuit of maintaining miracles, one crucial principle emerges - the importance of fostering a clean mental and spiritual environment. This principle calls for a vigilant examination of influences that may distort the purity required for miracles to thrive.

Maintaining miracles necessitates the demolition of influences that distort the purity of one's mental and spiritual landscape. This involves a proactive approach to identify and eliminate any sources of impurity.

i. LEWD AND EXPLICIT MEDIA

In the digital age, explicit media casts a shadow on our mental well-being and relationships. The constant exposure to explicit content can corrode the purity of our thoughts and emotions, affecting mental health and straining relationships. It is vital to advocate for a conscious decision to limit exposure to explicit media.

Rachel, a determined young professional, found herself at a crossroads. The explicit media that permeated her daily life began to take a toll on her mental well-being and relationships. Recognizing the need for change, Rachel made a conscious decision to limit her exposure to explicit content.

This transformative choice became the catalyst for a miracle in her life. As the negativity faded, so did Rachel's self-esteem flourished, leading to a newfound sense of self-respect and deeper, more meaningful relationships.

The carved images of negative thought patterns can become idols that hinder personal growth. Self-critical thoughts, when left unchecked, carve deep grooves in the mind, obstructing the path to personal miracles. To maintain miracles, exploring and dismantling these negative thought patterns is crucial.

STRATEGIES IN DEALING WITH EXPLICIT OR LEWD MEDIA

In our modern era, the pervasive presence of explicit or lewd media poses a significant challenge to maintaining a clean mental and spiritual environment. However, navigating this landscape and fostering mental purity is not only possible but imperative for those seeking to uphold the miracles in their lives.

- One effective strategy is to implement content filtering and blocking tools across digital devices. By restricting access to explicit content through these tools, individuals create a virtual barrier that helps in curbing inadvertent exposure.

- Familiarizing yourself with digital well-being practices and utilizing features provided by operating systems and apps adds another layer of protection. Setting up usage limits, notifications, and reminders contributes to better management of screen time, reducing the likelihood of stumbling upon explicit content.

- Curating the social media feed is a proactive step toward maintaining a positive and uplifting online environment. Unfollowing or muting accounts that share explicit content allows individuals to tailor their digital spaces to align with their values. This intentional approach to content consumption fosters a mindset that is conducive to personal growth and well-being.

- Engaging in positive hobbies serves as a powerful distraction from explicit content. By redirecting leisure time towards constructive pursuits, individuals reshape their mental landscape and reduce the allure of potentially harmful material.

- Setting clear boundaries, both personally and in interpersonal relationships, communicates a commitment to maintaining a clean mental environment. This clarity helps in managing expectations and reinforces the importance of mental purity.

- Seeking support from like-minded individuals or communities can be a valuable resource. Surrounding oneself with friends or groups that share similar values provides a supportive network that reinforces the commitment to avoiding explicit media. The power of collective accountability contributes to a sense of community and shared purpose.

- Mindfulness and meditation play a pivotal role in developing heightened awareness of one's thoughts. By cultivating a mindful approach to daily life, individuals gain the ability to recognize and redirect negative thought patterns. These practices contribute to a more centered and resilient mindset, fostering mental clarity.

- In instances where the challenge persists, professional counseling or therapy offers a personalized approach to overcoming addictive behaviors or patterns. Mental health professionals can provide guidance, support, and tools for navigating the complexities of digital environments.

"Therapy is not about 'what's wrong with you?'

but about 'what happened to you?'"

Gabor Maté

Creating a positive physical environment is another crucial aspect. Designing personal spaces with uplifting images, quotes, and colors contributes to an overall atmosphere that inspires a clean and wholesome mindset.

Additionally, scheduling regular digital detox periods encourages moments of disconnection from electronic devices, allowing individuals to focus on outdoor activities, hobbies, or connecting with loved ones.

Ultimately, dealing with explicit media requires a combination of intentional strategies, personal accountability, and a commitment to mental and spiritual well-being.

In the journey to maintain miracles, individuals have the agency to shape their digital and mental environments, fostering conditions that support personal growth, resilience, and a sense of purpose.

ii.   MOLTEN IMAGES

In the sacred journey of maintaining miracles, the symbolic weight of molten images transcends the confines of ancient sculptures. These representations, with their distorted features and association with false gods, echo the contemporary struggle against societal expectations, materialism, and unrealistic standards that obstruct the path to personal and spiritual growth.

In the modern landscape, equivalents to molten images manifest as societal expectations, materialism, and unrealistic standards. Societal expectations often create molds that individuals feel compelled to fit into, materialism can become a false god that dictates worth, and unrealistic standards act as distorted representations of success and beauty.

The pressure to conform to these expectations becomes a weight, hindering the authenticity required for personal miracles to flourish.

Consider the emotional journey of Emily Brown, who, under the constant gaze of societal expectations, found herself sculpting an outer shell that veiled her true essence. The process of maintaining miracles demanded a

209

courageous dismantling of these false molds, allowing Emily to emerge authentically, liberated from the burdens of societal conformity.

Materialism, akin to a false god, often becomes the focal point of worth and success. In the pursuit of material gain, the essence of personal miracles can be overshadowed.

James Fox, once entangled in the pursuit of wealth and possessions, experienced a profound awakening. His journey to maintain miracles led him to question the false god of materialism.

As he detached from the superficial allure of possessions, James discovered that true wealth resides in the intangible realms of inner peace and spiritual fulfillment.

Unrealistic standards, resembling distorted representations, permeate various aspects of modern life. Whether in beauty ideals, career benchmarks, or societal norms, these standards become molten images that individuals strive to emulate.

It is imperative to encourage individuals to reassess their beliefs and values. This involves a critical examination of societal expectations and their alignment with personal values.

Materialism must be confronted, and the pursuit of unrealistic standards questioned. The process of reassessment is likened to refining the inner sculpture, chiseling away false ideologies to reveal the true self.

"Too many people spend money they haven't earned,

to buy things they don't want,

to impress people they don't like."

Will Rogers

PRIDE IN EVERY SHADE: A JOURNEY OF BLACK EXCELLENCE

In the vibrant city of Harlem, where the rhythm of jazz echoes through the streets and the walls resonate with the voices of resilience, lived a young woman named Aisha. Raised in a community steeped in rich cultural heritage, Aisha's journey was a testament to the pride she carried in being Black.

Aisha's family, rooted in their African ancestry, instilled in her a profound sense of identity and pride. From an early age, her grandmother, Mama Zuri, regaled her with tales of their ancestors' strength and wisdom. Aisha would sit wide-eyed, absorbing the stories that wove a tapestry of resilience, innovation, and unyielding pride.

As Aisha grew, so did her understanding of the broader historical context. She learned about luminaries like Malcolm X, Maya Angelou, and Nelson Mandela, whose stories fueled the flames of her pride. Aisha saw each success, each triumph over adversity, as a brushstroke in a larger masterpiece of Black excellence.

However, Aisha's journey wasn't without challenges. In a world that sometimes tried to dim the brilliance of her melanin-rich skin, Aisha encountered moments of doubt. Yet, she remembered the stories of her ancestors, the words of wisdom from her elders, and the achievements of her heroes. These became the armor that shielded her against the forces that sought to diminish her pride.

One defining moment came during a school project on influential figures. Aisha chose to explore the life of Katherine Johnson, the brilliant mathematician whose calculations were pivotal to NASA's early space missions. As she delved into Katherine's story, Aisha felt a deep connection. It wasn't just a school project; it was an affirmation of the power and capability within her own Black heritage.

Aisha's pride extended beyond her personal journey. She became an advocate for celebrating Black excellence in all its forms. From organizing cultural events that showcased the diversity of Black art to speaking up in classrooms about the importance of inclusive education, Aisha became a beacon of inspiration.

In the heart of Harlem, Aisha's journey became a ripple that touched many. Her pride in being Black wasn't just personal; it was a rallying call for the community to stand tall, to celebrate their heritage, and to recognize that Black excellence was an indomitable force that had shaped the world in ways both seen and unseen.

Aisha's story is one of unapologetic pride, a narrative that echoes through the streets of Harlem and beyond. In every stride she took, in every word she spoke, Aisha celebrated the richness of her heritage, leaving an indelible mark on the tapestry of Black history—a tapestry that continues to unfold with each passing generation.

In the ongoing narrative of maintaining miracles, the exploration of molten images serves as a poignant guide. It calls individuals to embark on an emotional and practical journey of self-reflection, encouraging them to question societal constructs, detach from false gods, and reassess beliefs.

This transformative process is not just about sculpting a truer version of oneself; it is about unveiling the raw, authentic beauty that lies beneath the surface—a beauty that is integral to the miraculous unfolding of one's true potential.

In the realm of modern society, the Body Positivity Movement stands as a powerful example. This movement challenges unrealistic beauty standards that have become molten images, particularly for women. Influencers and advocates within the movement encourage individuals to reassess their beliefs about body image and beauty.

By promoting acceptance and celebration of diverse body types, the Body Positivity Movement fosters an environment where individuals can liberate themselves from distorted representations, embracing their authentic selves.

The Minimalism Movement in contemporary society exemplifies a collective reassessment of beliefs about materialism. Influenced by the desire for a more meaningful and intentional life, minimalists consciously detach from the false god of excessive material possessions.

By questioning the societal construct that equates happiness with consumerism, adherents of simplicity find freedom and purpose in reassessing their relationship with material wealth.

RISING ABOVE: A TALE OF BLACK PRIDE IN LONDON

In the bustling city of London, where the Thames River flowed beneath the shadows of historic landmarks, lived Adeola, a young woman whose journey embodied the unyielding pride of being Black in a European context.

Her narrative unfolded against the backdrop of a multicultural city, and her pride became a beacon for embracing diversity and challenging stereotypes.

Her roots traced back to Nigeria, and her upbringing in London was a fusion of vibrant cultures. From the spicy aroma of jollof rice in her home to the eclectic sounds of Afrobeat music, Adeola carried the richness of her heritage with grace.

However, her journey towards embracing her Black identity in a European context was not without its complexities.

As Adeola navigated the diverse streets of London, she encountered moments where her Blackness became a focal point. Stereotypes and misconceptions attempted to cast a shadow on her identity. Yet, her pride ran deep, nurtured by stories of her ancestors who had traversed continents and the strength she found within her cultural roots.

One transformative experience occurred during a summer internship at a prestigious British museum. Adeola was drawn to the African art section, where ancient artifacts spoke of a history that transcended borders.

In that space, she felt a profound connection to her ancestry. It became a catalyst for her to challenge the narrow narratives often associated with Black history in Europe.

Driven by her passion for storytelling, Adeola initiated a project to highlight the contributions of Black individuals to European history. From unsung heroes of the Renaissance to contemporary leaders breaking barriers, her project aimed to expand the narrative and celebrate the diversity woven into the fabric of European societies.

Adeola's commitment to her heritage extended beyond the confines of her own journey. She actively participated in community events that celebrated Black excellence, fostering a sense of unity among individuals from various backgrounds. In doing so, she became a trailblazer challenging preconceived notions and elevating the conversation around Black identity in Europe.

Her proudest moment came when she stood before an audience at a cultural festival, sharing stories that resonated with people from different walks of life. Adeola's narrative embodied the essence of being Black in Europe—embracing heritage, challenging stereotypes, and contributing to the mosaic of diversity that defined the city of London.

In the heart of Europe, Adeola's journey stood as a testament to the power of Black pride to transcend geographical boundaries. Her story resonated not only with those of African descent but with a diverse tapestry of individuals who recognized the importance of celebrating and embracing the richness that comes with a multicultural society.

"Diversity is not about how we differ.

Diversity is about embracing

one another's uniqueness."

Ola Joseph

iii.   DEMOLISH HIGH PLACES OF WORSHIP

In the expansive landscape of spiritual exploration, the concept of HIGH PLACES holds profound significance. As we consider this in the context of maintaining miracles, the metaphorical high places, reminiscent of locations where false worship rituals occurred, emerge as crucibles for spiritual integrity.

This point explores the intersection of spirituality and the modern world, urging individuals to ascend to genuine spiritual practices while navigating the potential pitfalls that compromise spiritual well-being.

The HIGH PLACES, in historical symbolism, were once arenas where false worship rituals unfolded—grounds for spiritual contamination. These high places represent the spiritual crossroads where individuals must make conscious choices to preserve their spiritual integrity.

The commitment to genuine spiritual practices becomes paramount, demanding a discerning eye to identify and eliminate influences that could compromise the sanctity of one's spiritual journey.

In modern life, high places manifest as contemporary challenges to spiritual well-being. These challenges could take the form of superficial rituals, materialistic pursuits masquerading as spiritual, or the blind adherence to doctrines that veer away from authentic connection with the divine.

It is essential to discuss these modern high places openly, recognizing that they pose potential threats to the spiritual integrity necessary for maintaining miracles.

Encouraging individuals to engage in authentic spiritual practices becomes a beacon in navigating these challenges. Whether through prayer, meditation, mindfulness, or other soul-nurturing activities, the emphasis is on fostering a genuine connection with the divine.

This commitment becomes a shield against the allure of high places that may lead to spiritual contamination. By elevating the soul through authentic practices, individuals fortify themselves against the spiritual pitfalls of the modern world.

The practical application extends to a conscious examination of one's spiritual landscape. It involves evaluating the influences, practices, and spaces that may compromise the sanctity of the spiritual journey. Just as ancient worshippers had to choose their places of devotion wisely, individuals today must discern where they invest their spiritual energy.

Furthermore, the call to eliminate practices that may lead to spiritual contamination underscores the importance of shedding superficial rituals or misguided beliefs.

This transformative process aligns with the overarching theme of maintaining miracles—purifying the spiritual path to create fertile ground for personal and collective growth.

In this ongoing chronicle of maintaining miracles, the exploration of high places becomes a pivotal juncture. It challenges individuals to ascend beyond the superficial and the misleading, to forge a connection with the divine that is both genuine and transformative.

The commitment to spiritual integrity becomes the cornerstone, ensuring that the journey towards miracles unfolds on sacred ground, free from the contamination of modern-day high places.

ECKHART TOLLE - EMBRACING PRESENCE OVER MATERIALISM:

In the heart of a bustling metropolis, Eckhart Tolle's journey unfolded against the backdrop of a society consumed by the relentless pursuit of material success.

Tolle, once caught in the throes of a mind dominated by desires and external validations, embarked on a transformative quest for a deeper understanding of existence.

Eckhart Tolle's awakening occurred during a period of intense inner turmoil. As a successful academic with a penchant for intellectual pursuits, he found himself grappling with a profound sense of emptiness despite outward accomplishments. It was in this existential crisis that Tolle experienced a profound shift—one that would shape his teachings for generations to come.

Retreating to the solitude of nature, Tolle underwent a period of intense self-reflection. It was during one fateful night, beneath the canopy of stars, that a realization dawned upon him—a realization that transcended the confines of materialistic pursuits.

Tolle discovered the transformative power of embracing the present moment, unburdened by the weight of past regrets or future anxieties.

By way of newfound clarity, Tolle began to share his insights with the world. His teachings emphasized the importance of cultivating a connection with the inner self and the present moment, urging individuals to rise above the allure of materialism.

In lectures, books, and spiritual gatherings, Tolle became a guiding light for those navigating the high places of consumerism.

Tolle's story serves as a testament to the transformative power of embracing presence over materialism. It illustrates that even in a world driven by external achievements, the path to maintaining miracles lies in the profound simplicity of being fully present and conscious in each moment.

REV. BILLY GRAHAM - SPIRITUAL INTEGRITY AMIDST GLOBAL FAME:

In the realm of Christian ministry, Reverend Billy Graham's life serves as a compelling example of maintaining spiritual integrity amidst global fame and the potential pitfalls that come with it. His journey unfolded in the spotlight of evangelical crusades, where the pursuit of genuine spiritual practices became a guiding force.

Billy Graham's rise to prominence as an evangelist coincided with an era marked by rapid societal changes. In an age dominated by materialism and shifting moral landscapes, Graham navigated the high places of fame and adoration with a commitment to authenticity and spiritual depth.

As his crusades drew massive crowds, Graham faced the temptation of becoming a charismatic figurehead rather than a messenger of timeless truths. Yet, his teachings consistently emphasized the centrality of a personal relationship with Jesus Christ and the transformative power of genuine faith.

One pivotal moment in Graham's journey came during the Civil Rights Movement. In a society grappling with racial tensions, Graham took a stand for racial equality, breaking down barriers and preaching a message of love and unity.

His actions illustrated the importance of eliminating influences that compromise spiritual well-being, even in the face of societal expectations.

Graham's commitment to fostering a connection with the divine transcended the boundaries of denominations and affiliations. He embraced humility, recognizing that true spiritual integrity required a continuous commitment to personal growth and a genuine love for others.

In the later stages of his life, as Graham's influence reached a global scale, he remained grounded in the simplicity of the Gospel message. His example encourages Christians to ascend beyond the high places of fame, recognizing that the path to maintaining miracles lies in unwavering faith, authenticity, and a dedication to a genuine relationship with God.

Rev. Billy Graham's life story echoes through the annals of Christian history as a testament to the enduring power of spiritual integrity.

In a world where the pursuit of miracles can be overshadowed by external pressures, Graham's example inspires believers to navigate the complexities of life with an unwavering commitment to their faith and a genuine connection with the divine.

"Faith is the bird that feels the light

when the dawn is still dark."

Rabindranath Tagore

THICH NHAT HANH - MINDFUL LIVING IN A FAST-PACED WORLD:

In the serene landscapes of Plum Village, a community founded by Thich Nhat Hanh, the teachings of mindful living unfolded as a sanctuary for those seeking solace in a fast-paced world.

A venerable Buddhist monk and peace activist, emerged as a beacon of wisdom, offering timeless insights into navigating modern complexities with mindfulness.

Thich Nhat Hanh's own journey began amidst the turbulence of war in Vietnam. Fueled by a deep compassion for humanity, he dedicated his life to promoting peace and mindfulness. In the face of the frenetic pace of contemporary life, his teachings provided a roadmap for individuals to reclaim a sense of calm and inner peace.

The story of Plum Village became a haven for those yearning to escape the cacophony of a society marked by constant connectivity. Surrounded by the gentle rustle of bamboo leaves and the fragrance of blooming flowers, individuals from various walks of life gathered to learn the art of mindful living.

Thich Nhat Hanh's teachings emphasized the transformative power of mindfulness—of being fully present in each moment, whether sipping tea, walking, or breathing. Through guided meditations and mindful practices, individuals discovered the antidote to the spiritual contamination induced by the relentless rush of the outside world.

Plum Village, under his guidance, became a living testament to the possibility of cultivating inner peace in a fast-paced world. The story of mindful living unfolded as a gentle revolution, inviting individuals to embrace authenticity, resilience, and a profound connection with themselves and the world around them.

Thich Nhat Hanh's example continues to inspire countless souls to embark on the journey of mindful living, finding miracles in the simplicity of each mindful breath.

3. TAKE POSSESSION OF THE LAND AND SETTLE IN IT...

In the intricate dance of life, the command to "Take possession of the land and settle in it, for I have given you the land to possess" unfolds as a profound directive in the context of maintaining miracles.

This imperative serves as the cornerstone that explores the practical and dramatic dimensions of claiming and settling into the abundance of miracles destined for each individual.

Just as a traveler navigates diverse terrains, individuals are invited to map their unique journey through the landscape of miracles. This involves a meticulous examination of your aspirations, desires, and the envisioned breakthrough awaiting you.

It's a whisper from the divine, a tender invitation to embark on a voyage where miracles cease to be distant dreams and become the very ground we walk upon.

In the practical dance of life, this call becomes a guide — an urging to consciously navigate towards the miracles awaiting our claim. This isn't a passive stroll but a deliberate journey, akin to charting a course through unexplored territories. It's a recognition that miracles aren't ethereal; they are tangible destinations waiting for us to step forward and claim them.

Imagine yourself as the hero in this insightful narrative, standing at the edge of a land teeming with promises and possibilities—a dramatic landscape where dreams meet reality.

The drama unfolds in your choice to take that bold step, embracing the uncertainties that come with the pursuit of miracles. It's your story — an epic of audacity, resilience, and the unyielding determination to script your own destiny.

Yet, this tale isn't confined to the realms of fantasy. It's a touching and relatable journey—a tale of everyday individuals facing doubts, fears, and external obstacles. It echoes the struggles inherent in our shared human experience, resonating in the collective history of people summoning the courage to claim their miracles.

The phrase "Take possession of the land and settle in it, for I have given you the land to possess" resonates as a pivotal moment in the divine covenant with the people of Israel. This was not a casual utterance but a solemn promise, a binding agreement forged between God and His chosen people.

Emerging from the crucible of slavery in Egypt, the Israelites found themselves on a journey guided by the threads of this covenant—a promise of liberation, guidance, and a destination filled with divine abundance.

The "land" in this saga transcends mere geography; it becomes a profound symbol woven with layers of meaning. It is more than a physical expanse; it is a canvas upon which God paints a picture of abundance, prosperity, and fulfillment. The Promised Land represents a sacred space where the promises spoken by the Creator find tangible expression.

It is a realm where the aspirations of a liberated people intersect with the providence of their divine guide, forming a landscape of hope and promise.

Central to the historical narrative is the notion of the land as a divine gift—an inheritance granted by divine grace. It wasn't a conquest driven by mere mortal ambitions; rather, it was an unfolding legacy bestowed upon the people by their Creator.

The land was a sacred bequest, a testament to the enduring love and fidelity of God. It signified more than territorial control; it was a tangible manifestation of the covenant—a gift given not as a reward for prowess but as an expression of divine benevolence.

The people were not just conquering land; they were receiving a sacred endowment, a bequeathal that echoed through generations.

CONQUEST AND SETTLEMENT

The historical journey embarked upon by the Israelites unfolded as a dynamic interplay of conquest and settlement. Under the stalwart leadership of figures like Joshua, the people were not passive spectators to their destiny; they became active participants in a military journey.

Conquest became the first act—a deliberate, strategic engagement with the challenges that stood between them and the Promised Land. It was a period marked by courage, resilience, and the tenacity to face adversaries head-on.

The Israelites, as architects of their fate, did not merely claim the Promised Land through wishful thinking; they engaged in military campaigns, a relentless pursuit of the divine inheritance.

It was a time of active possession, where the echoes of battle cries resonated in the air, and the clash of swords heralded a people's determined march toward their destiny.

Conquest, in this context, was the forging of a path through the wilderness of uncertainty, a testament to the indomitable spirit of a people driven by the promises of their covenant.

However, conquest was but the initial surge in this historical tide. Settlement emerged as the subsequent act—a nuanced, intricate process of transforming conquered territory into a home, a haven for a people on the brink of realizing their divine legacy.

Settlement required more than the physical claiming of land; it demanded the establishment of order, the formulation of laws, and the cultivation of a societal framework that would endure.

The Israelites, having crossed the threshold of conquest, now turned their attention to the meticulous art of settling—a task that involved not just the building of homes but the construction of a nation.

The historical context unfolds as a tapestry woven with threads of daring campaigns and the deliberate laying of foundations. The people of Israel, in their quest to possess the land, emerged not just as conquerors but as architects of a settlement that would resonate through the corridors of time—an enduring legacy of courage, perseverance, and the fulfillment of divine promises.

T.E. LAWRENCE: NAVIGATING THE SANDS OF DESTINY

Thomas Edward Lawrence, known as Lawrence of Arabia, became a legendary figure in the early 20th century. Born in 1888, Lawrence's dream was not of a nation's independence but of influencing the destiny of a people and region.

Lawrence's journey began with an archaeological background, but his destiny took a turn during World War I. Sent to the Arabian Peninsula, Lawrence immersed himself in the local culture, learning Arabic and understanding the complexities of tribal dynamics. His dream was not just about defeating the Ottoman Empire but about giving Arabs a say in their future.

Lawrence's skill development was unconventional. His mastery of guerrilla warfare and diplomacy became crucial in uniting Arab tribes against common enemies. His journey wasn't just about taking possession of territory; it was about navigating the intricate political landscape of the Arabian Peninsula.

The legacy of Lawrence of Arabia lies not only in the military victories but in his influence on shaping the post-war in Middle East. His dream of giving Arabs a voice and a role in determining their destiny showcases a historical example of "taking possession." Lawrence's story goes beyond traditional military conquests; it's about actively steering the sands of destiny.

SHAKA ZULU: A VISIONARY MILITARY LEADER

Consider the life of Shaka Zulu, a visionary military leader born around 1787 in what is now South Africa. Shaka's dream was to unite the various Zulu clans into a powerful and cohesive nation. His pursuit of this dream transformed him into one of the most influential military leaders in African history.

He actively pursued his dream by implementing innovative military strategies, introducing new weapons like the iconic short stabbing spear, and restructuring traditional formations. Through a series of military campaigns, he successfully forged a centralized Zulu kingdom.

His military conquest wasn't merely about territorial expansion; it was a deliberate effort to shape the destiny of his people. His dream of a unified Zulu nation became a reality, and his military innovations left an indelible mark on the history of Southern Africa.

Shaka Zulu's journey serves as a historical example of "taking possession" in the context of personal and collective dreams. His military prowess and strategic vision actively contributed to reshaping the destiny of the Zulu people and establishing a powerful and enduring legacy.

ESTABLISHMENT OF ORDER AND LAW

The journey wasn't solely defined by the clash of swords and the conquest of territories. It was equally characterized by the meticulous establishment of order and the formulation of a legal framework that would serve as the backbone of a nascent nation.

Moses, the venerable leader entrusted with guiding the Israelites through the wilderness, played a pivotal role in this unfolding narrative. On the sacred heights of Mount Sinai, he received more than just tablets of stone; he received a divine code—a set of laws that would govern the conduct of the people and shape the contours of their society.

The establishment of order, embodied in the Law, became an essential companion to the military endeavors. It wasn't merely about claiming land; it was about crafting a society anchored in justice, ethics, and a reverence for the divine.

This legal framework wasn't a rigid set of dictates but a dynamic guide—a compass steering the people toward a just and harmonious existence. The laws weren't arbitrary; they were a reflection of the divine wisdom, a blueprint for a society bound by principles that transcended the temporal.

Imagine these laws like a guidebook. They weren't just random rules; they were like a map showing the best way to live together. It was a bit like saying, "Hey, let's make sure everyone is treated well, and we do things in a way that's fair and right." So, alongside all the fighting for land, they were also figuring out how to create a fair and just society.

CULTIVATION AND STEWARDSHIP

Possession, in the divine economy, wasn't a license for exploitation; it was an invitation to cultivation and stewardship. The people of Israel weren't just tasked with claiming the land; they were called to be caretakers, stewards of a divine legacy entrusted to their care.

Cultivation wasn't restricted to the fields; it extended to the very fabric of their society. The land, viewed as a gift, demanded a reciprocal relationship—a commitment to nurture, preserve, and celebrate its fertility.

The people were summoned not just to extract from the land but to engage in a dance of reciprocity, recognizing the sacred bond between them and the earth beneath their feet. They were to add value to the land.

Stewardship, in this context, went beyond mere possession; it was a recognition of a shared responsibility with the divine. The people were not owners in the conventional sense; they were custodians, safeguarding the richness of the land for generations to come.

The act of cultivation became a sacrament—a spiritual practice echoing through the furrows of the fields and the alleys of their communal life. You don't just claim it; you water the plants, make sure they're healthy, and enjoy the beauty. That's a bit like what the people were asked to do with the Promised Land.

In the symphony of possession, the establishment of order and the call to cultivation and stewardship emerged as harmonious refrains. They were the nuances that transformed possession from a conquest of space into a legacy of justice, sustainability, and a sacred dance with the divine.

The idea was not just to take from the land but to work with it, make it better, and keep it healthy. It's like being a good friend to the land. They weren't owners who could do anything they wanted; they were more like helpers, making sure the land stayed amazing for everyone.

It was a bit like saying, "Let's take care of this place together, and make it a great home for us and future generations."

THEODORE ROOSEVELT: THE POLITICAL CONSERVATIONIST

Consider the political career of Theodore Roosevelt, the 26th President of the United States, born in 1858. Roosevelt's dream was to cultivate a nation that balanced economic progress with environmental conservation, setting the stage for modern environmental stewardship.

Roosevelt actively pursued his dream by championing the conservation movement during his presidency (1901-1909). He expanded the National Parks system, established the United States Forest Service, and signed into law the Antiquities Act, allowing the president to designate national monuments.

Roosevelt's approach was political cultivation—nurturing the nation's natural resources for the benefit of present and future generations.

His commitment to stewardship extended beyond policies. Roosevelt was an avid naturalist and explorer, using his influence to educate the public about the importance of preserving the environment.

His dream of a nation that balances progress with responsible stewardship actively shaped the political landscape, leaving a lasting impact on environmental policies.

Theodore Roosevelt's journey serves as a historical example of "taking possession" in the context of political cultivation and stewardship. His dedication to cultivating a nation mindful of its natural resources and his active role in environmental stewardship contributed to reshaping the political destiny of the United States and laid the groundwork for modern conservation efforts.

4. DISTRIBUTE THE LAND BY LOT, ACCORDING TO YOUR CLANS.

This speaks not merely of parcels of physical terrain but resonates as a universal decree urging us to navigate the intricate landscapes of our lives with equity and purpose.

This timeless wisdom forms a major keystone of our exploration into the heart of maintaining miracles. Beyond the literal allocation of land, it beckons us to delve into the essence of equitable distribution and purposeful allocation, guiding us on a journey where the preservation of miracles becomes an art—a conscious act of contribution to the harmonious symphony of life.

In the biblical context, the distribution of land by lot is prominently featured in the book of Joshua. After the Israelites crossed the Jordan River and entered the Promised Land, the allocation of territories among the twelve tribes became a crucial task.

Joshua, following the divine command, employed the casting of lots as a means to determine each tribe's inheritance.

Joshua 14:1-2 (NIV): "Now these are the areas the Israelites received as an inheritance in the land of Canaan, which Eleazar the priest, Joshua son of Nun and the heads of the tribal clans of Israel allotted to them. Their inheritances were assigned by lot to the nine and a half tribes, as the Lord had commanded through Moses."

This biblical account showcases the application of lots as a method ordained by God for the fair distribution of land among the tribes. The process involved seeking divine guidance to ensure impartiality and adherence to God's plan.

FAIRNESS AND IMPARTIALITY IN THE CASTING OF LOTS

The use of casting lots in the distribution of land among the tribes in biblical times was rooted in the principles of fairness and impartiality. This method was regarded as a divinely guided and unbiased approach to allocate territories, preventing any form of favoritism or human bias.

The casting of lots is mentioned in various biblical passages, including the allocation of land to the tribes of Israel in the book of Joshua. This method involved using tools or stones with markings to determine the divine will, and it was considered a way for God to guide the decision-making process.

It served as a safeguard against human interference and biases that might arise in the distribution process. In a society where tribal distinctions were significant, the potential for favoritism or unfair influence was a concern.

The casting of lots, being a process believed to be directly guided by God, eliminated any room for personal preferences or human manipulation.

The emphasis on divine providence in the casting of lots underscored the belief that God's will would be revealed through this method. It reflected a deep trust in the fairness of God's guidance, emphasizing that the allocation of resources, in this case, land, was not subject to human whims but rather directed by a higher, impartial power.

The use of casting lots aligns with broader biblical principles of justice and fairness. Throughout the Bible, there is a consistent call for just dealings and the avoidance of partiality. Proverbs 16:33 (NIV) captures the essence of casting lots: "The lot is cast into the lap, but its every decision is from the Lord."

This verse emphasizes that even seemingly random events, like casting lots, are under the sovereign control of God.

Historically, the distribution of land by lot played a pivotal role in the establishment of organized governance and the prevention of tribal conflicts.

Avoiding Tribal Strife:

This reflects the wisdom of using lots to prevent potential disputes among the tribes. By relying on a method perceived as impartial, the Israelites aimed to avoid internal conflicts over territorial claims, fostering unity and cooperation.

Organized Settlement:

The casting of lots facilitated the organized settlement of the Israelites in the Promised Land. It provided a systematic approach to dividing the land into distinct territories for each tribe, enabling efficient governance and resource management.

Preserving Ancestral Heritage:

The distribution according to ancestral tribes held historical significance by preserving family and tribal heritage. Each tribe received a portion of the land that aligned with its ancestral roots, reinforcing a sense of identity and continuity throughout generations.

In both biblical and historical contexts, the act of distributing land by lot emerges as a strategic and spiritually guided method. It reflects a harmonious blend of divine principles and practical considerations, ensuring the equitable allocation of resources while fostering unity and preserving the rich heritage of the Israelites.

LAND DISTRIBUTION IN ANCIENT ROME

In the heart of ancient Rome, a triumphant army returned from the frontlines, bearing the spoils of war and dreams of a new life. The Senate, conscious of the need for fairness and the prevention of undue influence, employed a method reminiscent of divine guidance: lot allocation.

Each veteran, regardless of rank or status, eagerly participated in the draw, the casting of lots determining their piece of the conquered land.

The lots fell with an impartial hand, bestowing fertile plains upon some and rugged hills upon others. The Roman state, by embracing the principle of casting lots, fostered a sense of equity among its veterans.

No longer bound by the whims of power or favoritism, each soldier became a landowner, securing a stake in the prosperity of the empire. This practice not only prevented internal strife but also contributed to the stability and unity of Roman society.

The notion that "to a larger group give a larger inheritance, and to a smaller group a smaller one" from the biblical verse emphasizes the concept of proportionate distribution based on the size or needs of the tribes.

This principle reflects a sense of fairness and equity, ensuring that each tribe receives an inheritance that aligns with its size or requirements.

HOMESTEAD ACTS IN THE UNITED STATES:

As the sun dipped below the vast expanse of the American frontier, a new chapter unfolded with the Homestead Acts. In the 19th and early 20th centuries, pioneers seeking a fresh start ventured westward, drawn by the promise of fertile lands.

The allocation of these lands, however, demanded a fair and impartial approach. The draw of lots, reminiscent of ancient practices, determined who would claim each parcel, ensuring an equitable distribution.

In the lottery of opportunity, families from diverse backgrounds eagerly awaited the outcome. The prairie breeze carried the dreams of settlers, and as lots were drawn, destinies were shaped.

The Homestead Acts, with their emphasis on fairness through lot allocation, became a beacon of hope, allowing individuals to forge new lives and contribute to the tapestry of the evolving American landscape.

This notion is part of the divine instructions given to guide the allocation of land among the tribes. The idea is rooted in the understanding that larger tribes, with more people, may require more resources or territory to sustain themselves, while smaller tribes may need proportionally less.

Historically, this principle helped in the practical and efficient settlement of the Israelites in the Promised Land. It acknowledged the diversity among the tribes and recognized that their varying sizes would necessitate different allocations to ensure their sustenance and well-being.

This concept is aligned with principles of justice and compassion, reflecting an intention to meet the unique needs of each tribe. It reinforces the idea that the distribution of resources, whether land or other blessings, should be tailored to the specific circumstances and requirements of the recipients.

In both settings, the notion of proportionate distribution serves as a guideline for just and considerate allocation, promoting a sense of balance and ensuring that each tribe's inheritance aligns with its size and needs. It contributes to the overarching theme of maintaining miracles by fostering an environment of fairness and harmony among the tribes.

"The true measure of any society can be found in

how it treats its most vulnerable members."

Mahatma Gandhi

AFFORDABLE HOUSING LOTTERIES

Amidst the towering structures of urban landscapes, where dreams of home ownership seem distant, the concept of affordable housing lotteries emerges as a beacon of fairness and opportunity.

In the hustle and bustle of city life, the scarcity of affordable housing poses a significant challenge for individuals and families striving to secure a place they can call home.

As the city skyline casts long shadows, municipal agencies conduct affordable housing lotteries as a means of equitable distribution. Eligible applicants, each harboring the hope for a stable abode, participate in this modern-day draw of lots.

The lottery becomes a leveller, ensuring that the allocation of these precious housing units is devoid of biases or undue influence.

Picture a diverse array of hopeful faces gathered in community centers or virtually connected through digital platforms, anxiously awaiting the outcome. The randomness of the lottery draw mirrors the unpredictability of life itself.

Families with varying backgrounds, occupations, and aspirations share a common desire for a fair chance at securing a home that aligns with their financial realities.

The drawing of lots transforms the housing application process into a democratic and impartial affair. Regardless of socioeconomic status or personal connections, everyone enters the lottery on an equal footing. In this modern narrative of housing scarcity and opportunity, the randomness inherent in casting lots becomes a symbol of justice and fairness.

Affordable housing lotteries stand as a testament to the commitment of urban planners and policymakers to address the pressing need for housing equity. By adopting this method, cities aim to create a pathway for individuals and families to break free from the constraints of skyrocketing real estate prices.

In the dance of chance and destiny, the lottery draws forth not just the names of prospective homeowners but also the promise of a more inclusive and just urban future.

The New York City Housing Connect program regularly conducts affordable housing lotteries to allocate housing units. Eligible applicants submit their entries, and a randomized selection process ensures fairness in awarding these coveted affordable homes.

In the context of "Maintaining Your Miracle," this emphasis on fairness and impartiality holds significance. It suggests that the preservation and distribution of wealth should be guided by principles that transcend personal biases and human influences.

By aligning with divine providence, individuals are encouraged to approach the stewardship of their blessings with a sense of justice and equity, fostering an environment where everyone has a fair share in the riches or wealth bestowed upon them.

In essence, the casting of lots as a symbol of fairness and impartiality in the biblical narrative offers a timeless lesson in the just distribution of resources and blessings, serving as a guiding principle for maintaining miracles with integrity and equality.

EDUCATIONAL OPPORTUNITIES THROUGH LOTTERY SYSTEMS

In the corridors of educational institutions, where the pursuit of knowledge intertwines with aspirations for a brighter future, the challenge of equitable access emerges.

In regions where the demand for quality education surpasses available slots, a modern approach reminiscent of ancient lotteries unfolds—a lottery system for educational opportunities.

Imagine a community where eager parents and hopeful students envision a transformative journey through education. However, the constraints of limited spots in sought-after schools or programs introduce an element of uncertainty.

To address this challenge, educational authorities turn to the impartiality of lotteries, ensuring that the allocation of coveted spots is devoid of external influences.

In the days leading up to the lottery draw, anticipation fills the air. Parents clutch applications and students visualize the possibilities that education can unlock.

The drawing of lots becomes the mechanism through which the community's aspirations are channeled into a fair and unbiased selection process.

The randomness inherent in the lottery system stands as a shield against favoritism, ensuring that educational opportunities are distributed based on chance rather than predetermined factors.

As the lots are drawn and names are announced, the community witnesses a transformation—a diverse group of students gaining access to educational paths that will shape their futures.

The lottery system becomes a symbol of equal opportunity, breaking down barriers that could otherwise hinder access to quality education.

The OneApp system in New Orleans, Louisiana, uses a lottery system for school admissions. Parents submit preferences for school placement, and a computerized lottery assigns students to schools, promoting fairness and preventing biased selection.

This modern application of lotteries in education underscores a commitment to fairness and inclusivity. It reflects a recognition that, in the pursuit of knowledge, chance should play a role in determining who gets to benefit from educational resources.

The lottery draw becomes a metaphorical gateway, opening doors to educational opportunities and laying the foundation for a more equitable and enlightened society.

"Fairness does not mean everyone gets the same.

Fairness means everyone gets what they need."

Rick Riordan

RESOURCE ALLOCATION IN HUMANITARIAN AID

In the aftermath of calamities, where devastation leaves communities in dire need, the orchestration of aid becomes a delicate dance of compassion and pragmatism. Humanitarian organizations, cognizant of the imperative for fairness, have adopted a method akin to casting lots in the allocation of resources.

This modern approach seeks to ensure that help reaches those most in need, guided not by favoritism but by the impartial hand of chance.

Imagine a landscape marred by the aftermath of a natural disaster or conflict, where basic necessities become elusive commodities.

In this dire setting, humanitarian aid organizations mobilize resources to provide assistance, whether in the form of food, shelter, or medical care. The challenge lies in determining who receives this aid, especially when needs surpass available resources.

In a bid to maintain fairness and objectivity, aid organizations turn to random selection methods. Through lotteries or other impartial mechanisms, individuals or communities are chosen to receive assistance. This process stands as a safeguard against potential biases, ensuring that aid is distributed based on need rather than subjective judgments.

Picture aid workers clustered around makeshift tables, preparing to draw lots or employ digital tools for a randomized selection. The names or locations selected become the focal points for targeted assistance. This method not only prevents undue influence or discrimination but also amplifies the principle of equal opportunity in times of crisis.

The randomness inherent in casting lots becomes a lifeline for those grappling with the aftermath of disasters. It signifies a commitment to fairness in the face of adversity, where the distribution of aid becomes a matter of chance rather than predetermined factors.

In this humanitarian narrative, the impartial draw of lots becomes a symbol of hope, ensuring that assistance reaches those who need it most, regardless of external factors.

Médecins Sans Frontières (Doctors Without Borders) employs a fair and impartial approach to resource allocation during humanitarian missions. Random selection methods, such as draws, help identify communities in need, ensuring aid reaches those most affected by disasters or conflicts.

The modern approach of casting lots in humanitarian aid embodies a commitment to justice, compassion, and the equitable distribution of resources, fostering a sense of collective responsibility in the global effort to alleviate suffering.

"Justice is what love looks like in public."

Dr. Cornel West

THE SCHOOL PLACEMENT SYSTEM IN GHANA

In Ghana, the school placement system is a crucial aspect of the educational landscape that aligns with the principles of maintaining miracles in a fair and equitable manner.

The process involves assigning students to various senior high schools based on their performance in the Basic Education Certificate Examination (BECE) and other relevant criteria.

This system serves as a reflection of the commitment to providing equal educational opportunities for all students, regardless of their backgrounds.

Fairness in Educational Access

The school placement system in Ghana is designed to ensure fairness in the distribution of educational resources and opportunities. Students from diverse socioeconomic backgrounds have an equal chance of gaining admission to reputable senior high schools.

This commitment to fairness aligns with the overarching theme of maintaining miracles, where access to quality education is viewed as a transformative and equitable force.

Impartial Allocation Based on Merit

The placement system in Ghana is merit-based, considering students' performance in the BECE. This impartial allocation of placements underscores the idea that individuals should be given opportunities based on their abilities and efforts rather than external factors.

The emphasis on merit aligns with the concept of maintaining miracles through hard work, dedication, and the pursuit of excellence.

Preventing Biases and Favoritism

By employing a transparent and standardized placement process, the Ghanaian educational system aims to prevent biases and favoritism in the allocation of school placements.

The randomized nature of the placement system ensures that external influences, such as personal connections or financial status, do not play a significant role in determining a student's educational destiny.

Equalizing Educational Outcomes

The goal of the school placement system is to equalize educational outcomes by providing students across the country with the opportunity to access quality education.

This aligns with the broader theme of maintaining miracles, where the transformative power of education is recognized as a pathway to personal and societal advancement.

Nurturing Future Leaders

The commitment to fair and equitable school placement in Ghana contributes to the nurturing of future leaders from various backgrounds.

By providing students with equal opportunities to access quality education, the system recognizes the potential for each individual to contribute meaningfully to the development of the nation, fostering a sense of collective responsibility for the future.

In the context of maintaining miracles, the Ghanaian school placement system serves as a beacon of fairness, equity, and the transformative power of education in shaping the destinies of individuals and the nation as a whole.

"Education is the most powerful weapon

which you can use to change the world."

Nelson Mandela

These examples illustrate how various organizations, from housing authorities to humanitarian aid groups and educational systems, have embraced the concept of casting lots or using lottery systems to ensure impartiality, fairness, and equitable distribution of resources or opportunities.

5. BUT IF YOU DO NOT DRIVE OUT THE INHABITANTS OF THE LAND... THEY WILL GIVE YOU TROUBLE IN THE LAND

In the spiritual sense, the instruction to *drive out the inhabitants of the land* emphasizes the need for individuals to remove negative influences and distractions from their lives.

These "inhabitants" could symbolize detrimental habits, toxic relationships, or any factors that hinder personal and spiritual growth. The notion of allowing them to remain suggests a lack of proactive effort in eliminating these hindrances.

Let's discuss some of the implications of this portion of the instructions given to the ancient people and draw inferences in context with our modern life:

Maintaining Purity and Holiness

Driving out the inhabitants is akin to maintaining purity and holiness in one's life. The analogy of these inhabitants becoming "barbs in your eyes and thorns in your sides" vividly shows the discomfort and challenges that arise when negative influences are allowed to persist.

To maintain miracles, individuals are encouraged to actively eliminate anything that hinders their spiritual and personal well-being.

Vigilance in the Modern Context

In modern setting, the call to drive out negative influences resonates with the need for spiritual vigilance. In a world filled with distractions and conflicting values, individuals must be proactive in maintaining spiritual purity.

Allowing negative influences to persist can act as spiritual barbs and thorns, causing discomfort and hindering the journey toward personal and collective miracles.

Symbolism of Trouble and Disruption

The phrase "They will give you trouble in the land where you will live" signifies that allowing detrimental influences to persist can lead to ongoing challenges and disruptions in one's life.

In the context of maintaining miracles, this involves creating an environment free from unnecessary troubles, allowing individuals to focus on their goals and aspirations without unnecessary hindrances.

Proactive Elimination of Obstacles

The instruction to drive out the inhabitants serves as a call to action —a reminder that maintaining miracles requires proactive steps in eliminating obstacles.

It implies a responsibility to identify and address issues that may hinder personal or collective progress. This proactive approach aligns with the overarching theme of emphasizing the importance of taking control of one's destiny.

Metaphor for Personal Growth

The symbol of inhabitants becoming *barbs and thorns* underscores the idea that allowing negative influences to persist can lead to discomfort and pain.

This serves as a powerful metaphor for personal growth, suggesting that the journey to maintaining miracles involves a commitment to removing elements that cause discomfort and impede progress in your life.

Symbolism of Barbs and Thorns in Daily Life

The symbolism of barbs in the eyes and thorns in the sides extends to various aspects of daily life. Barbs in the eyes represent the *blinding effects of negative influences on one's perception and clarity of purpose.*

Thorns in the sides symbolize the persistent discomfort caused by habits, relationships, or situations that impede progress. To maintain miracles in the modern world, you must be aware of these symbolic barbs and thorns and take deliberate steps to remove them.

Addressing Discomfort and Challenges

The metaphor of barbs and thorns serves as a strong reminder that allowing negative influences to linger can result in ongoing emotional and spiritual discomfort and challenges.

It urges individuals to address not only the visible manifestations of negativity but also the subtle, internal disruptions that can hinder spiritual growth.

Maintaining miracles requires a commitment to spiritual and emotional well-being and a willingness to confront and eliminate anything that obstructs the path.

Renewal and Cleansing

The metaphorical presence of barbs and thorns suggests the need for periodic psychological, emotional and spiritual renewal and cleansing. Individuals are encouraged to engage in practices that purify the mind, heart, and spirit.

This proactive approach aligns with the divine aspect of maintaining miracles, emphasizing the continuous effort to create an environment where growth and divine manifestations can flourish.

Creating a Sacred Space for Miracles

In the context of maintaining miracles, the symbolism of barbs and thorns underscores the importance of creating a sacred space for spiritual and mental growth. It involves cultivating an environment where positivity thrives, free from the entanglements of negativity.

This sacred space becomes a fertile ground for miracles to blossom, as individuals actively remove barriers to psychological, emotional and spiritual clarity and well-being.

REASONS FOR RELUCTANCE AND RESISTANCE TO THE RESOLUTION

In the unfolding drama of human life, there exists a pivotal command echoing through the ages: "drive out the inhabitants of the land." Yet, woven into the fabric of our existence are intricate threads that often lead individuals to resist or neglect this divine directive.

Come along as I embark on this exploration, unraveling the complex reasons behind the reluctance to heed this ancient call. These factors I find profound parallels in the modern pursuit of maintaining miracles.

From the comforting embrace of familiarity to the fear of facing confrontation, each thread weaves a unique story of human struggle and reluctance. Join me as we dissect the multifaceted reasons that hinder individuals from embracing the transformative journey of driving out the inhabitants in their own lands, unveiling a narrative that resonates across the eras of human experience and the pursuit of miraculous living.

Comfort Zone and Familiarity

In the historical narrative, the reluctance to *'drive out inhabitants'* is intertwined with the notion that these familiar figures are part of the known landscape.

The prospect of venturing into the unknown, displacing the accustomed order, and embracing uncertainty can be daunting. The status quo, even if less than ideal, provides a sense of stability and predictability.

Similarly, in contemporary contexts, individuals often grapple with the appeal of their comfort zones. The familiar, despite its shortcomings, exerts a powerful gravitational pull.

Whether it's habits, relationships, or work environments, the comfort zone becomes a stronghold, impeding personal and spiritual growth. Inertia and resistance to change foster a reluctance to venture beyond the familiar, even when stagnation and dissatisfaction persist.

Breaking free from this pattern involves recognizing the transformative potential that lies outside our comfort zone. It requires a conscious decision to embrace discomfort as a catalyst for growth and innovation.

Just as the Israelites had to face the uncertainty of the Promised Land, modern individuals must confront the unknown to realize their full potential.

OPRAH WINFREY AND THE O.W.N. NETWORK

Oprah Winfrey, a television icon, catapulted herself out of the comfort zone of her successful talk show to venture into uncharted territories as a media mogul.

After decades of dominating daytime television with "The Oprah Winfrey Show," Oprah faced the daunting challenge of launching her cable network, OWN (Oprah Winfrey Network), in 2011.

The network's inception was met with skepticism and faced initial struggles. Oprah encountered the complexities of managing a network, navigating through the uncertainties of programming, and building a brand from scratch. The comfort zone of daily talk show hosting was replaced by the demanding role of network executive and entrepreneur.

Despite early setbacks, Oprah's perseverance and strategic decisions gradually steered OWN toward success. The network evolved into a platform for inspirational and thought-provoking content, aligning with Oprah's vision for meaningful programming.

Oprah Winfrey's journey exemplifies the transformative power of stepping beyond one's comfort zone, embracing challenges, and achieving long-term success in uncharted professional territories.

SIR ERNEST SHACKLETON'S ANTARCTIC EXPEDITION (1914-1917)

In the annals of exploration, Sir Ernest Shackleton's Antarctic expedition stands as a testament to the courage required to step beyond the boundaries of the known into uncharted territories.

Shackleton, a seasoned explorer, envisioned traversing the Antarctic continent from sea to sea. His ship, the Endurance, set sail in 1914, aiming for a journey that would etch their names in the annals of exploration history.

However, adversity struck when the Endurance became trapped in the ice of the Weddell Sea. Shackleton and his crew found themselves marooned, far from any established outposts. The icy confines of Antarctica presented an unforgiving environment, pushing the crew to the brink of survival.

What set Shackleton apart was his ability to adapt and lead in the face of dire circumstances. Realizing that the Endurance was doomed, he made the audacious decision to abandon the ship, trekking with his crew across the treacherous ice.

Their journey on lifeboats and then a perilous open-boat voyage to South Georgia showcased Shackleton's leadership, determination, and willingness to leave the familiar, leading to the eventual rescue of his entire crew.

Fear of Confrontation

This highlights the potential for conflicts or challenges when confronting and driving out inhabitants. Fear of confrontation, be it physical or ideological, can deter decisive action. The avoidance of conflict may stem from a desire for peace or a reluctance to engage in battles that could have unforeseen consequences.

In modern situations, the fear of confrontation manifests in various aspects of life. Individuals may shy away from addressing negative influences due to the perceived discomfort of difficult conversations or conflicts.

The fear of upsetting the status quo or facing opposition becomes a barrier to resolving issues that hinder personal progress. This fear-driven avoidance perpetuates a cycle of stagnation.

Overcoming this fear requires a shift in perspective, viewing confrontation not as a threat but as an opportunity for growth and resolution. It involves developing effective communication skills, embracing discomfort as a natural part of change, and recognizing that addressing conflicts head-on is essential for personal and spiritual advancement.

Just as the Israelites had to confront challenges in claiming their Promised Land, modern individuals must confront their fears to navigate towards their own metaphorical land of promise.

"The only way to make sense out of change

is to plunge into it,

move with it, and join the dance."

Alan Watts

MALALA YOUSAFZAI AND GIRLS' EDUCATION ADVOCACY

Malala Yousafzai, a Pakistani activist for girls' education, confronted the oppressive policies of the Taliban in her native Swat Valley. In a region where the Taliban banned girls from attending school, Malala courageously spoke out against this injustice, advocating for the right to education for all children, irrespective of gender.

In 2012, Malala survived an assassination attempt by the Taliban, reinforcing her commitment to the cause. Instead of succumbing to fear, she intensified her advocacy efforts.

Malala co-authored the memoir "I Am Malala," became the youngest-ever recipient of the Nobel Peace Prize, and established the Malala Fund to promote girls' education globally.

Malala's fearless confrontation with the Taliban's oppressive policies garnered international attention and support. Her resilience and commitment to education as a fundamental right have elevated her to a global symbol of courage, demonstrating that confronting systemic injustices can lead to transformative change.

MARTIN LUTHER KING JR. AND THE CIVIL RIGHTS MOVEMENT

Martin Luther King Jr., an iconic figure in the Civil Rights Movement, fearlessly confronted the deeply entrenched racial injustice of his time. In the mid-20th century, racial segregation, discrimination, and systemic injustice were pervasive in the United States.

Driven by a vision of equality and justice, King emerged as a charismatic leader who fearlessly confronted the status quo.

King's approach to confrontation was rooted in nonviolent resistance and civil disobedience. He led massive peaceful protests, such as the *Montgomery Bus Boycott* and the *March on Washington*, demanding an end to racial segregation and the realization of civil rights for all Americans.

His powerful speeches, including the famous "I Have a Dream" speech, reverberated with a call for justice and equality.

Despite facing violent opposition, arrest, and personal threats, Martin Luther King Jr. persisted in his confrontation with injustice. His unwavering commitment and fearless confrontation catalyzed significant legislative changes, including the Civil Rights Act of 1964 and the Voting Rights Act of 1965.

King's legacy endures as a symbol of the transformative power of confronting societal ills with courage and nonviolent resistance.

Attachment to Unhealthy Relationships:

In the annals of history, a tribe found solace in unity, but this unity bore a double-edged sword—attachment to unhealthy relationships. As bonds strengthened within the tribe, emotional ties to certain inhabitants grew.

The divine command, though clear, faced resistance fueled by emotional connections. The struggle to sever these ties became a poignant saga, marking the historical landscape with the indelible ink of attachment.

In the bustling cityscape of today, Sarah, a beautiful young lady, grapples with a parallel dilemma. Entangled in relationships that no longer serve her growth, she faces the challenge of letting go.

The emotional attachments, much like the historical tribe, prove to be formidable barriers to her personal progress. Sarah's journey mirrors the ageless human struggle, where emotional ties hinder the expulsion of influences critical to maintaining miracles in the modern era.

"Letting go means to come to the realization that
some people are a part of your history,
but not a part of your destiny."
Steve Maraboli

RIHANNA'S COMPLEX RELATIONSHIP WITH CHRIS BROWN

Rihanna, a global music icon, found herself in a highly scrutinized and turbulent relationship with fellow artist Chris Brown. In 2009, the couple faced a public scandal when Brown physically assaulted Rihanna, leading to widespread condemnation.

Despite the severity of the incident and public pressure to sever ties, Rihanna's initial attachment to Chris Brown highlighted the complexities surrounding unhealthy relationships. The emotional intricacies, personal history, and societal pressures often complicate the process of leaving such relationships.

Over time, Rihanna distanced herself from Chris Brown, emphasizing the importance of prioritizing one's well-being. The public nature of her experience shed light on the challenges individuals face when attempting to detach from unhealthy relationships, even when subjected to public scrutiny.

QUEEN VICTORIA AND JOHN BROWN'S UNCONVENTIONAL FRIENDSHIP

Queen Victoria, one of the longest-reigning monarchs in British history, formed an unusual attachment to her Scottish servant, John Brown, in the mid-19th century. Following the death of her beloved husband, Prince Albert, Victoria found solace and emotional support in her friendship with Brown.

Their relationship faced intense public scrutiny and criticism, with rumors of a romantic involvement between the monarch and her servant. Despite societal norms and the disapproval of the royal court, Queen Victoria maintained her attachment to John Brown. His companionship provided her with a sense of comfort during a period of deep grief and loneliness.

While the nature of their relationship remains a subject of historical debate, Queen Victoria's steadfast attachment to John Brown challenges traditional expectations placed upon royalty. Her willingness to prioritize emotional well-being over societal expectations reflects the complexities of attachment, even in unconventional circumstances.

Short-Term Gain vs. Long-Term Pain:

In the shadows of ancient times, a community confronted the ageless dilemma of short-term gain versus the enduring sting of long-term pain. The allure of immediate benefits, much like the tempting fragrance of a fleeting blossom, captivated their senses.

The decision to permit certain inhabitants to linger proved akin to embracing the thorns willingly. What appeared as a momentary relief materialized into a saga of persistent discomfort and adversity till date.

The historical narrative unveiled with choices, where the short-lived joys of the present darkened the foresight needed to navigate the maze of the future.

The community, guided by the intoxicating allure of immediate benefits, unwittingly planted seeds of strife, witnessing the blooms of brief satisfaction metamorphose into enduring thorns.

In the modern rhythm of reality, Mark stood at the crossroads of decision, each path paved with its unique appeal. The promise of short-term gratification and immediate rewards beckoned seductively, whispering promises of comfort and convenience.

Mark, a young gentleman navigating life's labyrinth, found himself entangled in the echoes of the historical dilemma. His choices mirrored the timeless struggle—a testament to the innate human inclination to prioritize immediate gain while relegating the potential for long-term pain to the periphery.

Mark's narrative unfolds as a cautionary tale, a reflection of the modern human life, where the seeds sown in the fertile soil of the present bear fruits, either sweet or bitter, in the orchard of the future.

His story echoes across times, resonating with the perennial truth that decisions crafted in the proximity of today form the landscape of tomorrows yet to unfold.

"Don't sacrifice what you want most

for what you want now."

Zig Ziglar

TREATY OF VERSAILLES AND LONG-TERM GEOPOLITICAL TENSIONS

The Treaty of Versailles, signed in 1919 to formally end World War I, serves as a poignant historical example of prioritizing short-term gain over long-term stability.

The treaty imposed harsh conditions on Germany, including territorial losses, disarmament, and heavy damages. While intended to bring about immediate peace, the punitive nature of the treaty fueled resentment among the German populace.

The short-term gain of achieving peace after the devastating war came at the cost of long-term geopolitical tensions.

The punitive measures laid the groundwork for economic struggles and political instability in Germany, contributing to the rise of Adolf Hitler and the outbreak of World War II.

The treaty's focus on immediate solutions without considering the long-term consequences illustrates the challenges of balancing short-term goals with sustainable outcomes.

"Don't let short-term thinking

drive long-term consequences."

Victor Fung

FAST FASHION'S ENVIRONMENTAL IMPACT

The fast fashion industry's pursuit of short-term profits through rapid production and low-cost manufacturing has resulted in significant long-term consequences for the environment. The constant demand for new, inexpensive clothing has led to exploitative labor practices, environmental degradation, and a culture of disposability.

While fast fashion provides quick and affordable clothing options for consumers, the environmental toll is substantial. The industry contributes to pollution, water scarcity, and excessive waste. The short-term gains of affordable and trendy clothing come at the expense of long-term environmental sustainability.

These historical and modern instances underscore the challenges of prioritizing short-term benefits without considering the enduring consequences. Whether in post-war treaties or contemporary consumer practices, the pursuit of immediate gains can lead to far-reaching and sometimes unintended outcomes.

Resistance to Change

Throughout the tapestry of history, the fabric of human existence has often resisted the needle of change. In the hallowed corridors of the past, change, especially of profound magnitude, echoed with the footsteps of uncertainty and unfamiliarity.

The historical narrative bore witness to the age-old dance between tradition and transformation, where the inertia of the familiar contended with the winds of change. The resistance, an integral part of the human condition, stood as a testament to the struggle against the impending gusts of progress.

People with habits, anchored in the security of the known, view the prospect of change as an unwelcome visitor, unsettling the stability they cleave to.

In the bustling scope of the present, individuals grapple with the same innate resistance to change. The modern world, with its relentless pace, presents a myriad of opportunities for growth and evolution.

However, the vines of familiarity, woven into the fabric of routine, often resist the winds of change that seek to sculpt new landscapes.

People, bound to the comfort of the known, may find themselves reluctant to embark on the transformative journey required for personal and spiritual development.

The resistance to change, an enduring aspect of the human psyche, manifests as a barrier, hindering the exploration of uncharted territories that hold the promise of growth and transformation.

STEVE JOBS' IPHONE AND TECHNOLOGICAL DISRUPTION

In the early 21st century, Steve Jobs, co-founder of Apple Inc., introduced the iPhone—an innovation that transformed the mobile phone industry and disrupted established norms.

The iPhone represented a departure from traditional mobile phones, combining various functions into a single device and introducing the concept of a touchscreen interface.

Despite initial skepticism and resistance from competitors, the iPhone's success demonstrated the power of embracing technological change.

Steve Jobs' vision challenged the status quo, emphasizing the importance of innovation and user-friendly design. The iPhone not only revolutionized the smartphone market but also set a precedent for the rapid evolution of technology in the modern era.

THE LUDDITES MOVEMENT IN THE INDUSTRIAL REVOLUTION

During the early 19th century, the Industrial Revolution brought about significant technological changes in England. One such innovation was the introduction of automated weaving and textile machinery. However, these machines threatened the livelihood of skilled textile workers.

The Luddites were a social movement of English textile artisans who protested against the changes brought by the Industrial Revolution.

Named after Ned Ludd, a fictional character, the movement emerged in the early 19th century. The Luddites were particularly opposed to the introduction of mechanized looms and knitting frames.

In their resistance to change, the Luddites, often organized in secret, engaged in acts of sabotage, destroying machinery they perceived as threats to their traditional way of life. The movement represented a reaction to the fear of unemployment and the devaluation of their artisan skills due to technological advancements.

The Luddites' opposition to technological change reflected a deep-seated resistance to the unknown future that the Industrial Revolution promised. Their movement became synonymous with a reluctance to embrace new technologies and marked a historical example of people unwilling to shift from the known to the unknown easily.

Dependency on Negative Habits

The inhabitants may have provided a perceived benefit that became intertwined with the fabric of daily life. The historical community, perhaps unknowingly, found solace or advantage in the presence of these inhabitants. The dependency on the perceived benefit, even if detrimental, forged chains that bound them to the status quo.

The historical tale illuminated the delicate dance between perceived benefit and the unseen shackles it could weave. The inhabitants, though thorns in disguise, offered a semblance of advantage, creating a dependency that clouded judgment.

In the contemporary theater, people faced with addictions on negative habits—a parallel to the historical reliance on perceived benefits. The modern landscape, endemic with myriad of influences, harbors habits, addictions, or coping mechanisms that may provide momentary relief or pleasure.

The narrative unfolds in the lives of individuals ensnared by the twists of dependency, creating a cycle that becomes challenging to break.

Whether in the form of addictive substances, destructive relationships, or harmful coping mechanisms, these negative habits cloak themselves in the allure of perceived benefits, fostering a reliance that poses a formidable obstacle to the journey of personal and spiritual emancipation.

The modern person, like these historical counterparts, finds themselves entangled in the struggle to break free from the grasp of habits that masquerade as allies but conceal the barbs and thorns of lasting pain.

SIGMUND FREUD'S CIGAR DILEMMA

In the dimly lit study of Sigmund Freud, the father of psychoanalysis, the aromatic haze of cigar smoke wafted through the air. Freud, the genius unraveling the complexities of the human mind, found himself entangled in a seemingly innocent habit—his dependence on cigars.

The tobacco-filled rituals were more than a fleeting pleasure; they became woven into the fabric of Freud's daily life. Despite his profound insights into the human psyche, Freud struggled to break free from this dependency.

The very man who dissected the intricacies of the unconscious mind found himself in a tug-of-war with a habit deeply embedded in his routine. The cigars, initially a source of solace, transformed into a symbol of the universal human struggle against dependencies.

Freud's story is a reminder that even the most enlightened minds grapple with personal battles. In the intricate tapestry of his existence, the cigar smoke lingered as a testament to the complexities of the human condition—a narrative not devoid of struggles, even for those who unravel the secrets of the mind.

ROBERT DOWNEY JR.'S JOURNEY OF REDEMPTION

In the glitzy world of Hollywood, Robert Downey Jr. soared to fame, embodying iconic characters on the silver screen. Yet, beneath the glamorous facade lay a tumultuous journey marked by the shadows of substance abuse.

Downey's battle with negative habits became a very public odyssey—one that mirrored the struggles of countless individuals facing similar demons.

The actor's dependence on substances led to a downward spiral that threatened to overshadow his exceptional talent. However, Downey's narrative took an unexpected turn, one of resilience and redemption.

Through perseverance, rehabilitation, and a supportive network, he emerged from the grips of addiction, turning his life into a beacon of hope for others facing similar challenges.

Downey's story illustrates that the path to overcoming negative habits is both arduous and transformative. In the sprawling narrative of his life, the dedication to redemption stands as a testament to the human capacity for change and the possibility of reclaiming one's life.

"It is not the mountain we conquer,

but ourselves."

Sir Edmund Hillary

CONCLUSION

In conclusion, we have explored the profound wisdom embedded in the instruction to drive out the inhabitants of the land, both in historical and modern contexts. The metaphorical barbs and thorns that ensue when this directive is neglected serve as poignant reminders of the potential pitfalls in our lives.

From comfort zones to attachments and short-term gains, the factors hindering obedience are diverse, yet their consequences are universally impactful.

As you navigate the intricacies of maintaining your miracles, pay heed to the timeless guidance to drive out negative influences from your life. It's a call to awareness, challenging you to recognize the barbs and thorns that may be hindering your growth.

Embrace change, sever attachments to unhealthy relationships, and resist the allure of short-term gains that may lead to long-term pain. Let us actively drive out the inhabitants that impede our journey to personal and divine fulfillment.

The choice is yours: to live amidst thorns or to cultivate a field where miracles can flourish. May your actions echo through the modern world, weaving a narrative of resilience, growth, and the unwavering pursuit of the miracles that await you.

As we bring down the curtains on this chapter, let the lessons learned be engraved in the annals of your understanding. Maintaining miracles is not a passive endeavor; it is a dynamic dance — a dance with self-discovery, a journey through knowledge, an investment in growth, and a symphony of support.

May the words on these pages be more than ink on paper; may they be a guiding melody as you navigate the chapters of your own life. For, in the pursuit of maintaining miracles, the episodes are not just narratives; they are the very notes that compose the symphony of a life well-lived.

And so, as we turn the page to the final chapter of this book, let the resonance of "Maintaining Your Miracle" linger—a timeless melody guiding you through the passages of self-discovery, growth, and the harmonious dance of a life adorned with more miracles.

CHAPTER SIX

MORE MIRACULOUS MOMENTS:

THE MAJESTIC MELODY

In the twilight of our journey, as we stand on the precipice of the final chapter, we embark on a quest to unearth the extraordinary. This is not just the conclusion but a grand crescendo—a symphony of *More Miraculous Moments* that resonate beyond the pages and echo through the corridors of faith and daring dreams.

As we peep into the annals of history and delve into the heartbeat of the world, we encounter tales that transcend time and space—stories of miracles that have shaped civilizations, transformed lives, and left an indelible mark on the tapestry of humanity.

Yet, this grand narrative is not confined to distant eras or renowned figures; it weaves through the fabric of our everyday existence, beckoning us to witness and acknowledge the miracles that unfold in the most unassuming corners of our lives.

In these final pages, I invite you to journey with me through my personal experiences, woven with threads of miracles and transformative breakthroughs.

As I reflect on my own path, I am compelled to share moments of profound wonder, where despair transformed into triumph, and what seemed like the end marked the beginning of miraculous new chapters.

In the embroidery of life, our individual threads intersect and intertwine, creating a mosaic of shared human experiences. Here, I open the pages to not just my story but to the stories of many, each a testament to the resilience of the human spirit and the capacity for miracles to manifest.

Through the lens of my own encounters with the extraordinary, I offer glimpses into the power of perseverance, the unexpected turns that life takes, and the miracles that grace us even in the midst of adversity.

Yet, this narrative extends beyond my own journey. It extends to the stories of countless individuals who have faced their own trials, navigated their unique challenges, and emerged victorious in the face of adversity.

As you immerse yourself in these narratives, may you find inspiration and connection. May the shared tales of miracles and breakthroughs in my life and that of others become beacons of hope, illuminating the paths that others have forged through the darkness. Together, we weave a narrative of collective resilience and the enduring strength that resides within each of us.

This final chapter stands as a testament to the belief that, in sharing our stories, we not only illuminate our own journeys but also light the path for others.

Here, in the intersection of personal narratives and shared experiences, we discover that miracles are not isolated events but threads that run through the very fabric of our lives.

So, let the Majestic Melody guide us—a melody that is both timeless and ever-evolving, a melody that invites us to witness, celebrate, and contemplate the miracles that dance through the corridors of our existence.

The final chapter is not an endpoint but a gateway—a gateway to *More Miraculous Moments* that await us in the symphony of faith, daring dreams, and the enchanting melodies of life.

HARBOUR OF HOPE: FROM SHADOWS TO SUNLIGHT

In the heart of Asawase, Kumasi, where the sun struggled to pierce through the crowded alleyways, and dreams seemed to wither before they could even bud, I began my journey.

Born into a tapestry of financial struggles, my grandmother, a resilient soul, raised her ten children amidst challenges that would humble even the strongest. As the family grew, so did the hardships, and soon, her grandchildren found themselves nestled in the arms of adversity.

I was but one among the many, a little boy navigating the narrow pathways of the slums, where sleeping like sardines in a can was a nightly ritual, and the persistent hum of deadly mosquitoes was our lullaby.

The room, tainted with the scent of desperation and marked by the stains of childhood accidents, bore witness to our shared struggles. Yet, it was within this backdrop of seemingly insurmountable challenges that the miraculous began to unfold.

Divinity, it seemed, had singled me out from the crowded chaos. In the midst of countless grandchildren, I found myself chosen, plucked from the slums of Asawase, Kumasi, and destined for a city far beyond my humble beginnings.

The beacon of hope came in the form of an aunty Joana Charity Nketsiah, whose heart and arms opened wide to embrace a new chapter in my life.

As I left the slums behind, I stepped into the city lights of Accra with a heart heavy with both the weight of the past and the anticipation of the unknown. Life demanded that I start anew, and it was tough—oh, how tough it was!

But within those challenges lay the miracle, the question that lingered in the air like a divine whisper: Why me? Why was I the one chosen among the many, while others remained trapped in the cycle of hardship?

Some of my peers in society would later pass on mysteriously through accidents or strange diseases. Others became societal deviants and victims of various vices but divine grace and mercy kissed me.

Life demanded that I shed the layers of my past and emerge anew, and this metamorphosis was far from easy. The city of Accra presented its own set of challenges, and each hurdle seemed like a testament to the magnitude of the miracle that had brought me here.

From financial challenges at home to the threat of expulsion from school due to unpaid fees amid emotional and psychological turmoil, being a growing child was something I had to battle with daily.

There were days when I felt profoundly lost and distant, even though people were around me. I sometimes drenched my pillow and nearly broke down emotionally. In those moments, the weight of my emotional struggles felt unbearable, and the ache in my heart seemed to echo with every tear.

Where were the ones that brought me to this weird world in the first place and left me as a little fry in the vast ocean of life? I needed more than what money and material things could satisfy. My guardians I must say did their very best to provide me with the care and whatever they could glean from their meagre sources.

But, my soul yearned for more!

In the emotional tapestry of my journey, the miracle unfolded not only in my survival but in my ability to defy the odds. The crowded alleys I left behind could have been the breeding ground for a life lost—a statistic in the shadows, forgotten by society. Yet, here I stand, not only alive but thriving.

The miracle wasn't just a physical relocation; it was the rebirth of my spirit, the determination to rise above circumstance. Grace and mercy had kissed me on the cheeks and given me a rare opportunity to begin life all over again. Here I was in a city that drowned its citizens with both societal pressures and opportunities.

It could have been easy for me to become a statistic, another forgotten soul lost in the shadows of the slums. But instead, I stand here today, a testament to the miracles that unfold when one soul decides to uplift another.

I could have been a street boy, a casualty of circumstance, or worse. Yet, against the odds, I not only survived but thrived, breaking free from the chains of my past.

And as I share this emotional journey, I am haunted by the images of those who shared my childhood but did not share my fate. Some lie buried beneath the weight of life's struggles, casualties of a reality that refused to relent. Others linger on the fringes of society, grappling with the shadows that the slums cast over their lives.

In the face of this stark contrast, the magnitude of the miracle becomes even more poignant. The divine intervention that plucked me from the brink of obscurity and breathed life into my narrative.

The questions of "Why me?" evolve into a solemn acknowledgment that every step I take is a testament to the unseen forces that guided my path.

As I reflect on those early years, I see the miracle woven into the fabric of my existence. The divine intervention that plucked me from the slums and set me on a path of resilience and determination in a city of chances.

Today, I am alive, contributing to my family and the world, a living testament to the miracles that can emerge from the most unlikely places.

And as I share this story, I invite you to ponder the miracles in your own journey—the moments that, against all odds, propelled you forward and shaped the person you are today.

"Hard times may have held you down,

but they will not last forever.

When all is said and done, you will be increased."
Joel Osteen

EYES OF GRACE: A DIVINE INTERRUPTION

In the symphony of academic agility, where my mind danced to the rhythm of success, a discordant note entered the composition of my life. It started as a subtle discomfort beneath my left eye, a persistent reminder that even the brightest melodies could be disrupted by unforeseen chords.

Eight consecutive times, I stood at the zenith of my class, a testament to the grace that endowed me with intellectual prowess. Yet, in the quiet corridors of my existence, a silent intruder emerged — a cyst, a swelling beneath my left eye.

Medications, both modern and traditional, proved powerless against its persistent presence, casting a shadow over my social interactions and threatening more than just my physical comfort.

The discomfort was more than skin-deep; it reached into the depths of my guardian's heart. Fears whispered that this seemingly benign cyst could be a harbinger of darkness, a precursor to a future where the light in my eyes could be extinguished.

Desperation led us to medical centers and many prayer meetings, but the journey proved futile. The application of local remedies brought no relief, and the looming specter of a necessary surgical operation cast a cloud over our hopes.

As the clock ticked toward the proposed date of my eye surgery, my guardian shouldered the weight of a secret. A clandestine decision was made not to burden the family with the looming surgery, an operation that could decide the fate of my vision and academics.

The day arrived, and with unease, I ventured into the realm of uncertainty. To my bewilderment, the orchestrator of my fate, the doctor set to conduct the operation, was a no-show. It was a strange twist, an amnesty wrapped in an unexpected delay.

Undeterred, we rescheduled, bracing ourselves for the impending surgery. However, the cosmos had other plans. Just as we embarked on the journey

263

to the hospital, my estranged biological mother reached out through the community call center.

A voice from the past, resonating with concern and love, interrupted the journey to the operation theater. Her timing was divine, an intervention that defied the boundaries of reason.

Stunned and cut to the heart by the revelation of the impending surgery, my mother insisted on a different path. A path paved with faith, where prayers supplanted scalpels.

In a courageous act of defiance against medical convention, we declined the appointment, choosing to trust in the unseen hands that held the pillars of our lives.

Months passed, and the cyst that once threatened my sight vanished into the mists of the miraculous. The swelling receded, and the discomfort dissolved when my memory had almost forsaken the existence of such a problem.

The questions lingered, hanging in the air like unspoken prayers —what could have unfolded if the surgeon's knife had pierced the veil of my eye? Why did the doctor miss the initial appointment, and how did my mother's call coincide with our journey to the precipice?

Today, as I look into the mirror with both eyes unhindered, I am reminded of a divine interruption. A mother's call, a missed appointment, and a cyst's disappearance became chapters in a story of grace and resilience.

I stand, not only with academic accolades but with the vivid memory of a miracle that restored my academics, vision and preserved the light in my eyes.

"Your eyes show the strength of your soul."

Paulo Coelho

HEALED BY FAITH: FROM DEATH'S DOOR TO DIVINE RECOVERY

In the final year at KNUST, my world took a harrowing turn. What began as a seemingly simple illness morphed into a life-threatening situation that defied medical explanation. Prayer and conventional treatments proved futile, leaving me weak and clinging to life.

Desperate, I returned to my family house in Kumasi, where a relentless pursuit of both orthodox and traditional remedies yielded no relief. It was my paternal grandmother, affectionately known as Ebo (Elizabeth Nyame), who took my deteriorating health most dear to heart.

Determined to save her first grandson attending university, she embarked on a tireless quest for the best medical care in the entire city of Kumasi. We ended up in Obuasi, the AngloGold Hospital for more sophisticated treatment but all was not successful.

Ebo could not stand the thoughts of losing the first son of her first son who died mysteriously seven years down memory lane. Her first son passed away in a very bizarre manner and this brought a lot of pain to her heart. Seeing me, the first son of her deceased first son also showing signs of passing on, was a heart wrenching experience she could not accommodate.

Hospital after hospital, test after test, and all results came back normal, yet my condition worsened. Pox covered my body, and even the simplest acts, like sitting or sleeping, became excruciating. Normal water was like poison in my mouth and food was a piercing arrow to my weak heart.

In a moment of despair, I found myself dictating my will and handing over notes to close friends, convinced that returning to campus was an unattainable dream as they paid me visit.

With all hope seemingly lost, the final recourse was a spiritual one. A journey to a prayer camp in a remote village unfolded, where I underwent physical ordeals, spiritual rituals, and intense exercises. Nights were spent in prayers, spiritual exercises, spiritual baths were performed, and scriptures recited with unwavering faith in divine intervention.

My soul yearned for relief!

While my peers attended lectures, I battled for my life, spending nine weeks away from academia. Slowly, strength returned, and the once-debilitated body began to heal. Divine intervention smiled upon me, and after two weeks in the prayer camp, I was declared better.

I returned home, prepared for school, and faced mid-semester exams with an indomitable spirit. What I thought was a minor illness kept me away from campus for almost nine weeks, about half the semester.

Yet, against all odds, I caught up on lectures, notes, and exams with the help of a few mates. Miraculously, I didn't trail any paper or course. The grace of God and the unwavering support of my family, especially my grandmother Ebo, paved the way for my successful graduation with a second-class upper division.

It marked the beginning of my career in the banking sector, a testament to the miraculous journey from desperation to divine recovery.

The return to campus after those tumultuous nine weeks stands as an unequivocal testament to the miraculous intervention that defied all expectations. When all hope seemed lost, the academic landscape, once a distant dream, became the stage for a remarkable comeback.

As I stepped back into the lecture theatres, the very halls that witnessed my despair now bore witness to a resurrection of determination. The papers that could have lingered as haunting remnants of a challenging time were conquered with an unwavering resolve and a newfound appreciation for the fragility of life.

In the realm of academia, my second coming became a resounding proclamation of the extraordinary. The once-lost semester transformed into a canvas where the brushstrokes of resilience and faith painted a narrative of triumph over adversity.

The despair that once loomed over my academic pursuits gave way to the radiant glow of a second chance — a chance that, by all accounts, was nothing short of miraculous.

The lecture halls, once silent witnesses to my tribulations, now echoed with the footsteps of resilience, determination, and a spirit that refused to be vanquished.

The papers that could have been a stumbling block became stepping stones, each one a testament to the indomitable human spirit and the divine intervention that made the impossible possible.

Beyond the corridors of academia, this chapter in my life became a compass directing the trajectory of my journey. The miraculous healing, against all odds, propelled me into the professional realm of the banking sector.

What seemed like a detour in the script of my life turned out to be a plot twist authored by divine hands, steering me towards a destination I hadn't foreseen.

As I stand today, a graduate and a professional in the financial sector, every step on this journey is underscored by the resounding echoes of that miraculous second coming to campus.

It is not just a personal narrative but a proclamation of the extraordinary forces that shape the course of our lives — forces that can turn despair into triumph and transform what seemed like the end into a miraculous new beginning.

"You may encounter many defeats,

but you must not be defeated.

In fact, it may be necessary to encounter

the defeats so you can know who you are,

what you can rise from, how you can still come out of it."

Maya Angelou

I RUN WITH DRUG ADDICTS AND PROSTITUTES. NOW I SHARE THE GOSPEL WITH THEM:

SHARON DUTRA

I was born in Los Angeles to a family in turmoil. My father was an alcoholic and a womanizer, and he was married four times by the time I was 17. My mother left when I was about 5 years old, and I never saw her again.

Throughout my childhood, I was moved from foster home to foster home. I started using drugs when I was 13. I believe that's when I finally realized that I hated myself. Up until then, I had been able to ignore my feelings of worthlessness and the ongoing sting of rejection and abandonment.

At 15, I ran away from home, living on the streets until I was arrested. Thus began my life with the law.

On the run

At first, I ended up at Eastlake Juvenile Hall in Central Los Angeles (a facility to which I would return several times). Murderers, thieves, and gang members were lumped together with those who had only run away from home. As a white girl with long, blond hair, I immediately felt out of place.

Eventually, I was transferred to Florence Crittenton, an open-placement girls' home in East Los Angeles. Leaving the grounds was against the rules, but there were no bars or walls to prevent it.

During that time, I would ride buses across Los Angeles at night, unaware of the potential danger. Pimps, predators, and gangsters abounded in many neighborhoods.

But I was too restless to stay anywhere for long. After running away from the girls' home for the third time, I was arrested again and sent back to juvenile hall. At this point I was a ward of the court, since my father and stepmother had divorced, neither wanting to take me in.

The court placed me in a closed facility in Central Los Angeles called the Convent of the Good Shepherd. The neighborhood was so unsafe we had to move our beds away from the windows on holidays, because gang members had shot through them in the past.

The convent walls were 12 feet high. But I even ran away from there, climbing onto the roof of the laundry building and crawling up the ivy to escape. With each getaway, my self-hatred escalated, along with contempt for authority figures and mistrust of people in general. I was headed down a path of destruction.

At age 19, I started working for the California Conservation Corps. One of our responsibilities was to serve meals to firefighters and prisoners as they fought major fires.

This is where I met a man I'll call Bill, who was serving a prison sentence in Yreka, California. We wrote letters back and forth for months, and when he was released, we moved in together. Later, we married and had two children.

At the time, I was drinking heavily and smoking pot. For years, I had used every drug I could get my hands on. But little did I know that Bill was using cocaine and speed intravenously. And it didn't take much to get me doing likewise. I would spend the next six and a half years with a needle in my arm, racking up four near-death experiences when I overdosed.

Needless to say, I lost all interest in working and taking care of my kids, my husband, or my apartment. Over time, my veins were so scarred from injecting myself that I started shooting in my hands and feet.

On several occasions, I even had another stoned addict shoot drugs into my neck veins, which risked sudden death. Of course, none of this was remotely fun—I was just trying to deaden my pain.

Bill and I divorced less than a decade later. We had tried getting sober, but we didn't know who the other person was without the drugs. After a six-month attempt at sobriety, I abandoned my family and headed straight for the streets so I could continue feeding my addiction.

I never imagined that I would end up homeless for two years, looking every bit like the proverbial bag lady. During this period, I hung around a dangerous neighborhood, venturing into the projects at night looking for drugs. I occasionally scoured garbage cans for food, but usually I just sold my body so I could survive and maintain my drug habit.

I certainly had a death wish. Twice, guns were pulled on me, and once I told the attacker, "Shoot me and put me out of my misery." I even attempted suicide on several occasions. But miraculously, I survived every close call.

Water in the desert

By age 29, I had been arrested 13 times. One morning, when I was trespassing on Fort Ord, then an Army base near Seaside, California, six military police cars arrived, and a Seaside Police sergeant came busting through the door. Because of my lengthy criminal record, I was sent to a women's prison in Southern California, where I already knew some of the inmates from my time on the street.

Crowded by pairs into tiny cells in the receiving unit, we were on lockdown 23 hours a day, 7 days a week, so there was no privacy. Very few inmates were allowed out of their cells to work.

But God was preparing another miracle. My cellmate worked in the kitchen, which gave me significant alone time. While she was away, I started reading *Al Capone's Devil Driver*, a book about the mob boss's chauffeur. This man had killed many people and landed in prison, where he ultimately became a born-again Christian.

At the time, I wasn't even looking for God. All I knew was that I wanted to die. My whole life had been an unbroken stretch of misery, and the pain was unbearable.

After finishing the book, I realized that God was *exactly* who I needed. I got on my knees and cried out to him for over an hour, weeping for all the wrongs I had done. When I got up off the cell floor, I was a brand-new person.

After being placed in the general prison population a few weeks later, I immediately went to church. The chaplain befriended me and bought me an expensive Bible. I read it for hours every day. After a lifetime derailed by destructive lies, finding God's truth felt like discovering a cool stream in the desert.

The Scriptures spoke wholeness and hope to my heart. At first, I could hardly fathom that Jesus would love a sinner like me, much less that my sins were totally forgiven.

But the more I read, the more the Holy Spirit confirmed the shocking reality of the gospel. I drew special encouragement from Joel 2:25, which speaks of God "repaying you for the years the locusts have eaten."

Soon enough, I found myself wanting to share Christ with others in prison. So I began leading worship songs and eventually teaching Bible studies.

After my release, I had to go back to my hometown of Santa Cruz, California. But the only people I knew there were drug addicts and prostitutes.

I wondered why God had returned me to this kind of environment. How would I overcome my reputation there? But God graciously gave me many opportunities to witness to those I had run with.

Eventually, I returned to school and received my registered nursing degree. I also married the son of a California Highway Patrol captain, and together we started a ministry that helps people come to know Jesus and disciples them in the Christian faith.

For decades now, I have written Bible studies and taught them to diverse groups of women—some lifelong Christians, others fresh off the streets or recovering from addictions.

After so many years on the run—from home, from authority, from life itself—I praise God for giving rest to my weary soul. No life is too broken for God to heal. I am living proof.

Sharon Dutra is the cofounder of 'Be Transformed Ministries.'

I TOOK DRUGS TO A CHURCH CONFERENCE. THEN GOD FOUND ME:

FADY GHOBRIAL

I was born to religious, hard-working parents in 1990 in Cairo. At 40 days old, I was baptized by triple immersion like every good Coptic Orthodox Christian.

Growing up in this kind of religious atmosphere leaves its mark on your soul forever. I can still recall the routine—but much-dreaded—confession times with the priest. Those experiences were especially deflating. Even well into my teens, I remember finishing confession, being instructed to do some penance so that God would like me again—at least that's how it felt—and then inevitably returning to my same old sins.

My attitude toward God was that he was mean, like my teachers from the Jesuit school I attended who would physically punish me (and other students) for falling short of their academic or behavioral standards.

In 2002, my family moved to America. The middle-school years were rough for me: Imagine trying to make friends in the aftermath of 9/11 as a chubby Middle Eastern kid who spoke no English. To add to my school woes, I was bullied at the one place no one ever should be: the church.

Our family continued to attend Coptic Orthodox services, but my heart quickly soured on the church of my youth, which never appealed to me much to begin with. By the time I reached high school, I was so disillusioned with the faith that I swung from being a "good religious kid" to the opposite extreme.

A Different Breed of Christian

High school afforded opportunities to hang out with new friends, experiment with dating and drugs, and—after I got my driver's license—go wherever I wanted. Before long, I had given myself over to a lifestyle of partying, fornication, and drug addiction.

Things got so bad that I eventually found myself selling drugs. Perhaps saddest of all was the influence this had on my younger brother, Joe, who was only in middle school and who ended up venturing down similar paths.

I still recall arriving at home one night at around two in the morning as a high school senior. My mom was awake, crying to God and praying for Jesus to save me. Later on, I would discover that while I was running from God, he had been working on others close to me.

My best friend, George, who was something of a partner in crime, started going to a new church with his brother Mark. This church—Arabic Baptist Church, outside Boston—was not Coptic Orthodox, so naturally I was apprehensive about their sudden invitation to visit its youth group.

But Mark was relentless. Every Friday night, without fail, he would pick up me and Joe in his cool, red Mitsubishi Eclipse for the hour long drive to the church. Mark took me there for more than a year, at times against my will, until I was able to drive myself.

At Arabic Baptist, I found a very different breed of Christian. The people there sincerely loved God. They were kind and not hypocritical. They actually loved and welcomed me. *Wow*, I thought, *these Christians are having fun and enjoying their relationship with God. God seems so real to them.*

Around the same time my brother and I got connected with the youth group, the woman who would become my mother-in-law was praying and reading the Bible with my mom over the phone. I began noticing a different, more peaceful environment at home.

By late 2008, my whole family was attending this church together, and my parents and brother were getting quite involved. My dad began hosting a Bible study in our house, and I saw God change him during a study of the Book of Hebrews.

I was showing up to church meetings because I loved the people there and felt loved in return. But I was showing up under the influence of drugs. Even though I really needed Jesus, I was still looking for satisfaction in all the wrong places.

In July 2009, during the summer between my freshman and sophomore years in college, my dad forced me to attend the church's annual Fourth of July conference.

Dragging my feet, I went along, and I brought some drugs to help pass the time. I wasn't open to hearing from God. But I discovered that weekend that even the fiercest resistance or the coldest indifference is irrelevant once God decides to act in your life.

At the conference, I heard the gospel with new ears. I heard that God loves me so much that he sent Jesus to die for my sins. And I understood that by trusting in Jesus, all of my sins would be forgiven, and that I would be accepted by God and made right with him.

Surrendering to Jesus

I distinctly remember a feeling of internal struggle within my soul: How could God forgive all my sins? And how could he forgive me when I couldn't even forgive myself? At the time, I lacked the capacity to fathom God's lavish mercy and unmerited grace.

And yet I couldn't escape feeling like God had cornered me with his love and I had no choice but to lay down my resistance and surrender. I realized that what Jesus had done was sufficient to cleanse me from my sin and make me new.

I was born again in that moment when I finally saw and treasured Jesus by faith. Oh, what a glorious day it was! That Fourth of July conference changed my life forever.

My joy was doubled, however, because my brother Joe, who is now a pastor at our church, was also saved that same weekend. We both had a one-night rehab with Jesus and were miraculously set free from addiction to drugs.

In fact, when we returned to our car to leave the conference and realized we still had some weed left, we immediately tossed it out and said, '*We* can't go back.' Our parents were delighted with the two new sons they got back after that weekend. We were completely transformed.

Other radical and immediate changes took place as well. For example, I began to serve at church almost immediately with the worship team and with the youth group.

That was how I met my wife, who was the youth group and worship leader at the time. Our worship team traveled to different conferences and retreats, and during those trips, a sense of calling grew in my heart and I began pondering a future in ministry.

Meanwhile, I was devouring the Scriptures, Christian books, podcasts, sermons, and anything else I could get my hands on. I attended church services and midweek prayer meetings on a regular basis. And I was blessed to have a few mentors in the church who discipled me.

All this encouraged my pursuit of ministry as a full-time vocation, a journey that brought me to Gordon-Conwell Theological Seminary and eventually saw me ordained at Arabic Baptist Church, where my whole family had come to faith.

My life today is a testimony to God's goodness and grace. This past July, I celebrated another year of walking with and serving Jesus Christ at Arabic Baptist's annual One Name Boston conference.

I have been celebrating my spiritual birthday every Independence Day for the past 13 years, and the symbolic overlap isn't lost on me.

The very gathering where I once showed up under the influence, with the intention of keeping God at arm's length, is now a tangible reminder of his miraculous work in my life. Thank you, Jesus, for putting nothing to waste.

Fady Ghobrial is a Christian Union ministry fellow at Harvard University.

AL FADI: I WANTED TO DIE FOR ALLAH. NOW I LIVE FOR JESUS

I was born and raised in Saudi Arabia as part of a devout Muslim family. Growing up, I considered myself a devoted follower of Islam, one who applied its teachings to every aspect of his life. I believed that Islam was the only true religion and that those who didn't accept Allah as their God and Muhammad as his messenger were doomed to hell.

I had nothing but contempt for Christianity. I believed that Muslims were superior to all others; that all non-Muslims were infidels, and that Jesus was a prophet sent by Allah, not the divine Son of God. As far as I was concerned, he had never been crucified, never died on a cross, and never been resurrected.

I believed he had ascended into heaven, but only to be saved from his persecutors before coming back at the end of times to restore Islam as the true religion of Allah. All in all, I grew up harboring intense hatred for Christians, Jews, and all who refused Islam.

By age 12, I had memorized half of the Qur'an, and my goal was to memorize all of it—all 114 chapters, all 6,236 verses. At age 15, I was prepared to die on behalf of Allah, like so many young people who were journeying to Afghanistan to fight the Soviet Union alongside Osama bin Laden. (He was a hero to us at that time.)

Were it not for my mother, who pleaded with me to stay behind, I would have joined this "holy war." I believed that the rewards awaiting Muslims who died in the name of Allah were greater than any other a Muslim could receive. I was certain that by sacrificing my life in this manner, I would make it to paradise with all my sins forgiven.

Interacting with Christians

The more I grew up, however, the more notes of doubt began to creep in. As I gained a greater familiarity with the language of the Qur'an, I started seeing messages of hate within it, messages I could not understand and did not like at all. *How,* I wondered, *could God hate his own creation simply because they do not accept him?*

276

On some level, I thought God should be above that kind of petty vindictiveness. But sharing such thoughts and doubts with others would have caused me lots of trouble and likely jeopardized my safety, as the penalty for blaspheming Allah and leaving Islam was death.

After finishing college in Saudi Arabia, I went to the United States to pursue my graduate education in engineering. But I had a dilemma. Islam teaches its followers not to befriend Christians, and in the Muslim world people truly believe that the United States is a Christian nation—in other words, that everyone born in America is born a Christian.

In the summer of 1989, I arrived in the United States filled with fear and discomfort. In order to receive the best education, I knew it was imperative to attend an American university. But I was apprehensive because that meant having to interact with Christians.

After living in a dormitory for about a month, I began feeling the need to become more familiar with American culture and to sharpen my English language skills.

Around that time, I heard of something called the International Friendship Program, which paired students like me with local volunteers who would provide help and hospitality. I signed up for the program, not knowing it was a Christian ministry.

Almost two weeks later, a young couple from the program contacted me and indicated that they were the family assigned to work with me. And for the next seven months, this family showed me love that far exceeded my expectations, love of the sort I had never experienced among my fellow Muslims.

In November, this family invited me to their home for Thanksgiving dinner. Only then did I realize this was a Christian family, because they asked if they could pray before the meal. I admit that my heart sank at this moment. I had never realized that Christians are actually filled with love and not hate, as my Muslim upbringing had led me to believe.

This family had never shared the gospel with me, but they had shown me what the gospel looks like. And on that day, I walked out of their home with great doubts about my faith and its teachings. I vowed that I would do research on Christianity, hoping to learn more about how Jesus could make such a profound difference in someone's life, offering the kind of peace and joy I had never seen before.

Seeing the light

A few years later, after earning my master's degree, I joined a local engineering firm. There I met another born-again Christian. I was impressed by his faith—his joy, his peace, and the light that seemed to shine forth from him. And when he invited me to his home for Christmas dinner, I noticed that his wife and kids had the same qualities. They were just like the family I had met in college.

At this point, I couldn't hold back my curiosity any longer. I asked him why he was so different from those around him. He told me he was a born-again Christian, and he shared his testimony. Once again, I was gripped with the desire to know more about Jesus.

From that moment forward, God allowed me to go through numerous trials and adverse circumstances in my life, all of which increased my interest in Christianity. And in May 2001, going against everything my Muslim faith had taught me, I made my first visit to a Christian church. Over the course of the next six months, as the church studied the Gospel of John, I learned who Christ truly is.

In November 2001, without a shadow of a doubt, I accepted Christ as my Lord and Savior. But it wasn't easy at first. Within a matter of months, I lost my marriage due to unfaithfulness from my spouse, and I also lost my job.

It felt like Satan was actively trying to destroy my faith. But these months taught me invaluable lessons about having a personal relationship with Jesus and learning to depend on him through all circumstances. During this time, God revealed his awesome glory to me in ways I could not deny or doubt.

Since then, my life has changed forever, and I am no longer the man I used to be. Today I lead a global ministry called CIRA International, which I founded by God's grace in 2010. Our mission is to reach Muslims for Christ, to equip believers with practical tools for effectively sharing the gospel with Muslims, and to disciple new believers, especially those coming from Muslim backgrounds.

In addition, I teach classes and seminars on Islam at various churches, so that my brothers and sisters in Christ can learn how to better witness to their Muslim neighbors. And at my home church, I head up a newly established chapter of the International Friendship Program, the very ministry that planted the first seeds of gospel hope in my heart almost 16 years ago.

I came to know my beloved Jesus through simple acts of love. And I pray God will use my own simple acts of love to bring glory to himself by drawing others to a saving faith in him.

Al Fadi teaches courses in biblical theology, business, and comparative religion at Arizona Christian University.

AMELIA EARHART: BREAKING BARRIERS IN AVIATION

Amelia Earhart's journey towards the skies began in Atchison, Kansas, where she was born on July 24, 1897. Raised in a progressive household by her parents, Amy and Edwin Earhart, young Amelia was encouraged to explore the world around her, fostering a spirit of curiosity and independence.

The family faced financial challenges, with Amelia's father working various jobs to make ends meet. Tragically, Amelia's younger sister, Muriel, was born with a developmental disability, creating an environment that demanded adaptability and resilience from a young Amelia.

Despite financial constraints, the Earhart family instilled values of education and self-reliance in their children. Growing up, Amelia displayed an early affinity for adventure and unconventional pursuits, favoring activities typically deemed unconventional for girls in that era. As a teenager, she worked odd jobs to save money, hoping to eventually fulfill her dream of flying.

However, Amelia's path to aviation was not an immediate one. Initially, she attended college but had to leave due to financial constraints. Her first taste of flight occurred at an air show in 1920, where she experienced a plane ride that would forever alter the course of her life. The thrill of being airborne ignited a spark within Amelia, and she set her sights on conquering the skies.

After working odd jobs and saving every penny, Amelia took flying lessons in 1921. In 1923, she received her pilot's license, becoming one of the select few women in the world with this distinction. Despite facing societal norms that discouraged women from pursuing careers in aviation, Amelia pressed forward, determined to break barriers and chart her own course.

Amelia's early years were marked by a relentless pursuit of her dreams, a tenacity that would define her aviation career. Her experiences were not without challenges, but every obstacle served as a stepping stone toward her ultimate goal of pushing the boundaries of aviation.

The miraculous essence of Amelia's journey lies not only in her groundbreaking accomplishments but also in the resilience and determination she displayed.

Her flights were a dance with danger, as she braved treacherous weather conditions and navigated uncharted territories. The miraculous moments were not just in the successful landings but in the ability to rise above every obstacle and soar to new heights.

As Amelia Earhart's fame grew, she became a symbol of empowerment for women worldwide. Her impact extended beyond aviation, challenging the status quo and encouraging individuals to embrace their aspirations fearlessly.

Yet, even in the midst of her extraordinary achievements, the mystery of her disappearance during an attempted around-the-world flight in 1937 adds an enigmatic layer to her story.

Amelia's life was a testament to the miracles that unfold when daring dreams align with perseverance and a touch of divinity. Her legacy lives on as an inspiration for those who dare to dream beyond the constraints of societal expectations, reminding us that miracles often accompany those who push boundaries and challenge the ordinary.

Amelia Earhart's story is not just about breaking barriers in aviation; it is a saga of miracles, resilience, and the boundless possibilities that unfold when dreams take flight.

The early stages of Amelia Earhart's life were characterized by modest beginnings, financial struggles, and societal expectations that sought to confine her ambitions.

However, these challenges shaped her character, fueling a passion for defying expectations and a determination to prove that dreams could indeed take flight.

As Amelia embarked on her aviation journey, the miracles that would unfold in her life were already in motion, waiting to be written across the skies.

HELEN KELLER: A TRIUMPH OVER DARKNESS AND SILENCE

Born on June 27, 1880, in Tuscumbia, Alabama, Helen Keller's early life took an unexpected turn at just 19 months old when she was struck by a devastating illness. This mysterious affliction robbed her of both sight and hearing, plunging her into a world of profound darkness and absolute silence.

The challenges before her seemed insurmountable, and yet, within the cocoon of her silent world, a miraculous journey was about to unfold.

Faced with the daunting task of helping their daughter navigate a life without sight and sound, Arthur and Kate Keller sought the assistance of Anne Sullivan, a tenacious and devoted teacher. Anne's arrival marked a pivotal moment in Helen's life – a moment where the seeds of triumph over adversity were sown.

Anne Sullivan, herself visually impaired in her youth, embarked on the seemingly impossible task of breaking through the communication barriers that enveloped Helen. With innovative methods and unyielding patience, Anne introduced Helen to the tactile language of sign language.

Through touch and repetition, Helen began to associate words with objects and ideas, bringing a glimmer of understanding to her silent world.

The breakthrough, immortalized in the iconic moment at the water pump, encapsulated the essence of Helen's miraculous journey. As water flowed over her hand, Anne spelled out the word "water" into Helen's other hand. It was an epiphany – a moment of revelation that everything had a name, and words held the key to unlocking the mysteries of the world.

The journey towards knowledge was an arduous climb, with Helen surmounting challenges that seemed insurmountable. The tactile language expanded into a broader understanding of language, literature, and the vast realms of human expression.

Helen's relentless pursuit of education led her to Radcliffe College, where she achieved the remarkable feat of becoming the first deaf-blind person to earn a Bachelor of Arts degree.

Helen Keller's triumph over adversity extended beyond academic accolades. She emerged as a prolific author, captivating lecturer, and fervent advocate for the rights of the disabled. Her journey became a beacon of inspiration, illuminating the boundless possibilities within the human spirit.

The miracles in Helen's life were not confined to the academic realm. They echoed in the moments of connection, understanding, and the profound resilience she displayed against seemingly insurmountable odds.

Helen Keller's story stands as a testament to the miraculous potential residing within each individual – a potential waiting to unfold, flourish, and illuminate the darkest corners of our existence.

A TALE OF MIRACULOUS SURVIVAL IN THE AMAZON RAINFOREST:

JULIANE KOEPCKE

Born on October 10, 1954, in Lima, Peru, Juliane Koepcke grew up immersed in the rich biodiversity of the Peruvian rainforest. Her parents, Hans-Wilhelm Koepcke and Maria Koepcke, both renowned biologists, instilled in her a profound appreciation for nature.

Surrounded by the vibrant ecosystems of the rainforest, Juliane developed a deep understanding of its intricacies from an early age. Her childhood was marked by a unique blend of scientific exploration and a sense of wonder for the natural world.

The turning point in Juliane's life occurred on December 24, 1971, when tragedy struck during a routine flight to Pucallpa to reunite with her father for Christmas. Onboard LANSA Flight 508, severe thunderstorms wrought havoc, causing the aircraft to be struck by lightning. In a catastrophic turn of events, the plane disintegrated at 10,000 feet.

Juliane, miraculously strapped to her seat, found herself plummeting through the dense Amazonian canopy.

Surviving the fall was a testament to both luck and the sturdy structure of her seat. Despite suffering a broken collarbone, a gash on her arm, and minor injuries, Juliane emerged as the sole survivor of the crash. Alone in the heart of the Amazon rainforest, a perilous journey awaited her.

Battered and bruised, Juliane faced the daunting task of navigating the unforgiving terrain of the Amazon rainforest. Armed with limited survival skills, she battled hunger, exposure, and the constant threat of wildlife. Days turned into nights, each presenting a new set of challenges for the resilient teenager.

Juliane's tenacity and resourcefulness led her to a small stream, which she followed downstream in search of civilization. The stream became her lifeline, providing water and guiding her to a makeshift shelter where she discovered a bag of candies—a rare source of sustenance in her dire circumstances.

As her solitary journey continued, Juliane encountered a group of lumber workers who, to her immense relief, provided assistance and guided her to safety. Her incredible survival story captivated the world, symbolizing the strength of the human spirit in the face of unimaginable adversity.

Juliane Koepcke's survival saga serves as an enduring testament to the resilience of the human spirit. Beyond the physical challenges, her journey through the Amazon encapsulates the indomitable will to live.

Her story has inspired countless individuals facing adversity, reminding us all of the extraordinary strength that can emerge in the most testing of circumstances.

Juliane's life became a living testimony to the intricate dance between divinity and determination. Her ability to persevere through the darkest moments of despair has left an indelible mark on the annals of survival stories, making her a symbol of hope and tenacity for generations to come.

Juliane Koepcke's survival story offers several lessons, particularly emphasizing our belief in the miraculous or divinity during times of need:

Resilience in Adversity:

Juliane's ability to endure physical and emotional challenges in the midst of the Amazon rainforest showcases the incredible resilience of the human spirit. This resilience can be seen as a form of divine strength that emerges when faced with seemingly insurmountable obstacles.

Faith in the Unseen:

Juliane's survival against overwhelming odds encourages us to maintain faith in the unseen or the unknown. Even in the darkest moments, holding onto a belief that there might be a way forward or that help may come from unexpected sources can be a powerful source of strength.

Miracles in Ordinary Moments:

The discovery of a bag of candies in the jungle, providing Juliane with a source of sustenance, can be seen as a small yet significant miracle. It reminds us to appreciate the miracles that can manifest in seemingly ordinary moments, offering hope and sustenance even in the midst of challenging circumstances.

Guidance in Nature:

Juliane's navigation along a stream, leading her to safety, reflects the idea of finding guidance in the natural world. In times of need, a connection with nature can be perceived as a form of divine guidance, guiding individuals towards resources or paths that lead to safety.

Strength in Solitude:

Juliane's solitary journey underscores the strength that can be found in moments of solitude. It prompts us to reflect on our inner strength and resilience, which can be sources of divine fortitude during challenging times when external help may seem distant.

Embracing Divine Help through Others:

The encounter with lumber workers symbolizes the idea that divine assistance can come through the kindness of others. Being open to receiving help and support from fellow human beings can be an emotionally uplifting experience, portraying a shared connection that transcends the individual.

Purpose in Challenges:

Juliane's survival story suggests that challenges and hardships may serve a larger purpose in our lives. Viewing difficulties as opportunities for growth and refinement can be a way of finding meaning and purpose even in the face of adversity.

MOTHER TERESA: A LIFE OF SELFLESS SERVICE

On August 26, 1910, in Skopje, Macedonia, Agnes Gonxha Bojaxhiu entered the world, and little did anyone know that she would grow up to be Mother Teresa, a symbol of compassion, love, and selfless service. The miraculous undertakings of her life began long before she embarked on her mission of helping the destitute and ailing in Calcutta.

Agnes's childhood was marked by the influences of her parents, Nikola and Dranafile Bojaxhiu, who instilled in her a deep sense of faith and compassion. Early on, Agnes felt a calling to a life of service, a calling that would later manifest in her unwavering dedication to the poorest of the poor.

At the age of 18, Agnes left her home in Skopje and joined the Sisters of Loreto in Ireland. It was there that she took the name Sister Mary Teresa, marking the beginning of her formal journey into religious life. Her time with the Sisters of Loreto prepared her for her future mission, providing a foundation of education, discipline, and spiritual growth.

However, the true turning point occurred during a train ride to Darjeeling in 1946. On this seemingly ordinary journey, Sister Teresa experienced what she described as a "call within a call." She felt a divine urging to leave the convent and live among the poor, tending to their needs directly.

This spiritual revelation became the seed for the Missionaries of Charity, an order she founded dedicated to serving the most marginalized in society.

In 1948, after obtaining permission from the Vatican, Mother Teresa stepped out of the convent and into the streets of Calcutta, donning the simple blue and white saree that would become synonymous with her mission.

The miracles in her life were not marked by grandeur but by the transformative impact of love and compassion. She began by tending to the dying in the slums, picking up the destitute from the streets, and offering them solace in their final moments.

The Missionaries of Charity expanded rapidly, and Mother Teresa's unwavering commitment drew others to join her cause. She established hospices, orphanages, and centers for the poor and sick, emphasizing that every act of kindness, no matter how small, had the power to change lives. Her profound empathy and devotion became a beacon of hope for the suffering.

The recognition of Mother Teresa's extraordinary service extended beyond borders. She received numerous awards, including the Nobel Peace Prize in 1979. Despite the accolades, she remained dedicated to her mission, tirelessly working for the betterment of humanity until her passing on September 5, 1997.

Mother Teresa's life was a testament to the miracles that unfold when one person, driven by faith and love, decides to make a difference. Her legacy continues to inspire countless individuals to emulate the transformative power of compassion and selfless service.

Mother Teresa's life is considered a miracle for several compelling reasons:

1. Selfless Dedication: Mother Teresa's unwavering commitment to serving the poor, sick, and destitute in Calcutta is nothing short of miraculous. Her life was dedicated to alleviating the suffering of those in need, and her acts of compassion touched countless lives.

2. Founding the Missionaries of Charity: The establishment of the Missionaries of Charity, a religious congregation focused on serving the poorest of the poor, was a miraculous initiative. Mother Teresa founded this organization, providing care and comfort to those who were often neglected by society.

3. Compassion in Action: Mother Teresa's hands-on approach to helping others, irrespective of their background, religion, or social status,

showcased a level of compassion that transcended societal norms. Her ability to empathize and take practical steps to address the needs of the marginalized is a miracle in the realm of humanitarian work.

4. Impact on Global Consciousness: Mother Teresa's work significantly influenced global perceptions of poverty and social justice. By highlighting the plight of the impoverished and demonstrating that each individual can make a difference, she sparked a global movement towards empathy and compassion.

5. Recognition and Awards: The numerous awards and honors bestowed upon Mother Teresa during her lifetime, including the Nobel Peace Prize in 1979, are indicative of the extraordinary impact she had on the world. Such recognition is a testament to the miraculous nature of her contributions.

6. Miraculous Healings: In the eyes of many believers, there are accounts of miraculous healings associated with Mother Teresa. People have reported experiencing physical and emotional healings through prayers and interactions with her, contributing to the perception of her as a conduit for divine intervention.

7. Influence Beyond Borders: Mother Teresa's influence extended far beyond Calcutta. Her ability to inspire others to join her mission and the global resonance of her message speak to the miraculous nature of her impact, transcending geographical and cultural boundaries.

In summary, Mother Teresa's life is considered a miracle because of her selfless service, the establishment of the Missionaries of Charity, her impact on global consciousness, and the countless lives she touched. The profound influence she had on humanitarian efforts and her canonization by the Catholic Church further solidify her status as a miraculous figure in history.

"Not all of us can do great things.

But we can do small things with great love."

Mother Teresa

288

ELON MUSK: REVOLUTIONIZING SPACE EXPLORATION

Born on June 28, 1971, in Pretoria, South Africa, Elon Reeve Musk exhibited an early fascination with computers and technology. His childhood was marked by a voracious appetite for knowledge, and by the age of 12, he had taught himself how to code.

However, growing up in apartheid-era South Africa presented its own set of challenges, as Musk, being somewhat of a prodigy, often found himself at odds with his peers.

At the age of 17, Musk moved to Canada to attend Queen's University, later transferring to the University of Pennsylvania. It was during his time in the United States that Musk's entrepreneurial spirit began to emerge.

He and his brother Kimbal founded Zip2, a web software company that provided business directories and maps for newspapers. In 1999, Compaq acquired Zip2 for nearly $300 million, marking Musk's first major success.

The windfall from Zip2 allowed Musk to delve into his next ventures, including founding X.com, an online payment company. X.com eventually merged with Confinity, resulting in the formation of PayPal. In 2002, eBay acquired PayPal for $1.5 billion, further solidifying Musk's reputation as a tech mogul.

However, Musk's ambitions reached even greater heights as he set his sights on revolutionizing space exploration and sustainable energy. In 2002, he founded SpaceX (Space Exploration Technologies Corp.) with the audacious goal of reducing space transportation costs and making life *multiplanetary*.

SpaceX faced numerous challenges, including initial failures and financial struggles. At one point, Musk invested the last of his personal fortune into SpaceX, with only three launches left before bankruptcy.

Against all odds, SpaceX succeeded. The company developed the Falcon 1, the first privately developed liquid-fueled rocket to reach orbit. Subsequent achievements included the Falcon 9 and the Dragon spacecraft, the latter becoming the first commercial spacecraft to deliver cargo to the International Space Station.

Simultaneously, Musk set his sights on the automotive industry. In 2004, he founded Tesla Motors with the vision of producing electric vehicles that could compete with traditional automobiles.

The Tesla Roadster, introduced in 2008, became the first electric car with a range exceeding 200 miles per charge. Despite skepticism from the industry, Tesla went on to revolutionize electric vehicles and renewable energy solutions.

Elon Musk's journey is one of relentless determination, overcoming financial turmoil, industry skepticism, and technical challenges. His daring dreams of colonizing Mars and transitioning the world to sustainable energy sources continue to push the boundaries of what is deemed possible.

Musk's resilience in the face of adversity and his unwavering commitment to innovation make him a contemporary figure embodying the spirit of daring dreams and the pursuit of the seemingly impossible.

Elon Musk's life can be seen as a miracle to the world in various aspects:

1. Visionary Achievements: Musk's ability to envision and actualize groundbreaking projects, such as SpaceX and Tesla, demonstrates a level of innovation that many deemed unattainable.

The successful launch and recovery of reusable rockets by SpaceX, coupled with Tesla's transformative impact on the automotive industry, are testament to Musk's visionary miracles.

2. Resilience in Adversity: Musk faced numerous setbacks and financial challenges throughout his career, with moments where his companies were on the verge of bankruptcy. Despite these hardships, he persisted and overcame obstacles that would have deterred many. His resilience is a miraculous element in his journey.

3. Revolutionizing Industries: Musk's impact on the space exploration and automotive industries has been revolutionary. SpaceX has significantly lowered the cost of space travel, opening up new possibilities for space exploration. Tesla, under Musk's leadership, has accelerated the adoption of electric vehicles, driving the automotive industry toward sustainability.

4. Multiplanetary Vision: Musk's daring dream of making life *Multiplanetary* is an audacious and miraculous vision. The idea of colonizing Mars was once relegated to the realm of science fiction, but Musk's commitment to this goal has redefined the possibilities for humanity's future.

5. Influence on Renewable Energy: Through Tesla's innovations in electric vehicles and renewable energy solutions, Musk has played a pivotal role in reshaping the conversation around sustainable living. The impact of Tesla extends beyond automobiles, influencing the broader adoption of clean energy technologies.

6. Inspiring Future Generations: Musk's story serves as an inspiration for aspiring entrepreneurs and dreamers worldwide. His capacity to think beyond conventional boundaries and challenge the status quo encourages others to pursue their daring dreams, fostering a culture of innovation.

In essence, Musk's life is a miracle to the world because he challenges preconceived notions, breaks barriers, and exemplifies the transformative power of relentless determination and audacious vision. His impact extends beyond individual successes, influencing entire industries and inspiring a global shift toward a more innovative and sustainable future.

THE PURPOSE OF LIFE: A UNIVERSAL SYMPHONY

At the heart of our existence lies a quest for purpose, a yearning to understand our individual lives within the vast tapestry of existence. This philosophical inquiry transcends the mundane and invites us to contemplate the cosmic symphony in which our lives play a unique melody.

Our individual lives, like individual musical notes, may seem fleeting and isolated, yet they contribute to the composition of a grand symphony. The purpose, then, becomes a harmonious interplay of these unique notes, creating a melody that resonates through the corridors of time.

Viktor Frankl, a Holocaust survivor and existential psychiatrist, observed that "Life is never made unbearable by circumstances, but only by lack of meaning and purpose." The purpose of life, it seems, is intertwined with finding meaning amid the ebb and flow of experiences.

Miracles, those inexplicable interventions in our lives, emerge as the orchestration guiding us toward our destined purpose. Biblical narratives, such as the story of Joseph in Genesis, exemplify this notion.

Joseph's life was marked by adversities, yet the miraculous events, including his rise to power in Egypt, were integral threads weaving him into the larger purpose of saving his family during a severe famine. Miracles, therefore, become the spiritual instruments that fine-tune our individual melodies, aligning them with the universal rhythm.

Joseph, despite facing betrayal, slavery, and imprisonment, remained faithful to his dreams. The miraculous events, such as interpreting dreams in prison and eventually becoming Pharaoh's chief administrator, weren't merely strokes of luck.

They were intricately woven components of a purposeful life. In retrospect, Joseph acknowledged this, saying to his brothers, "You intended to harm me, but God intended it for good to accomplish what is now being done, the saving of many lives" (Genesis 50:20, NIV). His life, marked by miraculous turns, had a purpose far beyond personal ambitions.

BEETHOVEN'S DEAFNESS AND NINTH SYMPHONY:

Ludwig van Beethoven provides an extraordinary example in history. As he faced increasing deafness, many would have seen it as an impediment to his purpose as a composer. However, in this adversity, Beethoven created one of his greatest masterpieces – the Ninth Symphony.

His life, marked by the miraculous creation of symphonies amid deafness, illustrates that purpose transcends physical limitations.

In unraveling the purpose of life, we recognize that our individual narratives are not isolated; they are harmonious notes contributing to a cosmic symphony. Miracles, whether in the form of divine interventions or human resilience, align our melodies with a universal purpose.

Through the lens of biblical and historical narratives, we discover that the purpose of life is a melody that gains richness and depth through the orchestrated interplay of miracles in our journey.

The Role of Faith in Adversity: Finding Light in Tough Moments

Life is an unpredictable journey, filled with peaks of joy and valleys of adversity. Amidst the uncertainties, faith emerges as the unwavering compass, guiding us through the tumultuous seas of challenges.

In the face of adversity, faith becomes our guiding light. It's not merely a blind belief, but a profound trust in something greater than ourselves. Whether rooted in spirituality, philosophy, or personal convictions, faith provides the strength to endure, the courage to confront, and the hope to persevere.

Adversity, often perceived as an unwelcome guest, can be reframed as a sculptor shaping the intricate details of our character and destiny. Like a master craftsman chiseling away imperfections from a block of marble, challenges refine our resilience, patience, and tenacity. The trials we face, rather than hindrances, become essential elements in the intricate sculpture of our life's purpose.

Drawing inspiration from history and sacred writings, we find profound examples of individuals whose faith illuminated the darkest corners of adversity. Take Nelson Mandela, who endured decades of imprisonment with unwavering faith in justice and equality. His resilience turned a seemingly insurmountable challenge into a catalyst for societal transformation.

Biblically, the story of Job exemplifies the role of faith in adversity. Job faced unimaginable trials, yet his unwavering faith in God's plan sustained him through the storms. His story teaches us that faith not only helps us endure adversity but also leads to a profound transformation of our character.

In the crucible of challenges, faith emerges as a transformative force, reshaping our perspectives, fortifying our spirits, and guiding us towards the realization of a purpose far grander than we initially envisioned. It is in the darkest moments that the flame of faith burns brightest, illuminating the path to a brighter, more resilient version of ourselves.

"Miracles happen every day.

Change your perception of what a miracle is,

and you'll see them all around you."

Jon Bon Jovi

Faith: A Guiding Light in the Darkness

Miracles, often perceived as intensely personal, hold the power to reverberate through the collective consciousness. While the experience may be individual, its impact can extend far beyond personal boundaries.

Consider the story of Anne Sullivan and Helen Keller. Anne's unwavering dedication and Helen's triumph over darkness and silence not only transformed their lives but also inspired countless others facing seemingly insurmountable challenges. Miracles, it seems, are not isolated events but threads seamlessly woven into the fabric of shared humanity.

The role of faith in adversity becomes a luminous theme when examining historical and personal narratives. Think of the biblical story of Joseph, who faced betrayal and adversity yet emerged triumphant.

His unwavering faith in the midst of challenges not only shaped his destiny but also played a pivotal role in the larger narrative of the nation of Israel. Faith, it appears, acts as a guiding light that not only illuminates individual paths but also influences the trajectory of collective human stories.

Exploring the purpose of life on a universal scale invites reflection on the interconnectedness of our journeys. In the grand scheme of existence, each individual's story contributes a unique hue to the canvas of humanity.

This perspective can be exemplified by the historical account of individuals like Harriet Tubman, whose journey from slavery to freedom not only defined her purpose but also left an indelible mark on the broader narrative of human rights.

Our personal journeys are not solitary ventures; rather, they contribute to a broader, interconnected narrative. Take Elon Musk, whose daring dreams in space exploration have not only revolutionized industries but have become part of humanity's collective aspiration to reach new frontiers.

Musk's journey is a testament to the interconnectedness of individual ambitions and the collective human pursuit of the extraordinary.

As we navigate our individual journeys, let us recognize the intertwining threads of miracles, faith, and purpose. The interconnectedness of our stories forms a breathtaking tapestry, reflecting the resilience, triumphs, and shared aspirations of humanity.

In the words of Martin Luther King Jr., "Faith is taking the first step even when you don't see the whole staircase." May our collective journey be one of courage, faith, and the perpetual belief in the miraculous potential that lies within each of us.

CONCLUSION

In the harmonious symphony of life, each note plays a unique melody, weaving tales of faith, daring dreams, and the miracles that intertwine them. "Catch Your Miracle Today: Your Journey of Faith and Daring

Dreams" has been a pilgrimage through the landscapes of hope, adversity, and divine interventions.

As the final chords resonate, let us embark on an emotional reflection, celebrating the miracles that dance in the rhythm of time.

From the foothills of the "Mountain of Miracles," where whispers of divinity beckoned, to the valleys of "Meeting Miracle Monsters," where courage faced its fears, this journey has unfolded like a musical crescendo.

We confronted the shadows, battled our inner monsters, and discovered that miracles often wear disguises in the face of challenges.

The path wound through the terrain of "Managing Miracles Monsters," where the delicate dance of responsibility and faith took center stage. Miracles, it appears, thrive on the cultivation of our inner gardens—a symbiosis between action and trust.

In the final movement, the "Miraculous Melody" reverberated through stories of personal triumphs and shared victories. Inspirational figures both in history and in modern life emerged as beacons, guiding us through the ebbs and flows of life. This chapter served as an epiphany, reminding us that the greatest miracles often lie within the fabric of our shared humanity.

Through daily reflections, information gathering, investment in resources, and the unwavering support of a solid foundation, we became orchestrators of our miracles.

As we navigated the pages of this closing chapter, we found ourselves immersed in a journey that transcended the boundaries of time, connecting us with the eternal theme of miracles, faith, and daring dreams.

From the humble beginnings of a slum in Kumasi to the bustling city lights of Accra, the stories shared serve as testaments to the miracles that manifest in unexpected places. Each word is a brushstroke, painting a vivid picture of a life miraculously plucked from obscurity, guided by faith, and propelled by daring dreams.

Picture the gritty streets of Kumasi, a slum alive with dreams. Here, a young soul, amidst mosquito-laden nights and cramped quarters, found an unlikely ticket to a city's embrace. It's a narrative echoing from humble origins to the dazzling lights of Accra, a dance orchestrated by divine hands and fueled by relentless faith.

In a symphony of extraordinary tales, envision the roaring engines of Amelia Earhart's plane, the silence of Helen Keller's world, the selfless service of Mother Teresa, and Elon Musk's relentless pursuit of the cosmos.

Amidst these constellations in the night sky, we find the stories of Sharon Dutra, Beethoven, Al Fadi, and Fady Ghobrial. Their lives, like cinematic scenes, unfold with unique melodies.

Al Fadi and Fady Ghobrial, in particular, experienced profound religious encounters with Jesus, becoming pivotal moments that transformed the rhythm of their existence.

Pause for a moment and delve into the philosophical reflections. Why are we here, in this cosmic dance of existence? The purpose unravels, intertwined with faith and the pursuit of daring dreams.

The trials faced become not obstacles but sculptors shaping destinies. Interconnectedness reveals itself like a river merging into the vast ocean of shared humanity.

The rational reflections embedded within the narratives prompt you my precious reader to ponder the purpose of your own life, the role of faith in adversity, and the interconnectedness of your journeys. These tales are not just stories; they are harmonies that guide those who dare to dream and believe in the extraordinary.

We delved into the purpose of life, the cosmic dance of existence, we found solace in the notion that our individual stories contribute to a larger narrative, each miracle a stroke in the grand masterpiece of humanity.

The role of faith in adversity becomes a beacon of light, guiding us through the darkest nights and shaping the contours of our character and destiny. The network of our individual journeys, like rivers converging into an ocean, unveils the shared destiny that binds us all.

A CALL TO ACTION

In the concluding moments, I invite you precious reader to consider the profound and miraculous moments in your own life. The stories and reflections offered are not merely tales to be read but mirrors reflecting the potential for miracles within each individual.

The call-to-action is an invitation to embrace the unknown, to walk with faith through the uncertainties, and to dream daringly, knowing that miracles are not distant occurrences but threads woven into the very fabric of our existence.

As we turn the final page, may the resonance of these narratives linger, inspiring thought, stirring faith, and igniting the flame of daring dreams. For in this concluding pages, the book does not end but transforms into a catalyst for reflection, an anthem for those who seek the miraculous, and a testament to the boundless possibilities that await those who believe.

As we stand at the threshold of this narrative, let these words be more than an epilogue. Let them echo as a rallying cry—a call to action. Your journey is not confined to these pages; it is a living manuscript, continuously written with each heartbeat and every choice. The ink of your destiny is in your hands.

Dare to dream audaciously. Your dreams are the compositions that the universe yearns to play. In your dream lies the roadmap to miracles. Just as a radio tunes into frequencies, attune your soul to the melodies of faith. In moments of silence, listen closely—miracles often whisper.

Your life is a melody; make it resonate with acts of kindness. Extend a helping hand, share your miracles, and become a note in the symphony of collective well-being. When the music of life encounters discord, dance through it. Every step is a testament to your resilience, and miracles often unfold in the rhythm of perseverance.

As we lower the final curtain on "Catch a Miracle Today," remember that your journey is an unfolding symphony, with movements yet to be composed. Write your notes with inkwells of hope, and may your pages be illuminated with the miraculous glow of faith and daring dreams.

In the grand concert of existence, let your life be the resounding melody that catches miracles. The stage is yours, and the symphony is awaiting your unique composition. With faith as your conductor and daring dreams as your instruments, let your life's music soar. May you catch miracles in every chorus.

The final note has been played, but your symphony continues. Let the echoes of your miraculous melody resonate through the corridors of eternity. You are the composer, the conductor, and the audience. Catch your miracle, and may your life be a timeless and extraordinary masterpiece.